THE EVERYTHING®
SOUTHERN
COOKBOOK

Dear Reader,

My own experience with Southern cooking began with a move from New Hampshire to Mississippi nearly twenty years ago. I was fascinated with the many differences in dishes and ingredients, and delighted with the wonderful new tastes. I'll never forget my first meal; it was a sampler of sorts, and included fried chicken, fried green tomatoes, freshly cooked black-eyed peas, fried okra slices, chicken and dumplings, biscuits, and cornbread. And, of course, dessert was peach cobbler! Though there are many wonderful New England dishes and interesting regional foods throughout the nation, there is truly nothing in the United States quite like Southern cuisine.

As I began tasting these foods and new versions of vintage recipes, I found that I wanted to learn to cook them myself, not only to please my husband, who is a native Southerner, but also to satisfy my own culinary curiosity. I passed a personal cooking milestone when my husband approved of my fried green tomatoes, and another one when he liked my fried chicken and homemade biscuits. But I think my greatest personal achievement in Southern cooking came when my mother-in-law approved of my cornbread.

With this cookbook, I hope to do my own small part to preserve our Southern food culture and bring you a taste of many of the best-loved foods and recipes from regions throughout the South, along with some of my personal favorites.

Diana Rattray

Welcome to the EVERYTHING® Series!

These handy, accessible books give you all you need to tackle a difficult project, gain a new hobby, comprehend a fascinating topic, prepare for an exam, or even brush up on something you learned back in school but have since forgotten.

You can choose to read an Everything® book from cover to cover or just pick out the information you want from our four useful boxes: e-questions, e-facts, e-alerts, and e-ssentials.

We give you everything you need to know on the subject, but throw in a lot of fun stuff along the way, too.

We now have more than 400 Everything® books in print, spanning such wide-ranging categories as weddings, pregnancy, cooking, music instruction, foreign language, crafts, pets, New Age, and so much more. When you're done reading them all, you can finally say you know Everything®!

QUESTION

Answers to
common questions

FACT

Important snippets
of information

ALERT

Urgent
warnings

ESSENTIAL

Quick
handy tips

PUBLISHER Karen Cooper

MANAGING EDITOR, EVERYTHING® SERIES Lisa Laing

COPY CHIEF Casey Ebert

ASSISTANT PRODUCTION EDITOR Alex Guarco

ACQUISITIONS EDITOR Lisa Laing

ASSOCIATE DEVELOPMENT EDITOR Eileen Mullan

EVERYTHING® SERIES COVER DESIGNER Erin Alexander

Visit the entire Everything® series at *www.everything.com*

THE
EVERYTHING®
SOUTHERN
COOKBOOK

Diana Rattray

Adamsmedia
Avon, Massachusetts

This book is dedicated to my late grandfather,
Edward Bernard, the baker and chef who
introduced me to the world of cooking.

An Everything® Series Book.
Everything® and everything.com® are registered
trademarks of F+W Media, Inc.

Published by
Adams Media, a division of F+W Media, Inc.
57 Littlefield Street, Avon, MA 02322. U.S.A.
www.adamsmedia.com

Contains material adapted and abridged from *The About
.com Guide to Southern Cooking*, copyright © 2006 by
F+W Media, Inc., ISBN 10: 1-59869-096-5, ISBN 13: 978-1-
59869-096-5; *The Everything® Bread Cookbook* by Leslie
Bilderback, CMB, copyright © 2010 by F+W Media, Inc.,
ISBN 10: 1-4405-0031-2, ISBN 13: 978-1-4405-0031-2; *The
Everything® Cast-Iron Cookbook* by Cinnamon Cooper,
copyright © 2010 by F+W Media, Inc., ISBN 10: 1-4405-
0225-0, ISBN 13: 978-1-4405-0225-5; *The Everything®
Cookies & Brownies Cookbook* by Marye Audet,
copyright © 2009 by F+W Media, Inc., ISBN 10: 1-60550-
125-5, ISBN 13: 978-1-60550-125-3; *The Everything®
Hot Sauce Book* by Angela Garbes, copyright © 2012
by F+W Media, Inc., ISBN 10: 1-4405-3011-4, ISBN 13:
978-1-4405-3011-1; *The Everything® Ice Cream, Gelato,
and Frozen Desserts Cookbook* by Susan Whetzel,
copyright © 2012 by F+W Media, Inc., ISBN 10: 1-4405-
2497-1, ISBN 13: 978-1-4405-2497-4; *The Everything®
One-Pot Cookbook, 2nd Edition* by Pamela Rice Hahn,
copyright © 2009 by F+W Media, Inc., ISBN 10: 1-59869-
836-2, ISBN 13: 978-1-4405-836-7; *The Everything® Pie
Cookbook* by Kelly Jaggers, copyright © 2011 by F+W
Media, Inc., ISBN 10: 1-4405-2726-1, ISBN 13: 978-1-4405-
2726-5; *The Everything® Pressure Cooker Cookbook* by
Pamela Rice Hahn, copyright © 2009 by F+W Media,
Inc., ISBN 10: 1-4405-0017-7, ISBN 13: 978-1-4405-0017-6;
*The Everything® Quick and Easy 30-Minute, 5-Ingredient
Cookbook* by Linda Larsen, copyright © 2006 by F+W
Media, Inc., ISBN 10: 1-59337-692-8, ISBN 13: 978-1-59337-
692-5; *The Everything® Restaurant Recipes Cookbook*
by Becky Bopp, copyright © 2011 by F+W Media, Inc.,
ISBN 10: 1-4405-1125-X, ISBN 13: 978-1-4405-1125-7; *The
Everything® Salad Book* by Aysha Schurman, copyright
© 2011 by F+W Media, Inc., ISBN 10: 1-4405-2207-3, ISBN
13: 978-1-4405-2207-9; *The Everything® Slow Cooker
Cookbook, 2nd Edition* by Pamela Rice Hahn, copyright
© 2009 by F+W Media, Inc., ISBN 10: 1-59869-977-6, ISBN

13: 978-1-59869-977-7; *The Everything® Soup, Stew, &
Chili Cookbook* by Belinda Hulin, copyright © 2009 by
F+W Media, Inc., ISBN 10: 1-60550-044-5, ISBN 13: 978-1-
60550-044-7; *The Everything® Whole Foods Cookbook* by
Rachel Rappaport, copyright © 2012 by F+W Media, Inc.,
ISBN 10: 1-4405-3168-4, ISBN 13: 978-1-4405-3168-2; and
The Everything® Whole-Grain, High-Fiber Cookbook by
Lynnette Rohrer Shirk, copyright © 2008 by F+W Media,
Inc., ISBN 10: 1-59869-507-X, ISBN 13: 978-1-59869-507-6.

ISBN 10: 1-4405-8536-9
ISBN 13: 978-1-4405-8536-4
eISBN 10: 1-4405-8537-7
eISBN 13: 978-1-4405-8537-1

Printed in the United States of America.

10 9 8 7 6 5 4 3 2 1

Library of Congress Cataloging-in-Publication Data

Rattray, Diana.
  The everything Southern cookbook / Diana Rattray.
    pages cm
  Includes index.
  ISBN 978-1-4405-8536-4 (pb) -- ISBN 1-4405-8536-9 (pb)
-- ISBN 978-1-4405-8537-1 (ebook) -- ISBN 1-4405-8537-7
(ebook)
  1. Cooking, American--Southern style. I. Title.
  TX715.2.S68R37525 2014
  641.5975--dc23

                                    2014030609

Many of the designations used by manufacturers and
sellers to distinguish their products are claimed as
trademarks. Where those designations appear in this
book and F+W Media, Inc. was aware of a trademark
claim, the designations have been printed with initial
capital letters.

Always follow safety and commonsense cooking
protocol while using kitchen utensils, operating ovens
and stoves, and handling uncooked food. If children are
assisting in the preparation of any recipe, they should
always be supervised by an adult.

Photographs © iStockphoto.com.
Cover images © StockFood/Paul, Michael; StockFood/
Patrick, Dick; StockFood/Bronze Photography;
StockFood/Snowflake Studios Inc.

*This book is available at quantity discounts for bulk
purchases.*
For information, please call 1-800-289-0963.

Contents

Acknowledgments

Thanks to my mother, Grace Rattray, for always encouraging me in whatever I chose to do, and to my mother-in-law, Dorothy Lawhon, for answering so many cornbread and biscuit questions.

A special thank-you to my husband, Loy Lawhon, for his unwavering support and for tasting and testing whatever I made, whether he was hungry or not.

Last but not least, thanks to all of the wonderful people at Adams Media for their guidance and patience during the writing process.

Introduction

THOUGH THERE ARE MANY wonderful regional food specialties and dishes throughout the nation, there is nothing in the United States quite like Southern cuisine. Southern cuisine spans a large area and incorporates a variety of influences. The states with the richest history include Louisiana, Mississippi, Alabama, Georgia, Kentucky, Tennessee, Arkansas, Florida, North Carolina, and South Carolina. You'll also find Southern food traditions in parts of Texas and Oklahoma, Missouri, Virginia, West Virginia, and even Maryland.

African Americans have certainly had a big influence on Southern cuisine, but you'll also find Spanish and Caribbean influences in Florida; French in Louisiana and South Carolina; English, Scots, and Irish throughout the South; Moravian in North Carolina; German in Kentucky and parts of Tennessee; and the list goes on. Of course, the Native American influence is as pervasive in the South as anywhere else in the Americas. Without their influence, there would be no corn or hominy or grits, and Southern food wouldn't use pumpkin, squash, tomatoes, potatoes, chili peppers, peanuts, sweet potatoes, many types of beans, or a long list of other foods

Through the years, the basics of Southern cuisine have changed little, though with the availability of more ingredients and population changes in many larger cities, there is now much more experimentation, something all Southern cooks dearly love. Drop in on a conversation between most Southern cooks and you'll hear them talking about their chicken cordon bleu right along with their pinto beans and greens, and grilled tuna as well as catfish and hush puppies. Ask ten Southern cooks how they make their cornbread, and you'll get ten slightly different answers, but no complete recipe. The one thing they all have in common is the claim that their own personal recipe is the "best." Southern favorites, such as barbecue, vary widely according to which state you live in. In some cases, such as with North Carolina barbecue sauces and a regional Kentucky mutton barbecue, it can actually vary from one section of the state to another.

The Southern Foodways Alliance is one organization dedicated to preserving the heritage of this unique cuisine, and making sure through writings, events, chefs, and cooking demonstrations that it passes on from one generation to the next. Even as the years pass, traditional favorites will be remembered, and treasured recipes will hopefully change only slightly, depending on the region and the cook.

This cookbook will bring you a taste of many of the basics, some best-loved foods and popular recipes from regions throughout the South. Would you prefer creamy sausage gravy or muscadine jelly with your breakfast of hot buttered biscuits, pork sausage, eggs, and grits? A typical Southern Sunday dinner might include Fried Chicken Strips, Fried Green Tomatoes, freshly cooked Black-Eyed Peas with Ham, Crispy Fried Okra, Chicken and Dumplings, and more biscuits or Southern-Skillet Cornbread (with Southern-Style Ice Tea to wash it down, of course). The family next door might be eating Pulled-Pork Barbecue Sandwiches, Perfect Potato Salad, and Barbecue Baked Beans. Down the street someone might be dining on Fried Catfish, Hush Puppies, and Picnic Coleslaw. Or Country-Fried Steak, Savory Collard Greens, and Easy Fried Corn. Down on the coast, dinner might be Crispy Fried Oysters, Spicy Shrimp and Grits, or Cajun-Style Dirty Rice. Dessert might be Brown Sugar Pecan Pie, Peach Pie, Mississippi Mud Pie, or Pecan Praline Cookies. The options go on and on. In these pages you'll learn to cook all these Southern staples and much more.

CHAPTER 1

The Joy of Southern Cooking

Southern cuisine has a reputation that reaches all across the country, far surpassing the borders of the southern states. Even if you live on the opposite side of the United States, there is no doubt that you've heard of or seen recipes for homemade fried chicken, buttermilk cornbread, collard greens, grits, fried green tomatoes, and sweet tea. There are many other delicious food cultures and specialties in the United States, but no other region has such a storied and flavorful history as Southern cuisine.

The Basics of Southern Cooking

For many areas, the local cuisine or food culture is often based specifically on the foods that are cooked or cooking methods. But it's not simply the food that characterizes Southern cooking—it's the traditions in cooking styles, the cookware used, the dishes passed down through families, and the stories that are attached to the foods and regions.

If you've ever spent time with Southerners, you know that one of the most common conversation topics is food. People swap stories of new dishes they've made, changes they've tried in their classic dishes, or how they've used a new ingredient they found recently at the store or grew in their garden. In the South, the dinner table is the heart of the home, where families and friends gather together to share a meal or shuck corn or preserve food for the winter.

ESSENTIAL

The population of the southern United States is made up of a variety different groups who came to the region, each contributing to what is now known as Southern cooking. With influences ranging from the Caribbean, French, Spanish, English, German, Native American, and African American traditions, Southern cuisine and cooking is one of the most eclectic in the world.

If you ask Southern cooks how they make their biscuits, you'll probably get different answers from each person and no actual recipe or measurements. For the most part, cooking methods are passed down through families, and the act of cooking is often done by feel, not from a printed recipe or accurate measuring. Family recipes are taught in the kitchen and passed on through generations by telling and showing how dishes are made.

The basics rarely change in Southern cooking, which is what keeps the traditions and the identity of Southern cooking rich and recognizable. Greens are cooked low and slow, fried chicken is made in a cast-iron skillet, biscuits are patted out and cut by hand. While the tradition and know-how that is passed down stays fairly consistent, there is a good amount of experimentation happening recently as more ingredients become available in both restaurants and in the home kitchen.

Traditional Southern Dishes

During the 1800s, when many families lived on large plantations, guests would often come to visit for days or weeks at a time. Hospitality is very important to Southerners, and hosts prepare huge meals for their guests. This also explains why many Southern dishes make large amounts of food or are meant to feed people for a few days. Family, friends, and visitors are a large part of the Southern way of life, and always being willing to share a meal with people you love and new friends is one way that the South stands out.

The traditional Southern meal that most commonly comes to mind is pan-fried chicken, peas, greens (such as collard greens or mustard greens), mashed potatoes, cornbread, sweet tea, and some kind of pie for dessert—sweet potato, chess, shoofly, pecan, and peach are some of the most common—or a fruit cobbler. Many soups also originated in the American South and are staples of Southern cuisine.

FACT

The main meal of the day in the South used to be at midday and was called dinner, while the smaller evening meal was referred to as supper. More recently, the main meal has moved to the evening—as in most places—though some Southerners still call it dinner.

Some other foods and beverages with ties to the South are grits, country ham (or salt ham), hush puppies, succotash, mint juleps, chicken-fried steak, buttermilk biscuits (served with butter, jelly, fruit preserves, honey, gravy, or sorghum molasses, also called sorghum syrup), pimiento cheese, boiled or baked sweet potatoes, pit barbecue, fried catfish, fried green tomatoes, bread pudding, okra (fried, steamed, stewed, sautéed, or pickled), butter beans, pinto beans, and black-eyed peas.

Fried chicken is one of the region's best-known dishes. Thanks to the varied influences in Southern cuisine, you can thank the Scots for this dish, as they had a tradition of deep-frying chicken in fat, unlike the English who typically baked or boiled their chicken. Pork is also an integral part of the cuisine. Virginia ham is one example. A traditional get-together with a whole-hog barbecue is known in Virginia and the Carolinas as a pig pickin'. Green beans are almost always flavored with bacon or salt pork, biscuits served with ham often serve as breakfast, and ham with red-eye gravy or country gravy is a common breakfast or dinner dish for many families.

Today, a breakfast of buttermilk biscuits and sausage gravy is common throughout the region. Pork drippings from frying sausage, bacon, and other types of pan-fried pork are typically collected and used for making gravy and in greasing cast-iron cookware. Chicken and dumplings and fried chicken remain some of the most loved and popular dishes. Cornbread, hominy grits, cornbread pudding, and hominy stew are common foods, as corn is the primary grain grown in the Appalachian hills and mountains.

FACT

Fresh Georgia peaches are available only sixteen weeks each year, from mid-May to August.

The most popular fruits in this region are apples, pears, and berries. Sweetened fried apples are not only used in pies but are commonly a sweet side dish for supper or dinner. Wild morel mushrooms and ramps (similar to green onions and leeks) are foraged wherever possible. Along with sausage gravy, tomato gravy, a typical roux thinned with tomatoes, is very popular as well. A variety of wild fruits like pawpaws, wild blackberries, and persimmons are also commonly available in Appalachia.

While many dishes center around meat, other traditional Southern meals consist of only vegetables with no meat at all, although meat or meat products might be used in the cooking process. Beans and greens, which is usually either white or brown beans alongside dark, leafy greens, has always been popular in most parts of the South. Turnip greens are generally cooked with diced turnips and a piece of fatback. Another Southern staple is beans and cornbread—pinto beans, stewed with ham or bacon, and cornbread. This is sometimes served with greens and buttermilk.

Influences and Regional Differences

Each state, and sometimes even specific cities, has its own dishes and foods that represent that area, the traditions, and the influences that have helped develop Southern cuisine. The Southern cuisine region historically includes states south of the Mason-Dixon Line, which divides Pennsylvania from Maryland and Maryland from Delaware, as well as states south of the Ohio River.

The most notable influences come from English, Scottish, Irish, German, French, Native American, and African American cuisines. In recent history, some elements of Southern cuisine have spread farther north, affecting the development of other types of American cuisine as well.

Many items such as squash, tomatoes, corn and corn products (including grits), as well as the practice of pit barbecuing, come from southeastern American Indian tribes including the Caddo, Choctaw, and Seminole. Sugar, flour, milk, eggs, and baking or dairy products such as breads and cheeses are more associated with the European influence in the area. Black-eyed peas, okra, sorghum, and melons, as well as most spices, can be traced back to an African origin.

ESSENTIAL

Along with being famous for its spicy seafood cuisine, New Orleans has come to be known as the birthplace of jazz, which is still incredibly popular in the city today.

Thanks to the large area of the country that Southern cuisine covers, the dishes and characteristics vary widely by region:

- In southern Louisiana, there is both Cajun and Creole cuisine. Louisiana is a large supplier of hot sauces and is the largest supplier of crawfish in the country.
- Historically, rice was an important crop in the coastal areas of South Carolina, leading to local specialties like hoppin' John (a mixture of rice and black-eyed peas flavored with salt pork) and Charleston red rice. It is also one of the more prominent foods in Arkansas.
- Barbecue has many regional variations in the South. Barbecue sauce, if used, also varies by location. You may have tried different varieties, such as the typically vinegar-based North Carolina barbecue or the thicker, tomato-based sauces often found in Tennessee, Kentucky, and Georgia.

- Virginia produces Smithfield ham, one of the best-known foods from the state besides peanuts.
- Oklahoma has a reputation for many grain- and bean-based dishes, such as cornbread and beans or biscuits and gravy.
- Mississippi specializes in farm-raised catfish, found in fish houses throughout the state.
- Arkansas is the top rice-producing state in the nation, and is also noted for catfish and pork barbecue.
- Tennessee is known for its country ham, and Memphis, Tennessee, is the mecca of famous barbecue restaurants, as well a major barbecue competition held in May each year.
- Maryland is often recognized for its blue and soft-shell crabs.
- Florida is home of the Key lime pie and orange juice. Georgia is known for its peaches, pecans, peanuts, and Vidalia onions.
- The Appalachian areas have ramps (onions and their relatives—their arrivals each year are celebrated with festivals) and wild berries.
- Kentucky is famous for burgoo, a spicy stew typically served with cornbread.
- Texas is known for its barbecue and chili as well as their own variation of Mexican called Tex-Mex.
- Generally speaking, many parts of the upper South specialize more in pork, sorghum, and whiskey, while the low-country coastal areas are known for seafood (shrimp and crabs), rice, and grits.
- The western parts of the South like Texas and Oklahoma are more beef-focused and the eastern parts lean more toward pork.

Based on the geography, these distinctions make sense, as it shows how Southern cooks are putting their local ingredients to use.

Stocking Your Pantry

Southern cooking is often characterized by flavorful, hearty meals that are also easy to prepare. While some things like braised greens may take some time to cook, the actual process is very easy. Having a well-stocked kitchen will make planning and preparing a meal even easier. Here are some items you should try to keep on hand so you are ready to make a variety of Southern dishes.

Bacon Fat

Saving bacon fat is one practice that's fallen by the wayside recently in Southern cooking. But saving the grease left from cooking a batch of bacon isn't just frugal; it's a great way to add flavor to future dishes—and it makes cleaning the pan easier.

Instead of pouring the hot, melted fat into a container, it's easier (and safer) to let the pan sit on the stove and cool down until the fat solidifies into a softened-butter consistency. This makes it easy to scoop or scrape that fat out of the pan and into a jar to use later.

Wondering how you use leftover bacon fat? There really isn't anything you can't do with bacon fat, but some of the most popular ways of using it are:

- Using it in place of butter or oil when scrambling eggs or frying potatoes.
- Adding pork flavor to caramelized onions (using it in place of oil or butter).
- Using it as the fat for sautéing vegetables that will go into a frittata, quiche, or soup.
- Rubbing it on chicken breasts before roasting.
- Tossing it with herbs and some vinegar for a warm salad dressing.

Basically, bacon fat can be used anywhere you would normally use butter or another oil. It lends fantastic flavor to dishes, giving them a depth that you wouldn't have otherwise. It's also a great use of something you might normally throw away.

FACT

According to Bacontoday.com, the average American easts 17.9 pounds of bacon per year.

Buttermilk

Originally, buttermilk was the liquid left behind after churning butter from cream. This buttermilk is known as traditional buttermilk, as it was the original way buttermilk was made. Buttermilk also refers to a range of fermented milk drinks, common in warm climates (the Middle East, Turkey, Afghanistan, Pakistan, India, Sri Lanka, and the southern United States) where unrefrigerated fresh milk sours quickly, as well as in colder climates, such as Scandinavia, Finland, the Netherlands, Germany, Poland, Slovakia, and the Czech Republic. This fermented drink, known as cultured buttermilk, is made from cow's milk and has a characteristically sour taste caused by the bacteria found in lactic acid.

Buttermilk is often used as a refreshing drink (that is also known to help upset stomachs), and it can also be used in cooking. If you have buttermilk in the fridge, you have one of the best-kept secrets of Southern cooking at your fingertips. Buttermilk can be used in cornbread, pancakes, and biscuits. It also serves as a fantastic marinade for chicken, helping break down the protein (thanks to the acidity) and offering a tang of flavor that you can't get from other ingredients.

Buttermilk also lasts longer in the refrigerator than other dairy products, giving you more chances to cook with it and helping to make sure it doesn't go to waste.

Pork

In the South, where the environment is prime for raising hogs, pork is the supreme provider of meat. Cured pork products like ham and bacon are ubiquitous. Pork fat (lard) greases the cornbread dish, bacon fat adds "that certain something" to the fried chicken, and fatback and ham hocks are essential for greens, red beans and rice, and other typical Southern dishes.

Every part of the pig is used; nothing is wasted. From cracklings (pork skin) to pork belly (basically a large slab of bacon) to pickled pigs' feet, Southern cooks are extremely resourceful and have ways of using every bit of the pigs they raise. Some meals focus solely on the meat—ham, for example—while other meals stretch what they have, using just bits of pork to add flavor to a large pot of soup or greens or rice.

Greens

Greens are an inexpensive food and one that is also easy to grow in the garden or forage from your surroundings. Cooking greens with a bit of fat and protein makes for a hearty, balanced meal and is a great way to use up tidbits of protein you have in the refrigerator.

Collard greens are one of the oldest members of the cabbage family and are closely related to kale. They're available all year long, but their peak season is usually January through April. With the surge in greenhouses around the country, greens can be grown year-round if you can create the right environment.

Greens have been eaten for centuries, even dating back to prehistoric times. The ancient Greeks grew kale and collards, and the Romans grew several kinds of collards as well. It's commonly thought that the Romans or the Celts introduced the versatile green to Britain and France in the fourth century B.C.

When African slaves arrived in the Southern colonies, they brought the now Southern style of cooking collard greens. Like many other dishes that originated at the time, their way of cooking greens came out of a need to provide hearty, filling food for their families and satisfy their hunger with the scraps they had available. They would often have ham hocks, pigs' feet, and tops of greens, and they could easily turn these leftovers into a meal, which has now become known as the famous Southern greens.

In the South, there are some superstitious traditions associated with collard greens. On New Year's Day each year, those who believe in the tradition, or just like to play along, will serve up collard greens with black-eyed peas to ensure a year of good luck and good finances. Others might hang a fresh collard leaf over their door to keep bad spirits away, and a fresh leaf on the forehead is supposed to help cure a headache.

Even if the cooking style or ingredients changed, they kept at least one tradition from Africa—drinking the juice, called pot likker (or potlikker), left over from cooking the greens. Collard liquor, also known as pot liquor, is the leftover liquid from boiling vegetables, often greens; it is sometimes made with meat, especially pork, to add flavor. Pot liquor contains essential vitamins and minerals including iron and vitamin C. One of the most prevalent vitamins in greens, and in pot likker, is vitamin K, which aids in blood clotting.

Collard greens are quite unique to the southeastern region of the United States and have become a time-honored tradition in Southern kitchens. They have held an important place on the table for over a century now. A large amount of greens served in the home is commonly called a mess o' greens, but the exact amount varies from family to family. The traditional way to cook them is to boil or simmer them slowly with salt pork or ham hock to soften up the leaves and the bitter taste. The most common side to serve with collard greens is baked or fried cornbread.

Cast-Iron Cookware

One of the most commonly recognized items in a Southern kitchen is cast-iron cookware, specifically a cast-iron skillet or Dutch oven. Cast-iron pots and pans have been used for cooking for hundreds of years and were treasured for their durability and their ability to retain heat, which improved the quality of cooking meals. Before the introduction of the kitchen stove in the middle of the nineteenth century, meals were cooked in the hearth or fireplace, and cooking pots and pans were designed for this use. This meant that all cookware had to be designed to be suspended on, or in, a fireplace. Cast-iron pots were made with handles to allow them to be hung over the fire, or with legs so that they could stand up in the fireplace. Cooking pots and pans with legless, flat bottoms were designed when cooking stoves became popular; this period of the late nineteenth century introduced the first flat-bottom cast-iron skillet.

Cast-iron cookware was especially popular among homemakers and housekeepers during the first half of the twentieth century. The twentieth century also saw the introduction and popularization of enamel-coated cast-iron cookware.

Cast iron fell out of favor in the 1960s and 1970s, as Teflon-coated aluminum nonstick cookware was introduced and quickly became the cookware of choice in many kitchens. Today, a large selection of cookware can be purchased from kitchen suppliers, of which cast iron comprises only a small fraction. However, the durability and reliability of cast iron as a cooking tool has ensured its survival, and cast-iron cookware is still recommended by most cooks and chefs as an essential part of any kitchen.

What's the most important tool in the Southern kitchen?
Most Southern kitchens aren't outfitted with the latest kitchen gadgets. In fact, Southern kitchens typically work best when the tools you have can multitask rather than having a drawer full of items that can only do one thing. One tip that every cook should heed is to invest in some good knives—ones that will easily slice through a tomato, for instance, and ones that you can sharpen to keep them working well.

The most important part of keeping a cast-iron pan working for you for decades is to season it, and season it well. A seasoned pan has a stick-resistant coating created by oils and fats. Seasoning is the process where a layer of animal fat or vegetable oil is applied and cooked onto cast-iron cookware. New cookware should be washed in hot water with a strong detergent to remove any casting oils from the cookware's surface. A light coat of oil is applied and the cookware is placed upside down on a layer of newspaper to drain for 1 hour. The pan is then placed on the middle rack of the oven, set to 350°F, and baked for 30 minutes.

Some cookware now comes preseasoned from the factory. The seasoning layer protects the cookware from rusting, provides a nonstick surface for cooking, and prevents food from interacting with the iron of the pan. However, frequent use of acidic foods such as tomato sauce will remove the seasoning and the cookware will need to be reseasoned frequently. Even if your pan is seasoned well or if you have a preseasoned pan, reseasoning your cast-iron cookware each year is a great way to ensure you keep a nonstick surface and protect the surface from rust.

Canning

Home canning is a strong tradition in the South, and its popularity has also grown across the country over the past decade or so. Dried pinto beans are a major staple food during the winter months, used to make the ubiquitous ham-flavored bean soup usually called soup beans. Home-canned green beans is one of the most popular foods you'll find in Southern kitchens. Pears and apples are used to make pear butter and apple butter to slather on biscuits throughout the year. Bread and butter pickles, pickled beets, and chow-chow (commonly called "chow") and other relishes are popular. Tomatoes are canned in large numbers—crushed, whole, and in sauce—as well as sliced green tomatoes so fried green tomatoes can be made in the middle of winter.

Canning is a method of preserving food in which the food contents are processed and sealed in an airtight container. Canning provides a shelf life typically ranging from 1–5 years, although, under the right circumstances, it can be much longer.

Demand for canned food greatly increased during wars. Urban populations demanded ever-increasing quantities of cheap, varied, quality food that they could keep at home without having to go shopping daily, and this also offered options for food when everything fresh was being rationed. In response to the demands, companies like Nestlé and Heinz provided canned food for sale to the working class. The late nineteenth century saw a range of canned food available to urban populations greatly increase, as canners competed with one another using novel foodstuffs, highly decorated printed labels, and lower prices.

More than just a time-honored tradition and family activity, canning is a way of processing food to extend its shelf life. The idea is to make food available and edible long after the processing time. The heating process during canning has been studied and proven to preserve not only the foods themselves but also the vitamins and minerals present in the foods. Canned foods are a great way to preserve the harvest for the leaner times of the year.

A Waste-Free Culture

The American Civil War, from 1861 to 1865, had a major impact on the South and its food. Many plantations and farms were destroyed during this time. In order to survive, Southerners ate whatever they could grow or find, and nothing ever went to waste. When the economy began to recover, many people in the country were not allowed to share in the newfound wealth, so they continued to eat the simple foods that were available during the war. This simple way of cooking and eating, while using every bit of food you had available, is one of the biggest trademarks of Southern cooking. Nothing goes to waste; nothing is thrown away. If there's one thing Southern cooks know, it's how to stretch a meal and fill a table with delicious dishes, even when starting with what most people would consider meager ingredients.

CHAPTER 2

Appetizers and Breads

Spicy Cheese Straws

A Southern favorite, these cheese straws are spicy and delicious. Roll them into straw shapes or cut into narrow strips and gently turn to make cheese twists.

INGREDIENTS | MAKES 5–6 DOZEN

1¾ cups all-purpose flour

⅛ teaspoon salt

½ teaspoon ground cayenne pepper

14 tablespoons butter, at room temperature

3 cups shredded sharp Cheddar cheese

1 teaspoon Worcestershire sauce

Kitchen Lifesaver

A food processor is one tool that no cook—and definitely no Southern cook!—should be without. Your food processor will save you time in many recipes, and it can come in especially handy for this recipe. Combine the ingredients in the bowl of a food processor fitted with a metal blade. Pulse in short bursts until the mixture is just blended and clumping together.

1. Preheat oven to 300°F.

2. In a large mixing bowl, combine flour, salt, and cayenne pepper. Using 2 knives or a pastry blender, cut butter, cheese, and Worcestershire sauce into flour mixture until thoroughly blended.

3. Working with a small amount of dough at a time, roll into a long tube shape about the width of a straw and cut into desired lengths. Or, roll out dough on a floured surface to a thickness of about ⅛"–¼". Cut into strips and gently twist.

4. Arrange straws or twists on ungreased baking sheets. Bake for 20–25 minutes or until straws are crisp and just lightly browned.

5. Remove straws and let cool.

Crab-Stuffed Mushrooms

This is a delicious appetizer to fix for a Derby Day party, New Year's Eve, the Super Bowl, or just about any occasion.

INGREDIENTS | MAKES 20

20 large mushrooms (about 1 pound)
6 tablespoons butter, divided
4 green onions, finely chopped
2 tablespoons minced red bell pepper
1 cup fresh bread crumbs, processed until fine
4 ounces crabmeat
½ teaspoon Creole seasoning or seasoned salt
Dash ground black pepper
2 tablespoons freshly grated Parmesan cheese

Time-Saving Tip

Don't throw away day-old bread or rolls—use them to make homemade bread crumbs! Chop up the bread into smaller chunks, then run them through your food processor. Season as you like, and then freeze crumbs in small bags. Just pull what you need out of the freezer when you're ready to use it in a recipe. Some seasonings you might add to homemade bread crumbs include Parmesan cheese, dried parsley flakes, oregano and basil, garlic powder, onion powder, paprika, seasoned salt, or herb seasoning.

1. Preheat oven to 350°F.

2. Clean mushrooms. Trim ends, then twist to separate them from the caps. Chop stems finely and set aside.

3. Melt 2 tablespoons butter; brush over mushroom caps. Lightly butter a shallow 8" or 9" square baking dish or spray with a nonstick cooking spray.

4. Melt remaining 4 tablespoons butter in a medium skillet. Add chopped mushroom stems, green onions, and bell pepper. Sauté until vegetables are tender, about 6–8 minutes.

5. In a medium bowl, combine vegetables with bread crumbs, crabmeat, Creole seasoning, and ground black pepper. Fill mushroom caps, mounding slightly. Arrange in a single layer in the prepared baking dish. Sprinkle each mushroom with a little Parmesan cheese.

6. Bake until mushrooms are tender and stuffing is hot, about 15–20 minutes.

Fried Green Tomato Bruschetta

This recipe combines the best of Italy with the best of the Deep South.

INGREDIENTS | MAKES 12

1 cup olive oil

2 large eggs

1 cup all-purpose flour

1 cup dry fine bread crumbs,

4 medium green tomatoes, cut into ½" slices

1 tablespoon balsamic vinegar

¼ cup roughly chopped fresh basil

12 pimiento-stuffed green olives, halved

1 loaf crusty country bread, cut into 6 slices

¼ cup extra-virgin olive oil

1. Heat olive oil in a large skillet over medium-low heat.

2. Lightly beat eggs in a shallow bowl. Place flour in a shallow bowl and bread crumbs in another shallow bowl. Dredge tomato slices in flour, dip them in eggs, and then in bread crumbs, shaking off excess after each dip. Fry until golden and mostly tender, about 5 minutes per side. Place the still-hot tomatoes flat on a cutting board and dice them into ½" pieces.

3. In a large mixing bowl, gently toss diced tomatoes with vinegar, basil, and olives. Set aside.

4. Preheat oven to 400°F.

5. Brush bread slices with extra-virgin olive oil and place on a baking sheet. Toast in oven until lightly browned. Remove and top each slice with tomato mixture. Cut each in half. Serve warm or at room temperature.

Benedictine Spread or Dip

This light-green cucumber spread is a Kentucky tradition, named for Jennie Benedict, who ran a tearoom in Louisville, Kentucky, in the early 1900s. To make sandwiches, spread bread slices with mayonnaise, then a layer of Benedictine. To use as a dip for vegetables, stir in a little heavy cream or sour cream to thin slightly.

INGREDIENTS | MAKES ABOUT 1½ CUPS

1 large cucumber, peeled
½ small onion, peeled
8 ounces cream cheese, softened
1 tablespoon mayonnaise
Dash salt
Green food coloring (optional)

1. Grate cucumber and onion into a colander; drain well, pressing to remove all excess moisture.

2. Blend cream cheese and mayonnaise with a mixer or food processor; add salt and grated cucumber and onion. If desired, stir in a few drops of green food coloring.

Spicy Cheese Dip

This easy slow-cooker cheese dip is always a hit, and it's very flexible. Add a little diced hot pepper or ground cayenne to give it some extra heat.

INGREDIENTS | MAKES 7–8 CUPS

2 pounds pasteurized processed cheese food, cut into cubes
8 ounces cream cheese, cut into cubes
1 (4-ounce) can chopped mild green chili peppers
1 (1.25-ounce) envelope taco seasoning mix
16 ounces chunky salsa or canned Mexican-style diced tomatoes

1. Combine all ingredients in a 3- to 5-quart slow cooker.

2. Cover and cook on low setting, stirring occasionally, until cheese is melted and mixture is hot.

3. Serve warm from the slow cooker or a chafing dish. Stir occasionally to keep smooth.

Chili-Cheese Dip

You can substitute 3¾ cups homemade chili for the canned chili. For a thicker dip to serve with tortilla chips or celery sticks, stir in a pound of cooked and drained ground beef. This dip also makes a delicious topper for baked potatoes.

INGREDIENTS | SERVES 12

1 (15-ounce) can chili
1 pound Velveeta cheese, cut into cubes

Add the chili and cheese to a 4- to 6-quart slow cooker. Cover and cook on low for 2–3 hours or until the cheese is melted, stirring every 30 minutes. To serve, reduce the heat setting of the slow cooker to warm.

Deviled Eggs with Mustard

Honestly, it seems everyone loves deviled eggs. These have just a touch of mustard, and you can top them with an olive slice, a piece of pickle, or a sprinkle of paprika to give them a little color.

INGREDIENTS | SERVES 12

12 large hard-cooked eggs
2–3 tablespoons mayonnaise (enough to moisten yolks)
1 teaspoon prepared yellow mustard
1 scant teaspoon salt
3–4 tablespoons sweet pickle relish
Paprika
Olive slices or chopped pickles

1. Cut hard-cooked eggs in half lengthwise. Remove and mash yolks in a medium bowl; combine with mayonnaise, mustard, salt, and sweet pickle relish.

2. Refill the centers of egg whites with yolk mixture.

3. Garnish stuffed eggs with paprika and olive slices or chopped pickle.

Creamy Crab Dip

This flavorful dip is wonderful with assorted crackers or chips.

INGREDIENTS | MAKES ABOUT 2 CUPS

6 ounces cream cheese, softened

1 cup sour cream

2 tablespoons chopped green onion

Dash ground cayenne pepper

½ teaspoon paprika

1 (1.5-ounce) envelope ranch-style dressing mix

8 ounces crabmeat

Salt and ground black pepper

1 tablespoon chopped fresh flat-leaf parsley

1. In a medium bowl, beat cream cheese with sour cream until well blended. Blend in green onion, cayenne, paprika, and dressing mix. Stir in crabmeat.

2. Taste and adjust seasonings with salt and pepper.

3. Sprinkle chopped parsley over dip. Chill until serving time.

Dried Beef and Cheese Dip

This delicious dip is a festive addition to a holiday party.

INGREDIENTS | SERVES 10

4½ ounces dried beef (2 small jars), minced

2 (8-ounce) packages cream cheese, softened

8 ounces sour cream

¼ cup chopped red bell pepper

¼ cup chopped green bell pepper

3 tablespoons grated or minced yellow onion

1 cup chopped pecans

1. Preheat oven to 300°F.

2. Combine minced beef with cream cheese and sour cream in a medium bowl, blending well. Stir in chopped red and green bell pepper and grated onion.

3. Spread mixture in a 1½-quart baking dish; sprinkle chopped pecans evenly over the top.

4. Bake for 25–30 minutes until thoroughly heated.

Tangy Glazed Sausage Bites

These tangy sausage bites are a great alternative to meatballs. They're perfect for a game party, New Year's Eve, or any other special occasion.

INGREDIENTS | MAKES 5–6 DOZEN

2 pounds bulk pork sausage
2 large eggs, slightly beaten
1 cup fine dry bread crumbs, plain
½ cup whole milk
1 teaspoon ground sage
½ teaspoon dried thyme, crumbled
1 cup water
⅔ cup ketchup
¼ cup light brown sugar, packed
2 tablespoons apple cider vinegar
2 tablespoons soy sauce

Easier Mixing

Using a stand mixer or food processor for meat mixtures such as the one in this recipe is quicker and more efficient than mixing with a spoon and much less messy than using your bare hands. Try using your mixer for the next meatloaf, burger mixture, or meatball recipe you fix. Keep in mind that overmixing can make meatloaf tough and rather compact, so mix just until ingredients are well combined.

1. In a large bowl, combine sausage, beaten eggs, bread crumbs, milk, sage, and thyme. With an electric mixer or food processor, beat until well blended.

2. With wet hands, shape mixture into balls about 1"–1¼" in diameter.

3. In a large skillet over medium-high heat, arrange a batch of sausage balls in a single layer; brown on all sides. This will take about 12–15 minutes for each batch. When all sausage bites are browned, pour off excess fat and return to the skillet, or transfer to a large, heavy saucepan or Dutch oven.

4. Combine remaining ingredients in a medium bowl; pour over sausage bites. Cover and simmer on medium for 15 minutes, stirring occasionally.

5. Serve hot from a slow cooker or chafing dish, with toothpicks for spearing sausage bites.

Cheddar Sausage Balls

This is a popular appetizer in the South, and it is delicious served with dips. If you don't have time to make a dip, try store-bought ranch dressing or sweet-and-sour sauce.

INGREDIENTS | MAKES 36

1 pound bulk pork sausage, mild or spicy

2 cups finely shredded sharp Cheddar cheese

3 cups biscuit baking mix

½ cup minced green onion

Sausage Ball Dips

Here's a quick and easy dip to make for these sausage balls: Combine 1 cup mayonnaise with about 2 teaspoons prepared yellow mustard, 1–2 teaspoons Dijon mustard, and about ¼ teaspoon dried dill. Taste and adjust seasonings before serving. Or you can make a curried mayonnaise dip with about ½ cup each of mayonnaise and pineapple preserves and a little curry powder to taste.

1. Preheat oven to 350°F.

2. Combine all ingredients in a large bowl; mix well by hand or with a heavy-duty electric mixer.

3. Shape mixture into 1" balls; arrange on a 12" × 18" jelly-roll pan or large baking sheet.

4. Bake for 12–15 minutes or until the bottoms are browned.

Jalapeño Poppers

*These peppers aren't the deep-fried versions you'll find at bars,
but they're just as gooey, cheesy, and tasty.*

INGREDIENTS | MAKES 20

10 medium jalapeño peppers

8 ounces cream cheese, at room temperature

½ cup goat cheese, at room temperature

2 tablespoons finely chopped fresh cilantro

2 medium cloves garlic, finely chopped

½ teaspoon salt

Pinch ground cayenne pepper

Ground black pepper

Juice of ½ medium lemon

1. Preheat oven to 450°F and position an oven rack in the middle. Grease a baking sheet.

2. Slice jalapeños lengthwise down the center. Remove seeds and ribs from inside peppers and discard.

3. Combine cream cheese, goat cheese, cilantro, garlic, salt, cayenne, black pepper to taste, and lemon juice in a medium bowl. Stir until all ingredients are smooth and thoroughly mixed.

4. Spoon cheese mixture into each of the jalapeño halves. Place filled peppers on the prepared baking sheet about 2" apart.

5. Bake until peppers are starting to char and filling is browned and bubbly, about 12–15 minutes. Remove from oven and let cool for 5 minutes before serving.

Barbecued Chicken Wings

These chicken wings are sure to please your guests. If you like a spicier flavor, add a little ground cayenne to the sauce.

INGREDIENTS | MAKES 48

24 chicken wings (about 1 pound)

2 tablespoons prepared yellow mustard

⅓ cup apple cider vinegar

1 cup ketchup

¾ cup light molasses

3 tablespoons vegetable oil

1 tablespoon Worcestershire sauce

½ teaspoon salt

¼ teaspoon ground black pepper

¼ teaspoon garlic powder

Save the Tips

Instead of discarding the tips of the wings, put them in a food storage bag, and then seal and freeze for up to 6 months. When you need to make homemade chicken broth, add the wing tips along with any other chicken pieces, vegetables, and seasonings, and then strain them out of the finished broth. Use the broth in soup or any other recipe calling for chicken broth.

1. Preheat broiler to 500°F. Line a broiler pan with foil; brush with some oil to keep wings from sticking.

2. Cut each chicken wing through the joints to make three pieces; discard tip portion.

3. In a medium saucepan, combine remaining ingredients; blend well and bring to a boil. Remove from heat.

4. Arrange wing pieces on the prepared pan. Reserve about ⅓ cup sauce in a small serving bowl; refrigerate until serving time. Use remaining sauce for basting.

5. Broil chicken wings about 6" from heat for 12 minutes, turning frequently. Brush wings with sauce; turn and brush the other side. Continue broiling and turning, basting occasionally, for about 10 minutes longer, removing smaller pieces earlier as needed to keep them from burning.

Louisiana Hot Wings

If you're serving these at an evening-long party, add a little water and stir the wings every hour or so; then they won't dry out.

INGREDIENTS | SERVES 8

1 small yellow onion, peeled and diced

1 medium jalapeño pepper, seeded and diced

1 cup Louisiana red pepper sauce

2 tablespoons Worcestershire sauce

2 tablespoons Cajun seasoning, divided

1 cup barbecue sauce

5 pounds thawed chicken wings, tips removed

1. Preheat a 4- to 6-quart slow cooker on high.

2. Add onion, jalapeño, red pepper sauce, Worcestershire sauce, Cajun seasoning, and barbecue sauce to slow cooker and stir well.

3. Add chicken wings and stir until all wings are covered.

4. Cover and cook on high for 4 hours. Uncover and turn heat to low while serving.

Spiced Pecans

If spicy-hot Cajun seasoning isn't to your liking, you can use sweet-hot barbecue seasoning blend, savory Italian seasoning blend, or another seasoning mix instead.

INGREDIENTS | SERVES 16

3 pounds pecan halves

2 tablespoons extra-virgin olive oil or melted butter

2 tablespoons Cajun seasoning

1. Add pecans, oil or butter, and Cajun seasoning to a 4- to 6-quart slow cooker. Stir to combine. Cover and cook on low for 1 hour. Taste for seasoning and add more Cajun seasoning if desired. Stir the mixture.

2. Cover and cook for 2 more hours, stirring mixture again after 1 hour. Store in an airtight container.

Southern Skillet Cornbread

Most Southern cooks make cornbread so often that they don't need a recipe. Although a cast-iron skillet isn't absolutely necessary for this recipe, it makes the best, crustiest cornbread. If you don't have a skillet, use a 9" square baking pan and heat in the oven with oil before filling with batter.

INGREDIENTS | SERVES 8

1 tablespoon vegetable oil
2½ cups white or yellow cornmeal
1 cup all-purpose flour
2 teaspoons salt
2 teaspoons baking powder
1 scant teaspoon baking soda
2 large eggs
1 cup whole milk
1 cup buttermilk
2 tablespoons butter, melted

1. Preheat oven to 375°F. Add 1 tablespoon vegetable oil to a 10" cast-iron skillet and place in the oven.

2. In a large bowl, combine cornmeal, flour, salt, baking powder, and baking soda.

3. In a small bowl, whisk eggs. Lightly whisk in milk, buttermilk, and melted butter.

4. Pour egg mixture into dry ingredients. Mix until dry ingredients are just moistened.

5. Using pot holders, carefully take the hot skillet from the preheated oven; swirl gently to coat sides with oil. Pour batter into hot oil. Return to oven and bake for 35 minutes or until lightly browned on top.

6. Remove and let cool slightly on a wire rack. Cut into wedges or squares.

Cheesy Corn Muffins

Cheesy corn muffins are the perfect accompaniment to a steamy bowl of chili. Spice them up with a can of diced green chilies, or a minced fresh jalapeño, if you dare.

INGREDIENTS | SERVES 12

2 cups all-purpose flour
1 tablespoon baking powder
1 teaspoon salt
2 cups cornmeal
1 cup butter
2 tablespoons light brown sugar
2 large eggs
1½ cups shredded Cheddar cheese
2 cups buttermilk

1. Preheat oven to 375°F. Coat a 12-cup muffin pan with nonstick cooking spray or line with paper muffin cups. Sift together flour, baking powder, and salt in a large bowl. Stir in cornmeal and set aside.

2. Beat together butter and brown sugar in a medium bowl until creamy. Add eggs 1 at a time, then stir in cheese. Add dry ingredients to butter mixture alternately with buttermilk.

3. Fill prepared muffin cups to the rim with batter. Bake until risen and golden brown, about 20 minutes. A pick inserted into the middle of a muffin should come out clean.

4. Cool muffins in pan for 15 minutes before removing them.

Savory Bacon Cheddar Muffins

Delicious, savory muffins are wonderful with fruit for breakfast, or you can serve them with chili, baked beans, or a hearty vegetable soup.

INGREDIENTS | MAKES 10–12

12 slices bacon

1¼ cups all-purpose flour

¼ cup white or yellow cornmeal

2½ teaspoons baking powder

½ teaspoon baking soda

3 green onions, thinly sliced

½ cup shredded sharp Cheddar cheese

1 large egg

1 cup whole milk

2 tablespoons melted butter

Quick Muffins

Nowadays, people seem to be much busier, and they need to do everything more quickly. Southern cooks like to take their time with their recipes, but they also appreciate a good shortcut. If you need to make this recipe in a hurry, substitute ¾ cup of purchased crumbled real bacon or use diced cooked smoked ham in place of the bacon.

1. Preheat oven to 375°F. Coat a 12-cup muffin pan with nonstick cooking spray.

2. Cook bacon in a large skillet over medium heat until crisp; drain well and crumble.

3. In a large bowl, combine bacon with flour, cornmeal, baking powder, baking soda, green onions, and cheese.

4. In a small bowl, whisk egg with milk and butter. Blend egg mixture into dry ingredients, mixing until dry ingredients are just moistened.

5. Fill prepared muffin cups about ¾ full. Bake for 25–30 minutes until a toothpick inserted in the center of a muffin comes out clean.

Perfect Buttermilk Biscuits

These delicious biscuits won't disappoint you. Be sure not to overmix, and use your hands to gently knead and pat the dough into a circle.

INGREDIENTS | MAKES 10–12

2 cups all-purpose flour, stirred before measuring

2½ teaspoons baking powder

¼ teaspoon baking soda

1 teaspoon salt

¼ cup lard or vegetable shortening, chilled

2 tablespoons butter, chilled

¾ cup buttermilk, or more as needed

Use Southern Flour for Lighter Biscuits

Southern flours are typically lower in protein and gluten than most all-purpose flours. If you can find a brand milled in the South, give it a try. For light and flaky biscuits, also remember to cut the fats in with care, leaving some small pea-sized pieces. Handle the biscuits as little as possible to get the dough to clump together, then lightly pat—do not roll—into a circle before cutting.

1. Preheat oven to 450°F. Adjust oven rack to center position.

2. In a large bowl, combine flour, baking powder, baking soda, and salt. Cut in chilled lard or shortening and butter until you have pieces the size of small peas. Make a well in the center of dry ingredients and pour in buttermilk. With a wooden spoon, gently blend dry ingredients into buttermilk just until mixture clumps together. If necessary, add a few more teaspoons of buttermilk.

3. Transfer dough to a lightly floured board and knead gently just 4 or 5 times. Pat out in a circle about 8" in diameter and ½" thick. Using a 2½" biscuit cutter, cut out and place on an ungreased baking sheet. Bake for about 10–12 minutes until tops are browned.

Big Daddy Biscuits

These biscuits rise high and flaky, like down-home puff pastry.

INGREDIENTS | MAKES 15–20

3 cups cake flour

4 teaspoons baking powder

1 tablespoon graulated sugar

½ teaspoon salt

1 cup cold butter

1 large egg

1 cup cold whole milk

1 cup heavy cream

Flakiness

The size of the butter bits is directly related to the flakiness of the biscuit. In the heat of the oven, the water inside the butter is turned into steam. The steam rises and pushes up the dough around it. This creates pockets of air in the finished product. Those pockets are what we call flakiness. The bigger the butter bits, the flakier the biscuit.

1. Line a baking sheet with parchment paper. In a large bowl, sift together cake flour, baking powder, sugar, and salt. Cut in butter until it is broken down into pea-sized pieces.

2. Whisk together egg and milk. Make a well in the center of flour mixture and pour in wet ingredients. Using a fork, blend until dough just comes together.

3. Turn onto a floured surface and fold dough over onto itself 6–8 times. (Be careful not to knead or overwork.) Pat to 1" thickness. Cut into circles using a floured 2½" round cutter. Place biscuits 2" apart on the prepared pan and set aside to rest for 10–15 minutes. Preheat oven to 425°F.

4. Brush cream generously onto biscuits, then bake for 15–20 minutes until golden brown. Turn pan halfway through baking to promote even browning.

Drop Biscuits

These free-form biscuits are crispy on the outside, light on the inside, and are quick and easy to make.

INGREDIENTS | MAKES 8–10

1¾ cups cake flour
2 teaspoons baking powder
½ teaspoon salt
6 tablespoons cold butter
1½ cups cold whole milk

1. Line a baking sheet with parchment paper. In a large bowl, sift together cake flour, baking powder, and salt. Cut in butter until it is broken down into pea-sized pieces.

2. Make a well in the center of flour mixture and pour in 1 cup milk. Using a fork, blend flour and milk until dough just comes together.

3. Drop biscuits by heaping spoonfuls (about ¼ cup) 2" apart on the prepared pan. Set aside to rest for 10–15 minutes. Preheat oven to 425°F.

4. Brush remaining milk generously onto biscuits, then bake for 15–20 minutes until golden brown. Turn pan halfway through baking to promote even browning.

Angel Biscuits

Yeast, along with baking powder, makes these a light and airy favorite.

INGREDIENTS | MAKES 24

1 (¼-ounce) envelope active dry yeast

¼ cup warm water (about 110°F)

5–5¼ cups all-purpose flour

¼ cup sugar

2 teaspoons baking powder

1 teaspoon baking soda

1 tablespoon salt

¾ cup shortening, chilled

¼ cup butter, chilled

2 cups buttermilk, at room temperature

½ cup melted butter

Flavored Butter

Flavored butters can make a great alternative to butter and preserves or jelly. Soften ½ cup butter to room temperature, then stir until smooth and creamy. Stir in 1 heaping teaspoon of fine-grated orange zest and about 4 teaspoons of fresh orange juice. Put the butter on a sheet of waxed paper or foil, roll up in the shape of a cylinder, and then chill until firm.

1. In a small bowl, dissolve yeast in warm water. Set aside.

2. In a large mixing bowl, combine flour, sugar, baking powder, baking soda, and salt; stir to blend. Cut in shortening and butter until mixture resembles coarse meal, with some small pea-sized pieces remaining. Stir in yeast mixture and buttermilk, blending well.

3. Turn out dough onto a floured surface; knead a few times with floured hands, adding a little more flour if needed. Pat into a circle about ½" thick. Cut out rounds with a 2½" biscuit cutter. Place biscuits on a lightly greased baking sheet. Put the scraps of dough together, pat out, cut, and repeat until all of the dough is used. Cover uncooked biscuits with a dish cloth and let rise in a draft-free place for about 30–45 minutes.

4. Preheat oven to 400°F.

5. Bake for about 15–20 minutes until tops are browned. Remove from oven and brush with melted butter while biscuits are still hot.

Virginia Ham Biscuits

Nothing accompanies a plate of scrambled eggs better than these hammy biscuits. Add a handful of cheese if you're feeling really decadent.

INGREDIENTS | MAKES 15–20

3 cups cake flour

½ teaspoon ground nutmeg

4 teaspoons baking powder

1 tablespoon light brown sugar

1 teaspoon salt

1 cup cold butter

1½ cups diced ham

1 large egg

1 cup cold whole milk

2 tablespoons Dijon mustard

1 cup heavy cream

1. Line a baking sheet with parchment paper. In a large bowl, sift together flour, nutmeg, baking powder, brown sugar, and salt. Cut in butter until it is broken down into pea-sized pieces, then add ham.

2. In a small bowl, whisk together egg and milk. Make a well in the center of flour mixture and pour in wet ingredients. Using a fork, blend until dough just comes together.

3. Turn out onto a floured surface and fold dough over onto itself 6–8 times. (Be careful not to knead or over-work.) Pat out to 1" thickness. Cut into 2½" circles using a floured round cutter. Place biscuits 2" apart on prepared pan and set aside to rest 10–15 minutes.

4. Preheat oven to 425°F. Mix together mustard and cream and brush generously onto biscuits.

5. Bake for 15–20 minutes until golden brown. Turn pan halfway through baking to promote even browning.

Ham and Corn Fritters

These fluffy fritters are a great way to use leftover ham. Serve these fritters with beans or a hearty vegetable soup.

INGREDIENTS | MAKES 12–15

Vegetable oil
2 large eggs
¾ cup whole milk
1 cup canned cream-style corn
2 cups all-purpose flour
¼ cup cornmeal
2 teaspoons baking powder
1 teaspoon salt
½ cup chopped green onion
¾ cup finely diced ham

1. Heat oil to 375°F in a deep fryer or deep, heavy skillet.

2. In a large bowl, lightly whisk eggs; stir in milk and cream-style corn. Stir in flour, cornmeal, baking powder, and salt, stirring just until moistened. Fold in green onion and ham.

3. Using 2 tablespoons, drop scant tablespoons of batter into hot oil; fry until golden brown, about 4 minutes. Check the first few to make sure centers are cooked thoroughly and adjust size if necessary.

Dumplings

Nothing will cure your ills faster than a raft of fluffy dumplings floating in pot of homemade chicken soup.

INGREDIENTS | SERVES 8

1 cup all-purpose flour
2 teaspoons baking powder
½ teaspoon salt
1 large egg
⅔ cup whole milk
1 quart simmering broth

1. In a large bowl, sift together flour, baking powder, and salt. In a small bowl, whisk together egg and milk.

2. Make a well in the center of flour mixture and pour in milk mixture. Blend together just until a dough is formed.

3. Drop dough by heaping tablespoonful into simmering broth. Cover and simmer for 10–15 minutes. Serve immediately.

Hush Puppies

These hush puppies are delicious with fried catfish! If you don't have Creole seasoning, use ½ teaspoon seasoned salt and ½ teaspoon seasoned pepper. If you have bacon drippings, replace part of the butter with 1–2 teaspoons of that.

INGREDIENTS | MAKES 24

Vegetable oil
2 cups cornmeal
1 cup all-purpose flour
1½ teaspoons baking powder
½ teaspoon baking soda
½ teaspoon salt
1 teaspoon Creole seasoning
2 large eggs, beaten
½ cup buttermilk
½ cup whole milk
2 tablespoons butter, melted
½ cup chopped green onion

1. Heat oil to 375°F in a deep fryer or a deep, heavy skillet.

2. In a large bowl, combine cornmeal, flour, baking powder, baking soda, salt, and Creole seasoning.

3. In a small bowl, lightly beat eggs with buttermilk, milk, and melted butter. Stir milk mixture into dry ingredients just until moistened. Fold in green onions.

4. Carefully drop by teaspoonfuls into hot oil; do not crowd. The hush puppies will puff up and come to the surface. Fry until golden brown and cooked through. Check the first few and adjust size if hush puppies are browning but still soft in the center.

Spoon Bread

Spoon bread is more closely related to soufflés than it is to bread. It is delightfully light and flavorful, and makes a terrific change of pace from the usual dinner roll.

INGREDIENTS | SERVES 6

1 cup cornmeal
1 teaspoon salt
2 cups water
1 large egg yolk
1¾ cups whole milk
1 tablespoon butter, melted
2 large egg whites

1. Preheat oven to 350°F. Coat a 9" × 5" loaf pan with nonstick cooking spray.

2. Combine cornmeal, salt, and water in a medium saucepan. Bring to a boil over high heat, stirring frequently. Reduce heat to low and cook, stirring continuously, for 3–5 minutes until very thick. Remove from heat.

3. In a small bowl whisk together yolk, milk, and melted butter, then stir into cooling cornmeal. Whip egg whites in a medium bowl until stiff and gently fold in.

4. Transfer to prepared pan and bake for 30 minutes until golden brown. Serve warm.

CHAPTER 3

Breakfast

Light and Fluffy Pancakes

These pancakes are made light and fluffy with beaten egg whites.
Add chopped pecans to the batter for an extra crunch.

INGREDIENTS | SERVES 4–6

2 cups all-purpose flour

2 tablespoons sugar

½ teaspoon salt

1 teaspoon baking powder

½ teaspoon baking soda

1 cup buttermilk

¾ cup whole milk

2 large eggs, separated

¼ cup melted butter

Vegetable oil

Tips for Fluffy Egg Whites

Always separate eggs carefully to ensure none of the yolk breaks into the white. Even a tiny speck of yolk will prevent beaten egg whites from attaining a good volume. Because plastic tends to retain a film of grease, never beat egg whites in plastic bowls; use unlined copper, glass, or stainless steel bowls for best results. All beaters and utensils should be absolutely clean and grease-free. And as with most foods, fresh is best!

1. In a large mixing bowl, combine flour, sugar, salt, baking powder, and baking soda. In a small bowl, whisk together buttermilk, milk, egg yolks, and melted butter. Blend wet ingredients into dry ingredients until just moistened.

2. Beat egg whites in a medium bowl until stiff peaks form. Fold into batter until well incorporated.

3. Heat a small amount of oil in a large skillet over medium heat. When oil is hot enough for a drop of water to sizzle and pop, scoop pancake batter onto the skillet in about ¼-cup portions, spreading slightly. When the edges begin to look a little dry and bubbles on top are popping (after about 2–3 minutes), turn over and cook the other side until browned (about 2 minutes longer).

Apple Cinnamon Waffles

The aroma of these wonderful cinnamon-scented waffles will summon everyone to the breakfast table. Use whatever apples you have on hand. Golden Delicious work well, but you could use Fuji or Granny Smith.

INGREDIENTS | SERVES 6

2 cups sifted all-purpose flour
1 tablespoon baking powder
¼ teaspoon ground cinnamon
1 tablespoon sugar
½ teaspoon salt
3 large eggs, separated
1½ cups whole milk
4 tablespoons melted butter
1½ cups chopped apple

Better Than Eggos!

Did you know you can make waffles in big batches and freeze for those busy mornings? Just cool the cooked waffles and seal in plastic freezer bags; freeze for up to 6 months. To reheat, bake on a baking sheet for about 5 minutes in a 325°F oven or heat in the toaster.

1. Preheat a waffle iron.

2. Sift flour before measuring. Sift again into a large mixing bowl with baking powder, cinnamon, sugar, and salt; set aside.

3. In a medium bowl, beat egg yolks; stir in milk and melted butter. Pour into dry ingredients and whisk until smooth and well blended. Stir in chopped apple.

4. In another medium bowl, beat egg whites until stiff peaks form. Gently fold whites into apple batter until blended.

5. Spoon batter into each section of the hot waffle iron. Cook until crispy and browned.

Pain Perdu (French Toast)

French bread, a little sugar, and vanilla make this baked pain perdu, a Louisiana version of French toast, extra special. Serve pain perdu with melted butter and your favorite syrup or honey, or lighten them up with a light drizzle of butter and a sprinkling of powdered sugar.

INGREDIENTS | SERVES 4

8 slices day-old French bread
2 large eggs, slightly beaten
2 tablespoons sugar
⅓ cup whole milk
¼ teaspoon vanilla extract
⅛ teaspoon ground cinnamon

1. Preheat oven to 400°F. Lightly butter a 12" × 18" jellyroll pan or baking sheet with sides.

2. Remove crusts from bread; set bread aside.

3. In a small bowl, beat eggs with sugar, milk, vanilla, and cinnamon. Pour mixture into a shallow baking dish or pie plate. Put a few bread slices in the dish and let soak for several seconds, turning once. Place soaked bread slices on the prepared baking sheet; repeat with remaining bread. Spoon any remaining egg mixture over bread.

4. Bake for 15–20 minutes, turning after the first 10 minutes to brown on both sides.

Disappearing Peach Muffins

*If you prefer another kind of fruit, diced fresh pears or nectarines
instead of peaches would both work well in this recipe.*

INGREDIENTS | MAKES 12

1½ cups diced ripe peaches

2 teaspoons lemon juice

1½ cups all-purpose flour

½ cup light brown sugar, packed

2 teaspoons baking powder

¼ teaspoon salt

1 teaspoon ground cinnamon

½ cup melted butter

¼ cup whole milk

1 large egg

½ cup finely chopped pecans or walnuts

1 tablespoon sugar mixed with ½ teaspoon ground cinnamon

Make Your Own Cinnamon Sugar

If you'd like to have cinnamon sugar on hand for sprinkling on muffins, French toast, cakes, and other goodies, combine ½ cup sugar with 1 tablespoon cinnamon and store in a small canning jar or cleaned spice shaker. You'll be amazed at how often you reach for that jar.

1. Preheat oven to 400°F. Line a 12-cup muffin pan with paper or foil liners, or grease and flour the muffin cups.

2. Toss diced peaches with lemon juice. Set aside.

3. Combine flour, brown sugar, baking powder, salt, and 1 teaspoon cinnamon in a large bowl. In a small bowl, whisk together butter, milk, and egg. Stir milk mixture into dry ingredients and blend until just moistened. Fold in peaches and nuts.

4. Spoon batter into muffin cups, filling each about ⅔–¾ full; sprinkle each muffin with a little of the cinnamon sugar.

5. Bake for 25–30 minutes or until a cake tester or toothpick inserted in the center of a muffin comes out clean. Cool for 3 minutes in the pan on a wire rack, then remove muffins to the rack to cool completely.

Buttermilk Streusel Coffee Cake

Most bakers include a version of this cake in their repertoire. It's a delicious and popular coffee cake.

INGREDIENTS | SERVES 12

½ cup butter, softened
1 cup plus 3 tablespoons sugar, divided
2 large eggs
1 cup whole buttermilk or sour cream
2 teaspoons vanilla extract
2 cups all-purpose flour
1 teaspoon baking soda
1 teaspoon baking powder
½ teaspoon salt
1½ teaspoons ground cinnamon
½ cup chopped pecans

1. Preheat oven to 350°F.

2. Combine butter and 1 cup sugar in a large mixing bowl; cream with an electric mixer until light. Add eggs 1 at a time, beating after each addition. Beat in buttermilk or sour cream and vanilla. Sift together flour, baking soda, baking powder, and salt; stir into creamed mixture.

3. In a small bowl, combine cinnamon, 3 tablespoons sugar, and chopped nuts; set aside.

4. Grease and flour a 10" tube pan. Pour half of the batter into the prepared pan. Sprinkle with half of the nut mixture. Spoon remaining batter over nut mixture and then sprinkle with remaining nut mixture.

5. Bake for 35–40 minutes. Cool in pan on a wire rack; carefully loosen and remove from pan.

Fabulous Peach Bread

Peach schnapps gives this bread an incredible burst of flavor, but flavorful peach nectar can be used as a nonalcoholic substitute. Serve this bread with plain or flavored butter for brunch, breakfast, or dessert.

INGREDIENTS | SERVES 8

3 cups diced fresh peaches

¼ cup peach schnapps or peach nectar

1 teaspoon vanilla extract

½ cup butter, softened

1 cup sugar

3 large eggs

2¾ cups all-purpose flour

1½ teaspoons baking powder

½ teaspoon baking soda

1 teaspoon salt

1½ teaspoons ground cinnamon

Quick Breads

Quick breads are usually leavened with baking powder and/or baking soda, along with heat and eggs. In addition to typical quick breads that are baked in loaf pans, pancakes, muffins, and fried dough or fritters also fall into this category.

1. Preheat oven to 350°F. Grease and flour a 9" × 5" loaf pan.

2. In a medium saucepan, combine peaches with peach schnapps or peach nectar; simmer for 5 minutes or until peaches are tender. Remove from heat and stir in vanilla; set aside.

3. In a large mixing bowl with an electric mixer, cream together butter and sugar. Add eggs 1 at a time, beating after each addition.

4. In another large bowl, combine flour, baking powder, baking soda, salt, and cinnamon. With a wooden spoon, stir dry ingredients into creamed mixture, alternating with peach mixture. Mix well.

5. Spread batter into the prepared pan. Bake for 55–65 minutes or until a wooden toothpick inserted near the center comes out clean. Cool in pan on wire rack for 10 minutes. Remove from pan and cool completely.

Honey Pecan Rolls

The rich, sticky topping of these nutty rolls makes them irresistible.

INGREDIENTS | MAKES 12

1 cup light brown sugar, packed
½ cup honey, divided
1 cup butter, softened
¼ cup whole milk
2 tablespoons all-purpose flour
4 cups chopped pecans, divided
1½ cups water
1 (¼-ounce) envelope active dry yeast
3 large eggs
¼ cup canola oil
1 teaspoon salt
4–5 cups bread flour

1. Generously coat 2 muffin tins with nonstick cooking spray.

2. In a medium bowl, mix brown sugar, 2 tablespoons honey, butter, milk, all-purpose flour, and 2 cups pecans. Divide mixture evenly among muffin cups.

3. In another large bowl, combine water, remaining honey, and yeast. Stir to dissolve and let stand until foamy, about 10 minutes.

4. Add eggs, oil, salt, and enough bread flour to create a firm dough. Turn onto a floured surface and knead 8–10 minutes. Add flour only to reduce stickiness. Return dough to the bowl, dust the top lightly with flour, and cover with plastic wrap. Let rise at room temperature until doubled in volume, about 2–3 hours. Punch down dough, fold in half, and let rise again until doubled, about 45 minutes.

5. Turn out risen dough onto a floured surface and shape into a rope about 3" thick. Slice 2" pieces off the rope, then roll each into a tight ball. Place balls into the prepared muffin tins, dust with flour, cover loosely with plastic wrap, and proof for 30 minutes.

6. Preheat oven to 375°F.

7. Bake buns for 15–20 minutes until golden brown and bubbly. Remove from oven and cool for 10 minutes; while still warm, carefully invert onto a serving platter or tray. Cool before serving.

Beignets

These are very close in texture and flavor to the wonderful beignets found in the New Orleans French Market District. Sprinkle hot beignets heavily with powdered sugar and serve with coffee.

INGREDIENTS | MAKES ABOUT 4 DOZEN

1 (¼-ounce) envelope active dry yeast
1½ cups warm water (105°F–110°F)
½ cup granulated sugar
1 teaspoon salt
2 large eggs, beaten
1 cup evaporated milk
7 cups all-purpose flour
¼ cup shortening, at room temperature
Vegetable oil
Powdered sugar

1. In a large bowl, sprinkle yeast over water. Stir and let stand for 5 minutes. Add granulated sugar, salt, eggs, and evaporated milk. Whisk to blend well. Add 4 cups flour and beat until smooth. Beat in shortening, then gradually blend in remaining flour until a soft dough has formed. Cover and refrigerate for at least 4 hours.

2. Heat oil to 360°F in a deep fryer.

3. Roll out dough on a well-floured surface to about ⅛" thickness. Cut into 2½" squares.

4. Fry in hot oil a few at a time until golden brown on both sides, turning a few times. Drain on paper towels, then sprinkle generously with powdered sugar.

Banana Fritters

Are your bananas getting a little overripe? Try making tasty banana fritters instead of banana bread. Just before serving, sprinkle these fritters with a little cinnamon sugar or powdered sugar, and serve with vanilla sauce or maple syrup.

INGREDIENTS | MAKES 12

1⅔ cups all-purpose flour
2 teaspoons baking powder
2 tablespoons powdered sugar
¼ teaspoon salt
⅔ cup whole milk
1 large egg
3 medium ripe bananas, peeled and mashed
Vegetable oil

1. Sift flour, baking powder, powdered sugar, and salt into a large mixing bowl; set aside.

2. In a small bowl, combine milk and egg. Whisk to blend well. Add milk mixture to dry ingredients. Fold in mashed bananas. The batter should mound up in a spoon. If too thick, add a small amount of milk, or add flour if too thin.

3. Heat oil to 375°F in a deep fryer or deep, heavy skillet.

4. Drop batter by tablespoonfuls into hot oil, cooking about 4–6 at a time. As the fritters brown on the bottom, turn to brown on the other side. With a slotted spoon, move fritters to paper towels to drain. Keep warm.

Mississippi Breakfast Bake

This all-in-one breakfast casserole is such a snap to make, and you can prepare it the night before. Just refrigerate overnight and pop it into the oven when you get up in the morning. It's a great breakfast for a holiday or busy weekends.

INGREDIENTS | SERVES 4

1 pound bulk pork sausage

4 slices sandwich bread, crusts removed

3 green onions, sliced

1 small tomato, seeded and diced

1 cup shredded Cheddar cheese

¼ teaspoon salt plus more to taste, divided

⅛ teaspoon ground black pepper plus more to taste, divided

6 large eggs

1 cup whole milk

¼ teaspoon Creole seasoning or seasoned salt

Dash paprika

1. Preheat oven to 350°F. Grease a 2-quart baking dish with butter.

2. Brown sausage in a large skillet, breaking up chunks and stirring frequently. Drain well. Tear bread into pieces and spread over the bottom of the prepared baking dish. Evenly layer browned sausage over bread, then layer with green onion, tomato, and cheese. Sprinkle with salt and pepper to taste.

3. In a medium bowl, combine eggs, milk, Creole seasoning, ¼ teaspoon salt, ⅛ teaspoon pepper, and paprika. Whisk until well blended. Pour evenly over cheese layer.

4. Bake for 40–45 minutes or until set in the center. If refrigerated overnight, take the casserole out of the refrigerator about 30 minutes before baking.

Ham and Cheese Cornbread

The Cheddar cheese can be replaced with Swiss or pepper jack cheese. You can either use chopped cooked ham or thinly sliced boiled ham.

INGREDIENTS | SERVES 8

2 tablespoons butter or bacon grease

1 large yellow onion, peeled and thinly sliced

1 large clove garlic, minced

¼ teaspoon chili powder

½ cup chopped unsalted peanuts

Ground black pepper

1 (10-ounce) package cornbread mix

1 large egg, beaten

½ cup whole milk

½ pound cooked ham, diced

1 cup shredded Cheddar cheese

¼ cup sliced pimiento-stuffed green olives

1. Preheat oven to 350°F.

2. Melt butter or bacon grease in a 12" cast-iron or oven-proof skillet over medium heat. Add onion, garlic, and chili powder and sauté until onion slices are transparent, about 5 minutes. Remove from heat and stir in peanuts and black pepper to taste. Stir to mix well. Let cool slightly.

3. Once pan has cooled, add cornbread mix, egg, and milk to onion mixture. Spread evenly over the bottom of the pan and top with ham.

4. Bake for 15 minutes or until a toothpick inserted in the center comes out clean but cornbread is still moist. Top with cheese and return to oven; bake for 5 minutes or until cheese is melted. Garnish with olive slices before serving.

Bacon and Egg Casserole

This easy and convenient breakfast bake can be made without bacon for a delicious vegetarian version. Serve it with a warm fruit compote and sweet rolls or cinnamon buns.

INGREDIENTS | SERVES 4–6

10 slices bacon, diced

5 slices sandwich bread, lightly buttered

1 cup shredded Cheddar or Monterey jack cheese

6 large eggs, lightly beaten

2 cups whole milk

1 teaspoon salt

1 teaspoon dry mustard

½ teaspoon paprika

1. Cook bacon in a large skillet until crisp; transfer to paper towels to drain.

2. Preheat oven to 350°F. Lightly butter a 2-quart baking dish.

3. Tear buttered bread into small pieces. Layer torn bread, diced bacon, and cheese in the prepared baking dish (in that order). In a medium bowl, whisk together eggs, milk, salt, mustard, and paprika; pour over bread mixture.

4. Bake for 40–45 minutes or until casserole is puffy and a knife inserted near the center comes out clean.

Confetti Scrambled Eggs

This recipe is a flavorful version of everyday scrambled eggs. Allowing 2 eggs per person, you can easily adjust this recipe up or down.

INGREDIENTS | SERVES 4

8 large eggs

¼ cup whole milk or half-and-half

½ teaspoon salt

⅛ teaspoon ground black pepper

2 tablespoons butter

1 large tomato, seeded and diced

1 heaping tablespoon thinly sliced green onion, white part only

4 tablespoons finely chopped ham

1. In a medium bowl, whisk together eggs, milk, salt, and pepper until well blended.

2. Melt butter in a heavy skillet over medium-low heat. When butter is sizzling hot, pour in egg mixture.

3. Reduce heat slightly. As egg mixture begins to look set on the bottom and sides of the skillet, fold over toward the center with a spatula. Repeat until eggs are almost set, then fold in tomato, green onion, and ham. Heat through and serve hot.

Hard-Cooked Egg Casserole

Hard-cooked eggs are baked with a flavorful sherry cheese sauce.

INGREDIENTS | SERVES 4

8 large eggs

¼ cup butter

¼ cup all-purpose flour

¾ cup chicken broth

1¼ cups whole milk

½ cup shredded sharp Cheddar cheese

¼ cup freshly grated Parmesan cheese

2 tablespoons dry sherry

¼ teaspoon Worcestershire sauce

Dash Tabasco sauce

Salt and ground black pepper

½ cup soft buttered bread crumbs (see sidebar)

Chopped fresh flat-leaf parsley or green onions

Buttered Bread Crumbs

To make buttered bread crumbs for a casserole topping, tear or crumble day-old bread into small pieces, or whirl in the food processor, then drizzle the crumbs (about ½–1 cup) with a few tablespoons of melted butter. Like most toppings, you can personalize. A bread crumb topping on many casseroles would be delicious with a few tablespoons of Parmesan or other grated cheese, or you might toss the bread crumbs with a little sliced green onion, parsley, or other seasonings.

1. In a large saucepan, cover eggs with water. Cover and bring to a rolling boil over medium-high heat. Remove from heat and let stand, covered, for 20 minutes.

2. In a medium saucepan over low heat, melt butter. Stir flour into butter, cooking and stirring until well-blended and bubbly, about 1 minute. Gradually add chicken broth and milk, stirring constantly. Continue to cook, stirring constantly, until thickened. Stir in Cheddar and Parmesan cheeses, sherry, Worcestershire sauce, and Tabasco. Continue to stir until cheese is melted. Add salt and pepper to taste. Set sauce aside.

3. Preheat oven to 300°F. Drain eggs and peel; place in a greased 2-quart baking dish. Pour sauce over eggs and sprinkle with buttered bread crumbs.

4. Bake for 15–20 minutes or until heated through. Sprinkle with chopped parsley or green onion.

Fluffy Garden Omelet

This is a delicious 2-egg omelet, filled with a perfect combination of cheese, vegetables, and seasonings. You could easily add a little cooked sausage or sautéed mushrooms to the filling.

INGREDIENTS | SERVES 1

2 large eggs
2 tablespoons whole milk
¼ teaspoon salt
Few drops Worcestershire sauce
Dash Creole seasoning
Dash ground black pepper
2 teaspoons butter
2–3 tablespoons finely shredded Cheddar cheese
1 tablespoon chopped green onion
1 tablespoon diced tomato

How Fresh Are Your Eggs?

Try this trick to determine the freshness of eggs. Fill a deep bowl with cold water, enough to cover an egg, then place the egg in the water. If the egg lies on its side on the bottom, it's very fresh. If the egg stands up and bobs a bit on the bottom, it isn't quite as fresh. If it floats to the surface, you shouldn't use it. Fresh eggs are best in many recipes, but eggs that are about a week old are easier to peel when hard-cooked in the shell.

1. In a small bowl, beat eggs until frothy; whisk in milk, salt, Worcestershire sauce, Creole seasoning, and black pepper.

2. Heat a nonstick 8" skillet over medium heat; add butter and swirl around the pan to melt. When butter is hot, pour eggs into the pan and reduce heat to medium-low. Cook omelet slowly, gently lifting edges with a spatula several times to let uncooked egg run underneath. When omelet is almost cooked but still shiny on top, cover and cook for 1–2 minutes or until the surface is almost dry.

3. Sprinkle cheese, green onion, and tomato over the top of the omelet. Fold over and continue cooking to let cheese melt. Remove from heat and serve immediately.

Eggs Benedict with Tomato Slices

Garnish each plate of hot Eggs Benedict with a tomato slice.

INGREDIENTS | SERVES 6

2 large egg yolks

1 teaspoon lemon juice

½ cup butter

¼ cup boiling water

½ teaspoon plus a dash salt, divided

Dash ground cayenne pepper

3 medium tomatoes

6 slices Canadian bacon

6 large eggs

3 English muffins, split, toasted, and buttered

1. In the top of a double boiler, whisk egg yolks with lemon juice. Add 3 tablespoons butter. Place the pan over simmering water and cook, whisking constantly, until butter is melted and sauce begins to thicken. Add 3 more tablespoons butter. Stir until butter melts; then add remaining 2 tablespoons butter. Gradually whisk in boiling water. Continue cooking over simmering water, stirring constantly, until mixture thickens. Remove from heat and stir in dash of salt and cayenne. Set aside.

2. Heat broiler. Slice off tomato ends and cut in half. Place tomato halves and Canadian bacon on the rack of a broiler pan. Broil about 4" from heat for 3 minutes, or until meat begins to brown.

3. Meanwhile, pour about 2" of water into a large skillet along with ½ teaspoon salt. Bring water to a boil; reduce heat to maintain a light simmer. Carefully break 1 egg into a cup, then slip it into water. Repeat with remaining eggs. Continue to simmer, basting with water, for 3–5 minutes or until whites are thoroughly cooked and yolks are hot.

4. Top each English muffin half with a slice of Canadian bacon, a poached egg, and Hollandaise sauce. Serve with broiled tomatoes on the side.

Sausage Rolls

Cheese, sausage, thyme, and some puff pastry make delicious little rolls that are perfect for breakfast on the run. Bake them ahead of time, freeze them, then microwave each on high for 1–2 minutes until hot.

INGREDIENTS | SERVES 12

24 pork breakfast sausage links
1 (17.3-ounce) package frozen puff pastry, thawed
1 cup shredded Cheddar cheese
½ cup grated Parmesan cheese
1 teaspoon dried thyme, crumbled
1 large egg, beaten
¼ teaspoon salt

Puff Pastry

Puff pastry is found frozen near the pie shells and cakes in your supermarket. Follow the directions for thawing and using the pastry. Many brands require thawing overnight in the refrigerator so the butter that is encased in the layers of pastry doesn't melt. Keep a couple of boxes on hand to make easy snacks.

1. Preheat oven to 400°F. Line 2 baking sheets with parchment paper and set aside. In a heavy skillet, cook sausage links over medium heat until golden brown and cooked, about 5–7 minutes. Remove to paper towels to drain.

2. Unfold puff pastry sheet and place on a lightly floured surface. In a small bowl, combine cheeses and thyme and toss to combine. Sprinkle this mixture over puff pastry and gently press it into pastry; roll into a 12" × 18" rectangle. Cut into 3 (12" × 6") rectangles, then cut each rectangle in half to make 6 squares. Cut each square into 4 (3" × 3") squares. Place a cooked and drained sausage on the edge of each square and roll up to enclose sausage; press edges of pastry to seal.

3. In a small bowl, beat egg with salt and brush over sausage rolls. Place on prepared baking sheets.

4. Bake for 12–18 minutes until puffed and golden brown. Serve hot.

CHAPTER 4

Soups and Salads

Chicken Tortilla Soup

It's really easy to fry strips of fresh corn tortillas for this recipe, but you can use purchased tortilla chips in a pinch. This is a very flavorful soup that the whole family will enjoy.

INGREDIENTS | SERVES 4

4 cups chicken broth

Juice of 1 medium lime

1 (14.5-ounce) can diced tomatoes (undrained)

1 teaspoon finely chopped jalapeño pepper

1 (4-ounce) can diced mild green chilies

2 tablespoons chopped fresh cilantro

2 green onions, chopped

1 medium carrot, peeled and diced or thinly sliced

¾ cup fresh or frozen whole-kernel corn (thawed if frozen)

1½ cups diced cooked chicken

Salt and ground black pepper

Vegetable oil

3 (6") corn tortillas, cut into ½"-wide strips

½ cup shredded Monterey jack cheese or a Mexican cheese blend

1. In a large, heavy saucepan or Dutch oven, combine chicken broth, lime juice, tomatoes, jalapeño, green chilies, cilantro, green onions, carrot, and corn. Cook over medium heat for 40 minutes. Add diced chicken and cook for 5 minutes longer. Add salt and pepper to taste.

2. In a deep skillet or saucepan, heat about 1" of vegetable oil to 360°F. Add tortilla strips to hot oil in small batches, frying for just a few seconds until crispy. Drain on paper towels.

3. To serve, top each bowl of soup with a several crisp tortilla strips and a sprinkling of shredded cheese. Serve remaining tortilla strips on the side.

Chicken and Sausage Gumbo

This is a relatively easy version of gumbo, but it certainly won't disappoint.
Serve it with warm, crusty French bread and plenty of butter.

INGREDIENTS | SERVES 6

1 pound boneless, skinless chicken breasts

1 pound boneless, skinless chicken thighs

Salt and ground black pepper

1½ teaspoons Creole seasoning, divided

½ cup vegetable oil, divided

12 ounces smoked sausage, cut into ½" slices

½ cup all-purpose flour

1 cup chopped yellow onion

½ cup chopped green bell pepper

½ cup chopped red bell pepper

3 medium ribs celery, chopped

3 medium cloves garlic, minced

6 cups chicken broth

1 (14.5-ounce) can diced tomatoes in purée

½ teaspoon dried thyme, crumbled

1 cup sliced fresh or frozen okra (thawed if frozen)

4 green onions, thinly sliced

2 tablespoons chopped fresh flat-leaf parsley

3 cups hot cooked long-grain white rice

Dark or Light Roux?

In general, a roux is made to thicken a sauce or soup. As a roux becomes darker in color, its thickening properties diminish, but the roux becomes more flavorful. A roux for cream soup will generally be made quite light, since its purpose is to thicken the soup. A gumbo roux, meant to add complex flavor, is almost always cooked to a deep blond or dark reddish brown.

1. Trim chicken of fat and cut into small pieces; sprinkle with salt and pepper, then toss with ½ teaspoon Creole seasoning.

2. Heat 1 tablespoon oil in a heavy skillet over medium heat; add chicken. Cook, stirring, until browned. Transfer to a plate and set aside. Brown sausage; add to the plate with chicken.

3. In a large, heavy saucepan or Dutch oven, heat remaining oil; add flour. Cook, stirring constantly, until roux reaches a deep blond color, about the color of dark peanut butter. You can do this over medium to medium-high heat, but stir constantly and watch carefully. If it burns, you will have to start from scratch.

4. When roux has reached the color you want, add yellow onion, bell pepper, and celery and stir briskly. Continue to cook, stirring constantly, for about 3–4 minutes. Add garlic, chicken broth, tomatoes, thyme, chicken, and sausage. Season with salt and pepper to taste. Bring to a boil, then cook for about 1 hour, skimming fat off the top as needed.

5. Add okra and cook for about 20 minutes. Add green onions and parsley and cook for 10 minutes longer.

6. To serve, mound about ½ cup hot cooked rice in a bowl, then spoon gumbo around it.

Old-Fashioned Vegetable Beef Soup

Serve this classic soup with a tossed salad and crusty bread.

INGREDIENTS | SERVES 6

2 pounds meaty beef shanks

6 cups water

1 (10.5-ounce) can condensed beef broth

1 teaspoon salt

1 cup chopped yellow onion

3 medium ribs celery, chopped

¼ teaspoon ground black pepper

1 small bay leaf

1 (28-ounce) can diced tomatoes (undrained)

2 cups shredded green cabbage

2 medium carrots, peeled and thinly sliced

2 medium Yukon gold potatoes, peeled and diced

1 teaspoon sugar

2 teaspoons Worcestershire sauce

Beef Shanks

Beef shanks can be hard to find, so when you do, buy a few pounds extra to freeze. They make the most delicious soups and stews! If you can't get them from your local grocer, and you don't have a butcher shop in the area, use 1 pound of stew beef.

1. In a large stockpot, combine beef shanks, water, broth, salt, onion, celery, pepper, and bay leaf. Cover and simmer for 2–2½ hours until meat is tender.

2. Remove shanks and chop meat. Return meat to the pot. Add remaining ingredients and simmer for about 45 minutes or until vegetables are tender. Taste and adjust seasonings. Remove bay leaf.

Grilled Burger Soup

This soup makes a wonderful lunch, and it's hearty enough to serve as a main dish with crusty bread and a salad.

INGREDIENTS | SERVES 4–6

1 pound lean ground beef

4 cups beef broth

1 (14.5-ounce) can diced tomatoes (undrained)

2 medium carrots, peeled and diced

1 medium yellow onion, peeled and chopped

3 medium ribs celery, thinly sliced

1 large Yukon gold or white round potato, peeled and cubed

⅛ teaspoon ground black pepper

1 tablespoon chopped fresh flat-leaf parsley

½ cup frozen whole-kernel corn

¼ cup frozen peas

Salt

1. Form ground beef into burger patties. Grill burgers in a stovetop grill pan, on a charcoal or gas grill, or under the broiler, using a little oil in the pan or on the broiler rack.

2. In a large stockpot, combine beef broth with tomatoes, carrots, onion, celery, potato, and pepper. Bring to a boil. Reduce heat to low, cover, and simmer for 30–45 minutes or until vegetables are tender.

3. Cut cooked burgers into small pieces; add to soup. Add parsley, corn, and peas. Cover and cook for about 15 minutes. Add salt to taste before serving.

Hearty Salmon and Cheddar Chowder

This flavorful chowder is perfect for a first course or for lunch with a sandwich.

INGREDIENTS | SERVES 8

2 tablespoons butter
½ cup thinly sliced celery
2 tablespoons all-purpose flour
⅛ teaspoon ground black pepper
3 cups whole milk
2 cups cooked diced Yukon gold potatoes
1 cup frozen peas and carrots, cooked and drained
14–16 ounces canned salmon
2 cups shredded Cheddar cheese

1. In a large saucepan over medium-low heat, melt butter. Add celery and sauté until tender, about 5–6 minutes. Stir in flour and pepper; continue cooking, stirring constantly, until smooth and bubbly.

2. Gradually stir in milk. Continue to cook, stirring constantly, until bubbly and thickened.

3. Stir in cooked diced potatoes, peas and carrots, and flaked salmon. Heat through. Add cheese, gently stirring just until melted.

Pimiento Cheese Soup

This soup can be thinned with extra milk or turned into a cheese sauce by omitting the broth and cutting the milk in half.

INGREDIENTS | SERVES 6

2 tablespoons butter
2 tablespoons all-purpose flour
2 cups chicken broth or water
4 cups whole milk
3 ounces cream cheese
2 cups shredded mild Cheddar cheese
Dash Worcestershire sauce
½ teaspoon ground cayenne pepper
½ cup chopped pimientos
Salt and ground black pepper

1. In a large saucepan, combine butter and flour. Cook over medium-high heat, stirring constantly, until mixture forms a bubbly paste.

2. Slowly add broth or water; whisk until completely smooth. Bring to a boil; reduce heat to medium. Simmer for 10 minutes.

3. Add milk, cream cheese, and Cheddar cheese. Cook, stirring constantly, until soup is thick and cheese is completely melted. Add Worcestershire, cayenne, and pimientos; simmer for 3 minutes.

4. Season with salt and pepper to taste and remove from heat.

Corn Chowder

*Corn chowder is truly a comfort food. Serve this as a main dish
with crusty bread or crackers, or make it for lunch.*

INGREDIENTS | SERVES 6–8

8 slices bacon, diced

1 medium yellow onion, peeled and chopped

2 tablespoons all-purpose flour

2 cups diced Yukon gold potatoes

2 cups chicken broth

3 (8-ounce) cans cream-style corn

1 teaspoon salt

1 tablespoon chopped fresh flat-leaf parsley

2 cups half-and-half

Salt and ground black pepper

2 tablespoons thinly sliced chives

1. Cook bacon in a large, heavy saucepan or Dutch oven until crisp. Remove bacon from pan and drain on paper towels. Set aside.

2. Add onion to bacon drippings and cook for 1 minute. Stir in flour until well blended. Add potatoes. Gradually stir in chicken broth and bring to a boil, stirring constantly. Reduce heat to low and simmer for about 10–12 minutes until potatoes are tender.

3. Add corn, salt, and parsley. Simmer for about 1 minute. Add half-and-half; heat through. Add salt and pepper to taste. Top with chives and reserved bacon.

Ham and Bean Soup

*This old-fashioned ham and white bean soup is made with navy beans, but it's delicious with
Great Northern beans as well. Serve hot, with fresh cornbread or warm crusty bread.*

INGREDIENTS | SERVES 8

1 pound dried navy beans

8 cups water

1 ham hock or meaty ham bone

1 large yellow onion, peeled and chopped

¼ teaspoon ground black pepper

1 small bay leaf

2 medium carrots, peeled and diced

½ cup chopped celery

2 cups diced ham

½ teaspoon salt

1 (8-ounce) can tomato sauce

1. Rinse beans and discard any that are discolored as well as any stones you find. Cover with water in a large pot. Bring to a boil; boil for 2 minutes. Remove from heat, cover, and let stand for 1 hour.

2. Add ham bone or ham hock, onion, pepper, bay leaf, diced carrot, and celery to the pot. Bring to a boil. Reduce heat to low, cover, and simmer for about 1–1½ hours until meat is tender. Add water as necessary.

3. Remove ham bone or ham hock. Trim meat from the bone and chop; return meat to beans. Add diced ham, salt, and tomato sauce. Simmer for about 30 minutes.

4. Remove bay leaf before serving.

Alabama Peanut Soup

This is a creamy peanut soup, and the taste is just heavenly. Garnish with a bit of sliced green onion along with ground peanuts for a memorable presentation.

INGREDIENTS | SERVES 4

2 medium ribs celery, chopped

¼ cup chopped yellow onion

¼ cup butter

3 tablespoons all-purpose flour

4 cups chicken broth, warmed

1¼ cups creamy peanut butter

½ cup heavy cream

2 teaspoons lemon juice

½ teaspoon salt

¼ teaspoon celery salt

Sliced green onion

Ground unsalted peanuts

1. In a large saucepan over medium heat, sauté celery and onion in butter for 5 minutes or until tender. Add flour, stirring until blended and bubbly. Stir in warm chicken broth. Simmer over low heat for 30 minutes, stirring occasionally.

2. Stir in peanut butter, heavy cream, lemon juice, salt, and celery salt. Cook soup, stirring constantly, until hot.

3. If you would like a smooth soup, blend in batches until smooth. Ladle into soup bowls and sprinkle with sliced green onion and ground peanuts.

Crab and Shrimp Bisque

Tomato paste adds color and flavor to this seafood bisque recipe. Here, it's made with a combination of crabmeat and shrimp, but lobster would be very good in this bisque as well.

INGREDIENTS | SERVES 4–6

3 tablespoons butter

2 tablespoons finely chopped green onion

2 tablespoons finely chopped celery

3 tablespoons all-purpose flour

2½ cups whole milk

½ teaspoon ground black pepper

1 tablespoon tomato paste

1 cup heavy cream

8 ounces crabmeat

8 ounces small cooked shrimp

2 tablespoons dry sherry

1. In a large saucepan over medium-low heat, melt butter. Add green onion and celery; sauté until tender, about 5 minutes. Blend in flour. Cook, stirring constantly, for 1 minute.

2. Gradually stir milk into the saucepan. Cook, stirring constantly, until bubbly and thickened. Add pepper, tomato paste, and cream. Stir until smooth.

3. Stir in crabmeat, shrimp, and sherry. Bring to a simmer and cook until heated through, about 10 minutes.

She-Crab Soup

Authentic Charleston She-Crab Soup features the fatty meat of female blue crabs and crab roe. If you can't find crab roe, substitute crumbled hard-cooked egg yolks.

INGREDIENTS | SERVES 4

3 tablespoons butter

2 tablespoons all-purpose flour

3 cups half-and-half

½ small onion, peeled and very finely chopped

1 teaspoon Worcestershire sauce

¼ teaspoon ground cayenne pepper

¼ teaspoon ground mace

1 pound lump crabmeat

3 tablespoons crab roe or 2 crumbled hard-cooked egg yolks

Salt and ground black pepper

¼ cup sherry

¼ cup minced fresh flat-leaf parsley

1 teaspoon lemon zest

1. In a heavy soup pot over medium-low heat, melt butter; stir in flour and stir until blended into a smooth paste. Add half-and-half; whisk constantly until mixture begins to thicken. Add onion, Worcestershire, cayenne, and mace. Allow cream to begin to bubble around the edges of the pot; reduce heat to low.

2. Continue to simmer, not allowing it to boil, for 5 minutes. Stir in crabmeat and crab roe or crumbled egg yolks. Season with salt and pepper to taste and cook an additional minute.

3. Add sherry; remove from heat. Let stand briefly before serving. Ladle into bowls; garnish with parsley and lemon zest.

Crawfish and Wild Rice Soup

If you don't have access to crawfish, you can substitute peeled and deveined shrimp.

INGREDIENTS | SERVES 4

2 tablespoons butter

1 small sweet onion, peeled and minced

1 medium rib celery, minced

8 ounces fresh button or cremini mushrooms, sliced

2 tablespoons all-purpose flour

6 cups fish or shellfish broth

1 pound crawfish tails

1 cup cooked wild rice

1 cup heavy cream

Salt and ground black pepper

1. In a large, heavy soup pot, melt butter over medium-high heat. Add onion, celery, and mushrooms; sauté for 3 minutes.

2. Sprinkle with flour; stir until well blended. Slowly add broth. Bring to a boil; reduce heat to medium. Simmer for 15 minutes.

3. Add crawfish and wild rice; simmer for 15 minutes.

4. Stir in cream and salt and pepper to taste; cook for 5 minutes until heated through. Remove from heat and serve.

Seven-Layer Salad

This is a very popular salad throughout the South. It's often part of a festive holiday meal.

INGREDIENTS | SERVES 12

6 cups chopped iceberg or romaine lettuce

Salt and ground black pepper

6 large hard-cooked eggs, peeled and sliced

2 cups frozen peas, thawed

8 ounces bacon, cooked and crumbled

2 cups shredded mild Cheddar cheese

1 cup mayonnaise

3 tablespoons sugar

½ cup thinly sliced green onions

Paprika

1. Place 3 cups lettuce in bottom of a large bowl or serving dish; sprinkle with salt and pepper. Layer sliced hard-cooked eggs over the top and sprinkle with more salt and pepper. Continue to layer ingredients in this order: peas, remaining lettuce, crumbled bacon, and shredded cheese, along with light sprinklings of salt and pepper.

2. In a small bowl, combine mayonnaise and sugar; spread over the top of the salad, spreading to the edge of the bowl to cover entire salad.

3. Cover and chill overnight or up to 24 hours. Toss salad lightly before serving. Garnish with sliced green onion and a sprinkling of paprika.

Perfect Potato Salad

A waxy variety of potato makes the best salad because they hold their shape quite well. Potato varieties that work well in salads include Yellow Finn, boiling potatoes, red-skinned potatoes, round whites, purple potatoes, and new potatoes.

INGREDIENTS | SERVES 8

3 pounds potatoes

6 large hard-cooked eggs, peeled and chopped

¼ cup chopped red onion

½ cup chopped celery

¾ cup mayonnaise

1–2 tablespoons prepared yellow mustard

Salt and ground black pepper

Thinly sliced cucumber

1. Peel potatoes; cut in half or quarter. If using new potatoes, just scrub and cut in half or quarter. Cover with water and boil just until tender, about 15–20 minutes. Drain and let cool completely.

2. Cut cooled potatoes into small cubes. In a large bowl, combine potatoes with eggs, onion, and celery. Add mayonnaise, mustard, and salt and pepper to taste. Gently stir until combined and all ingredients are well moistened.

3. Garnish with sliced cucumbers.

Cajun Shrimp and Mango Salad

The easiest way to peel a mango is to cut away the cheeks, score the flesh, and peel away the skin.

INGREDIENTS | SERVES 4

1 pound large shrimp, peeled and deveined

2 teaspoons Cajun seasoning

3 tablespoons butter

2 medium cloves garlic, finely minced

2 cups diced mango

1 cup chopped celery

1 tablespoon lemon juice

4 cups torn romaine lettuce leaves

1. Place shrimp in a large mixing bowl. Sprinkle with Cajun seasoning and toss to coat.

2. Melt butter in a large skillet over medium heat. Add garlic and shrimp to skillet. Cook, stirring frequently, for 3–4 minutes until shrimp just turns pink. Pour contents of the skillet into a large mixing bowl.

3. Add mango and celery to shrimp. Drizzle lemon juice over salad. Toss to mix and coat. Split romaine lettuce between 4 plates. Split shrimp between plates and serve over lettuce.

Countryside Potato Salad

*This hearty recipe works as an entrée or side dish. If you don't
care for radishes, add a little white onion instead.*

INGREDIENTS | SERVES 8

2 pounds russet potatoes, peeled and chopped

1 (15-ounce) can whole-kernel sweet corn, drained

1 cup cubed smoked honey ham

½ cup chopped Roma tomatoes

¼ cup diced red bell pepper

¼ cup shredded radish

½ cup mayonnaise

2 tablespoons minced fresh chives

1 tablespoon minced fresh flat-leaf parsley

1 tablespoon white balsamic vinegar

½ teaspoon celery seed

¼ teaspoon dry mustard

¼ teaspoon salt

⅛ teaspoon ground black pepper

1. Place potatoes in a large pot filled with water. Bring to a boil over high heat, reduce heat to low, and simmer until tender, about 10 minutes. Drain water and return potatoes to the pan to cool for 5 minutes.

2. Place cooled potatoes in a large mixing bowl. Add corn, ham, tomato, bell pepper, and radish.

3. Stir together mayonnaise, chives, parsley, vinegar, celery seed, mustard, salt, and pepper in a small bowl. Pour into salad and mix well. Cover bowl with plastic wrap and chill in refrigerator for 30 minutes.

Hearty Chopped Salad

A delicious restaurant chopped salad was the inspiration for this recipe.
Serve this as a main-dish salad or with soup or a sandwich.

INGREDIENTS | SERVES 6

1 cup diced cooked ham

1 large head romaine lettuce, chopped

1/3 cup diced red onion

1/2 cup chopped pecans or roasted peanuts

1/2 cup cooked garbanzo beans or red kidney beans

1 medium cucumber, peeled, seeded, and diced

2 medium tomatoes, seeded and diced

1 cup diced Havarti or Cheddar cheese

1 tablespoon chopped fresh flat-leaf parsley

1/4 cup balsamic vinegar

1 teaspoon honey-Dijon mustard

1/2 cup extra-virgin olive oil

Salt and ground black pepper

Tortilla chips

1. Heat a small skillet over medium heat; spray with vegetable cooking spray or melt a little butter, then brown ham. In a large bowl, combine ham with chopped lettuce, onion, pecans or peanuts, garbanzo beans or kidney beans, cucumber, tomato, cheese, and parsley; toss to mix well.

2. In a measuring cup or small bowl, combine balsamic vinegar and honey mustard. Gradually whisk in olive oil; season with salt and pepper to taste.

3. Arrange tortilla chips on individual salad plates. Top with a mound of salad and serve with dressing on the side.

New Orleans–Style Oysters and Shrimp Salad

You can serve the pasta and the salad separately, but the contrast between the warm, soft pasta and the cool, crisp salad makes for a delightful dish.

INGREDIENTS | SERVES 8

1 pound dried penne pasta

2 tablespoons peanut or vegetable oil

2 tablespoons all-purpose flour

1 large yellow onion, peeled and diced

1 teaspoon anchovy paste

1 cup whole milk

1 cup heavy cream

Tabasco sauce

1 teaspoon Worcestershire sauce

Pinch dried thyme, crumbled

1 quart small fresh shucked oysters

2 pounds medium shrimp, cooked, peeled, and deveined

Salt and ground black pepper

8 cups mixed salad greens

8 green onions, chopped

1. In a large Dutch oven, cook penne according to package directions; drain, set aside, and keep warm.

2. Wipe out Dutch oven; add oil and heat over medium heat. Stir in flour and cook it until it begins to turn light brown. Add onion; sauté for 3 minutes or until limp. Whisk in anchovy paste, milk, and cream. Bring to a simmer and stir in Tabasco sauce to taste, Worcestershire sauce, and thyme; simmer for 10 minutes.

3. Drain oysters (reserving liquor if desired) and stir oysters and shrimp into cream sauce. Simmer just long enough to bring seafood to temperature, then stir in pasta. If pasta mixture is too thick, stir in a little extra milk, cream, or the liquid drained from oysters. Taste for seasoning and add salt and pepper if needed.

4. To serve, spread 1 cup salad greens over the top of a plate, ladle pasta mixture over salad greens, and garnish with chopped green onion.

Creamy Cabbage Slaw

This version of coleslaw is tangier and sweeter than the typical basic coleslaw made with mayonnaise, salt, and pepper.

INGREDIENTS | SERVES 8

1 medium head green cabbage, shredded

1 medium carrot, peeled and shredded

1 tablespoon minced or grated onion

1¼ cups mayonnaise

⅓ cup sugar

¼ cup apple cider vinegar

¼ teaspoon celery seed

Salt and ground black pepper

Coleslaw Tips

When it comes to shredding cabbage for coleslaw, cut the cabbage into quarters first and remove the core. For the crispest slaw, soak the shredded cabbage in ice water for 20–30 minutes before preparing. Coleslaw will develop more flavor if refrigerated for at least 1 hour before serving. You can use a blender for mixing the dressing, but a clean jar with a screw-on top will do an excellent job and cleanup is a breeze. Just shake ingredients until well blended and then pour over the vegetables.

1. In a large bowl, combine cabbage, carrot, and onion.

2. In a medium bowl, combine mayonnaise, sugar, vinegar, and celery seed. Whisk to blend well. Add salt and pepper to taste. If too sweet for your taste, add a little more mayonnaise.

3. Add dressing to cabbage mixture and stir until well moistened.

4. Refrigerate slaw for at least 2 hours until thoroughly chilled.

Picnic Coleslaw

*This coleslaw isn't made with mayonnaise so it keeps very well for about
1 week in the refrigerator and also travels nicely for a picnic.*

INGREDIENTS | SERVES 8

8 cups shredded green cabbage

1 cup finely grated peeled carrot

1 cup chopped sweet onion

1 cup chopped green bell pepper

12 green olives, chopped

⅓ cup light brown sugar, packed

½ teaspoon salt

1 teaspoon celery seed

1 teaspoon Dijon mustard

⅛ teaspoon ground black pepper

4 teaspoons olive oil

⅔ cup balsamic vinegar

1. Combine cabbage, carrot, onion, bell pepper, and chopped olives in a large bowl.

2. Combine brown sugar, salt, celery seed, mustard, pepper, oil, and vinegar in a small saucepan. Bring to a boil over high heat. Reduce heat and simmer for 3 minutes.

3. Pour warm dressing over cabbage mixture. Toss gently, coating evenly.

4. Cover and refrigerate for at least 6 hours before serving. Toss coleslaw a couple of times while it's chilling. Serve chilled.

Tangy Coleslaw with Cooked Dressing

*This particular coleslaw makes a great topping for pulled-pork sandwiches.
It's tangy and delicious, and lighter than the mayonnaise version.*

INGREDIENTS | SERVES 8

1 medium head green cabbage, shredded

1 medium red onion, peeled and thinly sliced

1 cup sugar

1 teaspoon salt

1 teaspoon dry mustard

1 teaspoon celery seed

1 cup apple cider vinegar

⅔ cup vegetable oil

1. Add cabbage and onion to a large bowl and mix to combine.

2. Combine remaining ingredients in a medium saucepan; bring to a boil. Pour hot dressing over cabbage mixture; toss.

3. Chill thoroughly before serving.

Muffaletta Salad

This cold pasta salad is a twist on the big, round muffaletta sandwiches of New Orleans, which contain Italian meats and cheeses.

INGREDIENTS | SERVES 4

24 slices pepperoni
2 ounces sliced salami
4 ounces sliced ham
4 ounces sliced turkey
1 cup sliced celery
¼ cup chopped green onion
1 cup roasted red peppers
¼ cup sliced black olives
½ cup chopped green olives
1¼ pounds spiral pasta, cooked
3 tablespoons Italian dressing
1½ cups mixed salad greens
¼ cup julienned spinach leaves
1 cup diced Roma tomatoes
1 cup shredded Italian cheese blend
¼ cup shredded Asiago cheese

1. Cut pepperoni, salami, ham, and turkey into thin julienne strips. Place meats in a large salad bowl. Add celery, green onion, and roasted peppers to the bowl.

2. Chop both types of olives and add to the bowl.

3. Add cooked pasta. Pour Italian dressing on pasta and toss everything together gently.

4. Place salad greens and spinach on a cold serving platter, leaving a space in the middle for pasta salad. Pile salad mixture high in the center of the platter. Top salad with tomatoes and cheeses.

Wilted Spinach Salad with Bacon

This popular salad can be found in many Southern restaurants, sometime with the name Killed Salad. It's the bacon drippings that give it such great flavor.

INGREDIENTS | SERVES 4

2 tablespoons bacon drippings

2 tablespoons all-purpose flour

¼ cup minced sweet onion

1 cup water

½ teaspoon dry mustard

2 tablespoons apple cider vinegar

1 pound fresh spinach, chopped

Salt and ground black pepper

1 large hard-cooked egg, peeled and thinly sliced

1. Heat bacon drippings in a large saucepan over low heat. Stir in flour until smooth. Add minced onion, stirring until well blended.

2. Add water, dry mustard, and vinegar. Cook over low heat, stirring constantly, until thickened and smooth.

3. Put spinach in a large bowl; pour hot dressing over spinach. Toss to mix. Season salad with salt and pepper to taste.

4. Garnish with sliced hard-cooked egg.

Broccoli Salad with Raisins and Pecans

This classic broccoli salad is a great dish to take along to a potluck or family dinner.

INGREDIENTS | SERVES 8

8 ounces bacon

1 bunch fresh broccoli, cut into bite-sized pieces

¼ cup chopped red onion

½ cup raisins

1 cup mayonnaise

3 tablespoons apple cider vinegar

2 tablespoons sugar

¾ cup coarsely chopped pecans

Use Florets

Broccoli florets are great in this salad, and you can buy them already separated and cleaned in the produce section of the supermarket. Use 1 pound of broccoli florets, or about 4–5 cups.

1. In a large skillet, cook bacon over medium heat until browned and crisp. Drain on paper towels. Crumble into a cup or bowl, cover, and refrigerate.

2. In a large serving bowl, combine broccoli, onion, and raisins. In a small bowl, combine mayonnaise, vinegar, and sugar. Whisk to blend well. Pour dressing over broccoli mixture and stir to combine. Refrigerate for 2–4 hours.

3. Just before serving, add crumbled bacon and pecans. Toss to combine.

Bacon, Lettuce, and Tomato Salad

This classic combination makes a great sandwich, but it also makes for a super salad. Use a French dressing, vinaigrette, or your own favorite dressing.

INGREDIENTS | SERVES 4

6 slices bacon

2 medium tomatoes, quartered

4 cups mixed salad greens

French dressing or your favorite dressing

Salt and ground black pepper

3 large hard-cooked eggs, peeled and quartered

1. In a large skillet over medium heat, cook bacon until browned and crisp. Transfer bacon to paper towels to drain, reserving 1 tablespoon of bacon drippings. Crumble bacon.

2. In a serving bowl, combine tomatoes, crumbled bacon, reserved drippings, and salad greens. Toss with dressing. Add salt and pepper to taste. Arrange quartered eggs on top of salad.

Traditional Three-Bean Salad

One of the most important ingredients in a traditional bean salad is the sugar, as it not only sweetens everything up but also helps bond the different flavors together.

INGREDIENTS | SERVES 8

½ cup sugar

⅔ cup white wine vinegar

⅓ cup vegetable oil

½ teaspoon salt

⅛ teaspoon ground black pepper

1 (14.5-ounce) can French-cut green beans, drained

1 (14.5-ounce) can yellow (wax) beans, drained

1 (15-ounce) can red kidney beans, drained

1 large white onion, peeled and thinly sliced

1. In a small bowl, whisk together sugar, vinegar, oil, salt, and pepper.

2. In a large bowl, combine beans, onion, and dressing. Mix well. Chill at least 4 hours or overnight, stirring occasionally. If desired, salad can be drained before serving.

Black-Eyed Pea Salad with Basil Dressing

Use fresh basil in this delicious, nutritious salad for the best flavor. Serve this salad on your New Year's Day table for good luck. Red and yellow peppers make the dish look more colorful, but you can use all red.

INGREDIENTS | SERVES 6

3 cups cooked black-eyed peas

½ teaspoon salt, divided

½ cup finely chopped red onion

½ cup finely chopped celery

¼ cup finely chopped red bell pepper

¼ cup finely chopped yellow bell pepper

¼ cup apple cider vinegar

3 tablespoons chopped fresh basil (or 1 tablespoon dried basil, crumbled)

3 medium cloves garlic, crushed

1½ teaspoons sugar

¼ teaspoon ground black pepper

1 cup extra-virgin olive oil

Small fresh basil leaves

1. In a large serving dish, combine black-eyed peas, ¼ teaspoon salt, onion, celery, and bell peppers.

2. In a small, deep bowl, combine vinegar, basil, garlic, sugar, pepper, and remaining ¼ teaspoon salt. Slowly whisk in oil until well blended.

3. Pour dressing over black-eyed pea mixture and toss to combine. Cover and refrigerate for at least 2 hours. Garnish with basil leaves before serving.

Fried Tomato and Corn Salad

This dish is good served cold, which makes it great for taking to a summer barbecue.

INGREDIENTS | SERVES 6

1 pint cherry or grape tomatoes

1 medium poblano pepper

1 tablespoon olive oil

Kernels from 2 ears sweet corn or 2 cups frozen whole-kernel corn, thawed

1 small yellow onion, peeled and diced

2 teaspoons dry sherry or rice wine vinegar

⅓ cup chopped fresh cilantro

Salt and ground black pepper

Protect Yourself

Wear an oven mitt around your wrist or use a splatter screen to protect yourself if the tomatoes pop in this recipe.

1. Place tomatoes in the freezer for at least 2 hours or overnight.

2. Use long tongs to hold pepper over a burner set on high heat. Rotate and move pepper until all of the skin has blackened and bubbled. Wrap it in a paper towel and roll it tightly in foil for 2 minutes. Remove the foil and rub the skin off pepper. Remove stem and seeds from pepper and dice it finely.

3. Place a large skillet over high heat and add oil. Once it starts to smoke, add tomatoes to the skillet. Shake the skillet back and forth frequently. Once tomatoes start to thaw and release their juice, drain juice from the skillet. Add corn to the skillet. Toss to combine and cook for 2–3 minutes. Drain again if necessary and add onion and pepper; cook for an additional 2–3 minutes. The onions should be soft.

4. Stir in sherry or vinegar and cilantro. Season with salt and pepper to taste. Serve hot, warm, or cold.

Southern Cornbread Salad

The toasted cornbread is crisp on the outside and tender on the inside, providing wonderful texture to this beautiful salad.

INGREDIENTS | SERVES 6

Southern Skillet Cornbread (see recipe in Chapter 2)

1 (15-ounce) can black beans, rinsed and drained

1 pint grape tomatoes

1½ cups cubed pepper jack cheese, divided

1 cup spicy ranch salad dressing

Bread Salads

Many cultures use leftover or stale bread in salads. In America, cornbread salad is probably the most well known. Italians make a bread salad called panzanella with stale bread, and Lebanese make fattoush with crisp pieces of flatbread or pita bread.

1. Preheat oven to 400°F. Cut cornbread into 1" squares and place on a baking sheet. Bake for 5–8 minutes until toasted, watching carefully. Remove to a wire rack and let stand for 5 minutes to cool slightly.

2. Place cornbread in a serving bowl. Add black beans, tomatoes, and 1 cup cheese to cornbread and toss gently. Drizzle with salad dressing, toss again, then top with remaining cheese. Serve immediately or cover and chill for 2 hours before serving.

Dot's Strawberry Pretzel Salad

*Make this delicious salad for a holiday dinner or take the salad
along to a potluck dinner or summer get-together.*

INGREDIENTS | SERVES 10

3 cups sliced strawberries

1¼ cup plus 3 tablespoons sugar, divided

2 cups crushed pretzels

¾ cup butter, melted

1 (6-ounce) package strawberry-flavored gelatin

2 cups boiling water

1 (8-ounce) package cream cheese, softened

1 (8-ounce) container whipped topping, plus extra for garnish

6–8 whole strawberries

1. In a medium bowl, combine sliced strawberries with ¼ cup sugar. Set aside for 15 minutes.

2. Preheat oven to 400°F.

3. In a medium bowl, combine crushed pretzels with melted butter and 3 tablespoons sugar. Press mixture evenly over the bottom of a 9" × 13" baking pan. Bake for 8 minutes. Set aside to cool.

4. Add strawberry-flavored gelatin to boiling water. Cool for 10 minutes, then add sliced strawberries. Chill in the refrigerator until slightly thickened, about 45 minutes.

5. In a large bowl, beat cream cheese with remaining 1 cup sugar. Fold in whipped topping. Spread over cooled pretzel layer.

6. Spoon partially thickened gelatin mixture over cream cheese layer. Garnish with fresh strawberries and more whipped topping if desired.

Millionaire Fruit Salad

This delicious fruit salad is an old-fashioned classic, with a few updates. It's a good salad with an Easter ham dinner, but you'll find it's a great fit with other holiday dinner menus as well.

INGREDIENTS | SERVES 8

3 ounces cream cheese, softened

3 tablespoons half-and-half or light cream

¼ cup mayonnaise

2 tablespoons lemon juice

2 tablespoons sugar

1 (8-ounce) can pineapple tidbits, drained

1 (8-ounce) container peach chunks, drained

1 (11-ounce) can mandarin orange sections, drained

½ cup drained halved maraschino cherries

½ cup halved seedless green grapes

½ cup coarsely chopped pecans

1 cup miniature marshmallows

1 cup heavy whipping cream

1. In a large bowl, combine cream cheese with half-and-half, mayonnaise, lemon juice, and sugar. Beat until smooth.

2. Stir in pineapples, peaches, mandarin oranges, cherries, grapes, pecans, and marshmallows.

3. In a medium bowl, beat heavy whipping cream until stiff. Fold into fruit mixture until well blended. Transfer to an 8" square baking dish.

4. Chill or freeze salad before serving.

Lighten it up!

There are many products on the market these days that can take the place of higher-fat foods. Use light cream cheese and light mayonnaise and substitute fat-free or reduced-calorie whipped topping for the heavy whipped cream. You could even replace the sugar with Splenda and cut back on the pecans or leave them out altogether.

Sweet and Creamy Peach Fruit Salad

This light salad takes peaches and cream to a whole new level and can serve as a breakfast entrée, side dish, or dessert.

INGREDIENTS | SERVES 4

2½ cups diced peaches
1 cup diced nectarines
½ cup toasted almond slices
3 ounces cream cheese, softened
3 tablespoons whole milk
2 teaspoons water
¼ teaspoon vanilla extract

1. Combine peaches, nectarines, and almond slices in a large mixing bowl.

2. Mix together cream cheese, milk, water, and vanilla in a small bowl. Mix thoroughly.

3. Pour cream cheese mixture over fruit and mix well. Serve immediately or chill up to 1 hour before serving.

CHAPTER 5

Sandwiches

Pimiento Cheese Sandwiches

The pimiento cheese sandwich is a classic in the South. Use this delicious cheese spread as is or add a few tomatoes and a little bacon or sliced ham to the sandwich.

INGREDIENTS | SERVES 6

1 (2-ounce) jar diced pimientos, drained

1 cup finely shredded sharp Cheddar cheese

¼ cup mayonnaise

2 teaspoons lemon juice

⅛ teaspoon salt

Dash garlic powder

Few drops hot sauce

12 slices white or whole-wheat bread

1. Drain and mash pimientos. In a large bowl, combine pimientos, cheese, mayonnaise, lemon juice, salt, garlic powder, and hot sauce. Mix until well blended.

2. Refrigerate until ready to serve. Spread on sliced bread to make sandwiches.

Pimiento Cheese Add-Ins

Vary the flavor of your spread with your favorite additions. Try a little Parmesan cheese, a small amount of minced jalapeño pepper, and some coarsely ground black pepper.

New Orleans–Style Roast Beef Po'Boy

Use good French bread and your favorite meat or seafood for these delicious sandwiches. Roast beef makes a classic po'boy, but fried oysters, shrimp, ham, and sausage are other popular fillings.

INGREDIENTS | SERVES 4

4 French bread rolls or 2 baguettes
Mayonnaise
1 cup shredded lettuce
1 pound roast beef, thinly sliced
1 cup thick beef gravy
2 medium tomatoes, thinly sliced
Dill pickle slices

1. Split rolls lengthwise. If using baguettes, cut into 12" lengths, then split lengthwise.

2. Warm or toast bread in the oven or under the broiler.

3. Spread bottom half of bread with mayonnaise, then layer with lettuce and sliced roast beef; spoon gravy over the top, then add tomato slices and dill pickles. Finish with top piece of bread. Repeat with remaining bread.

Oyster Po'Boys

The soft interior and crackly crust of French bread is perfect for this sandwich.

INGREDIENTS | SERVES 4

¾ cup cornmeal
¼ cup all-purpose flour
⅛ teaspoon ground cayenne pepper
Salt and ground black pepper
¾ cup vegetable oil
1 quart small fresh shucked oysters, drained
4 crusty French bread rolls
1 cup Rémoulade Sauce (see recipe in Chapter 12)
Shredded lettuce
Sliced tomatoes

1. In a medium bowl, combine cornmeal, flour, cayenne, and salt and pepper to taste.

2. Heat oil in a medium skillet over medium-high heat.

3. Pat each oyster dry with a paper towel. Dip them in cornmeal mixture, then lay gently into the skillet.

4. Fry oysters in batches until golden brown, turning once, about 5 minutes total. Set aside to dry on a plate lined with paper towels to absorb excess oil.

5. Spread rolls with Rémoulade Sauce. Add oysters, then top with lettuce and tomato.

Catfish Po'Boy with Stone Fruit Slaw

*Cornmeal, nectarine, plum, celery, and celery seed provide enough fiber
to indulge in a fried-fish po'boy and feel good about it.*

INGREDIENTS | SERVES 2

2 large catfish fillets (about ½ pound)
½ cup yellow cornmeal
¾ teaspoon salt, divided
⅛ teaspoon ground cayenne pepper
¼ cup canola oil
2 teaspoons mayonnaise
1½ tablespoons plain yogurt
2 teaspoons lemon juice
1 teaspoon lemon zest
1 teaspoon grated fresh ginger
1 teaspoon celery seed
¼ teaspoon ground black pepper
1 small nectarine, pitted and finely diced
1 small plum, pitted and finely diced
2 tablespoons minced celery
2 crusty French bread rolls
½ cup shredded lettuce

1. Rinse fillets and pat dry with a paper towel.

2. Mix together cornmeal, ¼ teaspoon salt, and cayenne pepper in a medium bowl.

3. Heat canola oil in a large skillet over medium-high heat. Dip fillets into cornmeal mixture, then carefully place in hot oil. Cook for 3 minutes, then turn and cook until fish can be flaked with a fork, about 2 minutes. Drain fillets on paper towels.

4. In a medium bowl, mix together mayonnaise, yogurt, lemon juice, lemon zest, ginger, celery seed, remaining salt, and pepper; add nectarine, plum, and celery and toss to combine.

5. Break catfish into pieces and place them in rolls. Top catfish with fruit slaw and lettuce.

Peach and Goat Cheese Panino

Sweet peaches make this grilled sandwich an unusual delight.

INGREDIENTS | SERVES 1

2 ounces goat cheese, at room temperature
¼ teaspoon ground ginger
¼ baguette, sliced in half
1 peach, peeled and sliced

1. In a small bowl, mix goat cheese with ginger.

2. Spread mixture on a baguette slice. ·

3. Layer peach slices on top of cheese. Top with the other baguette slice.

4. Heat a panini press to medium and press until cheese is soft and sandwich is hot.

French Toasted-Ham Sandwiches

In these ham sandwiches with a twist, the bread is dipped in an egg batter like French toast, giving this sandwich more flavor and character.

INGREDIENTS | SERVES 6

Prepared yellow mustard
12 slices firm white bread
12 thin slices cooked ham or smoked turkey
6 slices Swiss cheese
2 large eggs, lightly beaten
½ cup whole milk
¼ teaspoon salt
Ground black pepper
3 tablespoons butter

1. Spread a thin layer of mustard over each slice of bread. On each of 6 slices, place 2 slices of ham or turkey and 1 slice of cheese. Top with remaining 6 slices of bread, mustard side down.

2. In a shallow bowl, whisk eggs with milk, salt, and pepper.

3. Melt butter in a large skillet over low heat.

4. Dip sandwiches in egg mixture, turning to coat well. Depending on the size of the skillet, cook 2 or 3 at a time. Place sandwiches in the hot skillet and brown well on each side.

Kentucky Hot Brown

This hot turkey sandwich was created by Louisville's Brown Hotel in the 1920s. This is a version with a Parmesan cheese sauce, but it is also frequently made with Cheddar cheese.

INGREDIENTS | SERVES 6

5 tablespoons butter

⅔ cup all-purpose flour

1½ cups chicken broth

1½ cups whole milk

½ teaspoon salt

⅛ teaspoon ground black pepper

1 cup freshly grated Parmesan cheese, plus extra for garnish

6 slices firm white bread

12 slices roast turkey

Paprika

12 slices tomato

6 slices bacon, cut in half crosswise and cooked

1. Preheat oven to 400°F. In a large saucepan over medium-low heat, melt butter. Blend in flour, stirring until incorporated. Gradually whisk in broth, then slowly add milk, whisking until smooth. Stir in salt, pepper, and Parmesan cheese. Reduce heat to low and cook, stirring frequently, for 5 minutes. The sauce will be thick.

2. Toast bread and arrange on a baking sheet. Top each piece of toast with 2 turkey slices, then cover turkey with sauce. Sprinkle paprika over sauce, then top each with 2 tomato slices. Arrange 2 halves of cooked bacon in an X shape on tomato.

3. Bake for 10 minutes or until sauce is bubbly. Garnish with grated Parmesan before serving.

Pulled-Pork Barbecue Sandwiches

Long, slow cooking in the oven is the way most people cook the pork. Serve hot with split buns, coleslaw, and beans, if desired. A potato salad also goes well with this for a bigger meal or party.

INGREDIENTS | SERVES 8

1 large (7- to 9-pound) pork shoulder or butt roast

3 medium cloves garlic, minced

1 teaspoon Creole seasoning

½ teaspoon salt

½ teaspoon ground black pepper

1 large yellow onion, peeled and sliced

2 teaspoons vegetable oil

1 large yellow onion, peeled and chopped

1 cup barbecue sauce

½ cup apple cider vinegar

8 split rolls

1. Preheat oven to 350°F. Rinse pork and pat dry.

2. Spread a large sheet of heavy-duty foil across a roasting pan. Place pork roast on foil. Rub pork with minced garlic, Creole seasoning, salt, and pepper. Arrange sliced onion over the top of the roast. Bring foil up around roast, wrapping well. Bake pork for 4–5 hours or until a meat thermometer registers about 185°F. The meat should be tender, almost falling apart.

3. Let roast cool slightly. Shred with 2 forks or chop meat, discarding excess fat and bone as you find it.

4. In a small skillet, heat oil over medium heat; sauté chopped onion until tender, about 5 minutes. Put onion and pork in a 4- to 5-quart slow cooker, a large saucepan, or a Dutch oven. Stir in barbecue sauce and vinegar.

5. Heat on low setting or over low heat on the stovetop for 20–30 minutes or until thoroughly heated.

6. Serve pulled pork hot on split rolls.

Chicken Sandwiches with Curried Mayonnaise and Golden Raisins

This makes a delicious sandwich, but you could also serve it on lettuce leaves for a lighter luncheon dish.

INGREDIENTS | SERVES 4

¼ cup mayonnaise

2 tablespoons fruit chutney

1 tablespoon curry powder

¼ cup chopped celery

1 tablespoon chopped green onion

⅓ cup chopped golden raisins

2 tablespoons chopped pecans

1½ cups diced cooked chicken

2 tablespoons heavy cream

8 slices whole-wheat or oatmeal bread

4 large lettuce leaves

1. Combine mayonnaise, chutney, and curry powder in a small bowl.

2. In a medium bowl, combine celery, green onion, raisins, pecans, and chicken. Stir in mayonnaise mixture and cream.

3. Toast bread if desired; top 4 slices of bread with 1 lettuce leaf, then spread 3–4 tablespoons of the chicken mixture on lettuce. Top each with another slice of bread.

Other Ways to Dress Up Chicken Salad

Jazz up a cup of plain chicken or turkey salad with a few tablespoons of chopped apple or tasty chopped, dried cranberries or a few chopped toasted pecans. Dark or golden raisins are also delicious, and do try some herbs, such as a little dried tarragon or basil. Roasted red peppers make a nice addition, too, as do sliced ripe or stuffed green olives, or try some chopped capers or a little pickle relish or chopped pickles. The possibilities are endless!

Chili Beef Burgers

These burgers pack a lot of flavor! You can make these with more beef and no beans, but the beans make them interesting. These are super for parties.

INGREDIENTS | SERVES 6

2 pounds extra-lean ground beef

1 large sweet onion, peeled and chopped

½ cup chopped red bell pepper

½ cup chopped green bell pepper

1 (15-ounce) can pinto beans, drained and rinsed

2½ cups water

2 cups ketchup

2½ tablespoons prepared yellow mustard

4 teaspoons light brown sugar, packed

2½ tablespoons chili powder

⅛ teaspoon garlic powder

½ teaspoon salt

⅛ teaspoon ground black pepper

6 large hamburger buns or similar rolls, split

1. In a large skillet over medium heat, brown ground beef with onion and bell peppers. Drain off excess fat. Stir in beans.

2. Combine water, ketchup, mustard, brown sugar, chili powder, garlic powder, salt, and pepper in a medium bowl. Blend well, then add to beef and bean mixture. Simmer until thickened. Taste and adjust seasonings.

3. Toast split buns if desired. Spoon beef and bean mixture over split buns.

Out-of-the-Ordinary Burgers

Herbs help to flavor this lean ground-round mixture. You'll love these delicious grilled burgers. To top the burgers off, try sautéed mushrooms or onions, barbecue sauce, prepared chili, peppers, or cooked bacon.

INGREDIENTS | SERVES 4

1 slice crusty bread

¼ cup whole milk

1½ pounds ground round or ground sirloin

2 tablespoons finely chopped fresh flat-leaf parsley

½ teaspoon dried oregano, crumbled

½ teaspoon dried tarragon, crumbled

½ teaspoon dried thyme, crumbled

½ teaspoon seasoned salt

1 teaspoon salt

¼ teaspoon ground black pepper

1 large egg, lightly beaten

4 hamburger buns, split

1. Heat grill. In a medium bowl, soak bread in milk for a few minutes.

2. Squeeze bread to drain off milk. Put bread back in the bowl; add ground beef, parsley, oregano, tarragon, thyme, seasoned salt, salt, and pepper. Use your hands to combine. Mix in beaten egg.

3. Shape beef mixture into 4 large patties, about 1" thick. Place burgers on the hot, oiled grill about 4" above the heat source. Grill for about 10–15 minutes on each side or until cooked through and juices run clear.

4. Toast split hamburger buns if desired. Serve burgers on buns.

Five Burger Tips

(1) Mix the ground beef mixture lightly. (2) Add a little tomato juice or vegetable broth for flavor and moisture. (3) Add chopped leftover vegetables to the mixture. (4) Add a little diced bacon for a smoky flavor. (5) Freeze shaped burgers, separated with plastic wrap.

CHAPTER 6

Beef, Veal, and Lamb

Beef and Sweet Onions with Rice

This is an easy everyday skillet recipe your family will ask for again and again. Use sweet Vidalia onions if you can get them.

INGREDIENTS | SERVES 6

2 pounds beef sirloin

2 tablespoons vegetable oil

1 tablespoon butter

2 large sweet onions, peeled, quartered, and sliced

3 tablespoons all-purpose flour

1 teaspoon salt

½ teaspoon ground black pepper

¼ teaspoon dried thyme, crumbled

2 cups beef broth

2 tablespoons red wine vinegar

1 tablespoon ketchup

3 cups hot cooked long-grain white rice

Sweet Onions

There are a number of varieties of sweet onions on the market these days, and you're likely to find them at almost any time of the year. Some of these include Vidalia, Maui, Walla Walla, Texas Sweets, Sweet Imperial, Mayan, Grand Canyon, and a few others. For best results, these onions should be stored in the refrigerator, individually wrapped in paper towels. Another effective way to store these onions is to put them in the legs of panty hose, making a knot between each onion. Hang in a cool, dry, well-ventilated place. To use, cut an onion off just below the next knot.

1. Trim sirloin of excess fat; cut into bite-sized cubes. Set aside.

2. In a large skillet, heat oil and butter over medium heat until hot. Add onions and cook, stirring constantly, until tender and lightly browned, about 5–7 minutes. Add beef to the skillet with onions. Increase heat to medium-high and sauté until beef is browned. Reduce heat to medium.

3. In a small bowl, combine flour, salt, pepper, and thyme; add to the skillet, stirring to incorporate and blend well. If necessary to moisten flour, add a little more butter.

4. Add beef broth, vinegar, and ketchup. Stir to blend. Reduce heat to low; cover and cook for about 1 hour or until meat is very tender.

5. Serve with hot cooked rice.

Beef and Biscuit Pie

This easy family recipe is a tasty meal in one dish.

INGREDIENTS | SERVES 4

1½ pounds sirloin steak, about ¾" thick

1 tablespoon vegetable oil

8 ounces fresh button or cremini mushrooms, sliced

1 medium sweet onion, peeled, quartered, and sliced

1 medium clove garlic, minced

¼ cup beef broth or water

1½ cups beef gravy

1½ cups frozen peas and carrots, thawed

¼ teaspoon dried thyme, crumbled

1 (12-ounce) tube refrigerated buttermilk biscuits

1. Preheat oven to 400°F.

2. Trim steak of excess fat. Cut into ½" × 3" strips.

3. Heat oil in a large skillet over medium-high heat. Add beef, working in batches, stirring to brown all sides. Remove beef strips from the skillet with a slotted spoon and set aside.

4. Add mushrooms, onion, garlic, and broth or water to the same skillet; cook, stirring constantly, for about 3 minutes or until onion is tender. Stir gravy into the skillet (use 1½ cups of thick leftover gravy, if you have it) along with peas and carrots and thyme. Bring mixture to a boil; simmer for 1 minute. Stir in browned beef.

5. Spoon beef and vegetable mixture into a 2-quart baking dish. Separate biscuits; cut in half. Arrange biscuits, cut side down, on top of beef mixture. Bake for 12–14 minutes or until biscuits are browned.

Vegetable Beef Stew

This stew is loaded with vegetables, and if you have some fresh from the garden, so much the better! Serve with crusty bread.

INGREDIENTS | SERVES 8

2 pounds stewing beef, cut into small cubes

4 cups beef broth

3 medium russet potatoes, peeled and cubed

1 small rutabaga or turnip, peeled and cubed

2 medium carrots, peeled and thinly sliced

1 small yellow onion, peeled and chopped

2 medium ribs celery, sliced

1 cup sliced button or cremini mushrooms

½ cup cooked lima beans or butter beans

¼ cup dry red wine

½ teaspoon salt

¼ teaspoon ground black pepper

¼ teaspoon dried thyme, crumbled

½ cup frozen mixed vegetables, thawed

3 tablespoons all-purpose flour

¼ cup cold water

1. In a large stockpot or Dutch oven over medium-high heat, combine beef and beef broth; bring to a boil. Reduce heat; cover and simmer for about 1½ hours.

2. Add potatoes, rutabaga or turnip, carrots, onion, celery, mushrooms, lima beans, wine, salt, pepper, and thyme. Cover and simmer for about 25–35 minutes or until vegetables are tender. Add mixed vegetables to stew about 10 minutes before it's done.

3. Combine flour and water in a small bowl; stir until smooth. Slowly stir flour mixture into simmering stew. Continue cooking for a few more minutes, stirring until thickened.

Slow Cooker Variation

Replace the 4 cups of beef broth with a 10.5-ounce can of condensed beef broth. Combine all the ingredients, except the flour and water mixture and frozen vegetables, in a 4- to 5-quart slow cooker. Cook on low for about 8–9 hours, until meat and vegetables are tender. Cook the frozen vegetables slightly before adding them to the stew. Stir in the flour and water mixture and cook on high for a few minutes, until thickened.

Beef and Chili Bean Stew

Serve this flavorful stew on game day, or for any hearty fall or winter meal. Try it with freshly baked hot cornbread.

INGREDIENTS | SERVES 8

2 pounds lean stewing beef, cut in ½" cubes

2 tablespoons vegetable oil

1 large yellow onion, peeled and chopped

1 medium green bell pepper, seeded and chopped

2 medium ribs celery, chopped

2 medium cloves garlic, minced

2 tablespoons chili powder

1 (14.5-ounce) can diced tomatoes (undrained)

1 (4-ounce) can diced mild green chilies

1 cup beef broth, warmed

1 teaspoon salt

2 tablespoons all-purpose flour

¼ cup cold water

2 (15-ounce) cans red beans or kidney beans, drained and rinsed

1 (11-ounce) can whole-kernel corn, drained

1. In a large Dutch oven over medium-high heat, brown beef in vegetable oil, stirring frequently. With a slotted spoon, remove beef to a plate and set aside. Drain off all but 2 tablespoons of the drippings or add oil to make 2 tablespoons.

2. Add onion, bell pepper, celery, and garlic to the pan; sauté until vegetables are just tender. Stir in chili powder and cook for about 1 minute, stirring. Add tomatoes and green chilies. Stir in warm beef broth. Add salt and return beef to the pan. Reduce heat to low; cover and simmer for about 1½–2 hours until beef is tender.

3. In a cup, blend flour with cold water. Gradually stir into stew. Cook stew, stirring constantly, until thickened.

4. Add beans and corn to stew and heat through.

Grillades and Grits

This is a delicious Louisiana-style dish, traditionally served for brunch or breakfast.

INGREDIENTS | SERVES 6

1½ pounds lean beef steaks

¼ cup plus 2 tablespoons all-purpose flour, divided

½ teaspoon salt plus more to taste, divided

¼ teaspoon ground pepper plus more to taste, divided

4 tablespoons vegetable oil, divided

1 large yellow onion, peeled, quartered, and sliced

3 medium ribs celery, chopped

½ cup chopped red bell pepper

½ cup chopped green bell pepper

2 medium cloves garlic, minced

1 cup beef broth

1 (14.5-ounce) can diced tomatoes (undrained)

½ teaspoon dried thyme, crumbled

½ teaspoon dried basil, crumbled

¼ teaspoon crushed red pepper

2 tablespoons red wine vinegar

2 tablespoons chopped fresh flat-leaf parsley

4 cups hot cooked grits

1. Flatten steaks to ½" thickness; cut into 2" pieces. Combine ¼ cup flour, ½ teaspoon salt, and ¼ teaspoon pepper in a food storage bag. Add beef and toss gently to coat.

2. Heat 2 tablespoons oil in a heavy skillet over medium-high heat. Cook steak pieces, turning to brown both sides. Remove beef to a plate and set aside.

3. Add onion, celery, and bell pepper to the skillet and sauté until tender, about 5–7 minutes. Stir in garlic. Transfer vegetables to a plate and set aside.

4. Add remaining oil to the skillet. Stir remaining 2 tablespoons flour into oil and cook, stirring constantly, until light to medium brown. Do not let mixture burn. Add cooked vegetables back to the pan along with beef broth. Stir until well blended and bubbly.

5. Add steak back to the pan along with tomatoes. Sprinkle with thyme, basil, and crushed red pepper. Stir in vinegar. Reduce heat to a simmer and cook for about 45 minutes or until beef is tender. Taste and add salt and pepper as needed. Stir in chopped parsley.

6. Serve beef over hot cooked grits.

Home-Style Pot Roast

Dried herbs and condensed beef broth give this pot roast great flavor.

INGREDIENTS | SERVES 6–8

2 tablespoons vegetable oil

1 (3-pound) beef pot roast (chuck, top round, rump, etc.)

1 medium yellow onion, peeled, quartered, and sliced

1 medium clove garlic, minced

1 teaspoon dried thyme, crumbled

1 teaspoon dried marjoram, crumbled

1 teaspoon salt

¼ teaspoon ground black pepper

1 (10.5-ounce) can condensed beef broth

6 medium carrots, peeled

12 small white onions, peeled

1 small rutabaga, cut into 1" pieces

3 tablespoons all-purpose flour

¼ cup cold water

What Are the Best Beef Cuts to Use for Pot Roast?

There are a number of beef cuts that make great pot roasts, like chuck arm, chuck fillet, and top round. Rump and blade roasts also make great pot roasts.

1. Heat oil in a large stockpot or Dutch oven over medium heat. Brown beef roast well on all sides.

2. Add sliced onion, minced garlic, thyme, marjoram, salt, and pepper. Stir to combine.

3. Add beef broth and bring to a boil. Reduce heat to low; cover and simmer for 1½–2 hours or until pot roast is tender.

4. Slice carrots in half crosswise, then cut in half lengthwise. Add to broth. Add white onions and rutabaga. Cover and simmer until vegetables are tender.

5. Move roast to a warm platter. With a slotted spoon, arrange vegetables around roast. Cover and keep warm.

6. Combine flour with cold water in a small bowl; whisk until smooth. Gradually stir flour mixture into simmering broth. Continue cooking, stirring constantly, until broth is thickened. Serve gravy with pot roast and vegetables.

Country-Fried Steak

Serve the gravy over the top of the steak, with mashed potatoes and your favorite vegetable on the side.

INGREDIENTS | SERVES 4

1½ pounds round steak

1 cup plus 3 tablespoons all-purpose flour, divided

¾ teaspoon salt plus more to taste, divided

¼ teaspoon ground pepper plus more to taste, divided

1 large egg, beaten

Vegetable oil

2 tablespoons butter

1 cup whole milk

½ cup water or beef broth

No-Mess Cutlets

When thinning pieces of beef, veal, chicken, and other cuts of meat, put the piece of meat in a large, heavy-duty food storage bag, then gently pound until flattened. The bag is strong enough to resist tearing, flips over easily so you can pound on the other side, and it should stand up through several pieces of meat, probably all of the meat in your recipe. You'll also have much less mess!

1. Cut steak into 4 portions. Place between 2 pieces of plastic wrap. Using a meat mallet, flatten to about ½" thickness.

2. In a large, shallow bowl, combine 1 cup flour with ¾ teaspoon salt and ¼ teaspoon pepper. Dredge steaks in seasoned flour. Dip in beaten egg, then dredge again in flour mixture.

3. Heat 1" of vegetable oil in a large, heavy skillet. Using tongs, put steaks in oil. Cook steaks, turning once to brown both sides. Lower heat to medium-low, cover, and continue to cook for about 3–4 minutes until steaks are cooked through. Move steaks to paper towels on a warm platter; cover with foil.

4. Drain off all but 1 tablespoon of the oil and add butter. Add 3 tablespoons of flour, stirring and scraping the bottom of the skillet to loosen any browned bits. Cook flour, stirring for 1 minute. Stir in milk and water or broth; cook, stirring constantly, until thickened and bubbly. Season gravy with salt and pepper to taste.

Beef Tenderloin with Mushroom-Wine Sauce

Beef tenderloin is a perfect choice for a very special dinner. The mushroom-wine sauce is the perfect accompaniment.

INGREDIENTS | SERVES 4

2 pounds beef tenderloin roast

1 large clove garlic, halved

Salt and ground black pepper

2 tablespoons olive oil

1 cup thinly sliced button or cremini mushrooms

2 green onions, white part only

1 small clove garlic, minced

3 tablespoons all-purpose flour

1½ cups dry red wine

2 cups beef broth

¼ teaspoon dried thyme, crumbled

Roasting Pans

Every Southern cook needs a good roasting pan! A roasting pan should have a heavy bottom and should be about 2" in depth, deep enough to allow juices to accumulate yet shallow enough to let dry heat surround and cook the roast. For best results, match the size of your roasting pan to the size of the roast.

1. Preheat oven to 400°F. Rub roast with cut sides of garlic halves. Sprinkle with salt and pepper and place in a shallow roasting pan.

2. Roast for about 1 hour for medium rare or 75 minutes for medium, or when a meat thermometer registers 135°F (for medium rare) or 150°F (for medium). Transfer meat to a warm platter. Let stand for 15 minutes. The temperature will rise another 10°F or so.

3. Place the roasting pan over medium heat; add olive oil, mushrooms, green onion, and minced garlic. Sauté until mushrooms are tender, about 5–8 minutes. Stir in flour until well incorporated, then stir in red wine and beef broth. Simmer until reduced by about ⅓. Add thyme. Sprinkle with salt and pepper to taste.

4. Slice tenderloin and serve with mushroom sauce.

Standing Rib Roast

This is a terrific oven roast for a special family dinner, and it's relatively easy to fix. Serve this roast with baked or mashed potatoes and a wilted spinach salad, along with your favorite special vegetable side dish.

INGREDIENTS | SERVES 8

1 (6-pound) standing rib roast of beef
2 teaspoons salt
¾ teaspoon ground black pepper
¼ teaspoon garlic powder

Beef au Jus

For beef au jus, add ½ cup beef broth to the drippings; bring to a boil. Season the jus with salt and pepper to taste.

1. Preheat oven to 450°F.

2. Rub roast all over with salt, pepper, and garlic powder.

3. Place on a rack in a shallow pan and roast for 25 minutes. Reduce heat to 350°F and roast for about 15 minutes per pound, or to an internal temperature of about 135°F for medium rare. Cover loosely with foil and let stand for 10 minutes before carving.

Corned Beef and Cabbage

Many Southerners have Irish roots, and corned beef and cabbage is a popular dish throughout the region. This recipe will leave you with plenty of delicious leftover corned beef for sandwiches or a casserole.

INGREDIENTS | SERVES 4–6

4 pounds corned beef brisket, with spice packet
1 medium bay leaf
¼ teaspoon ground black pepper
1 medium head green cabbage, cut into wedges
2 small rutabagas, cut into large chunks
8 medium carrots, peeled and halved
12 small whole white onions, peeled
6 medium russet potatoes, peeled and halved

1. Put corned beef in a large stockpot with spice packet, bay leaf, and pepper and cover with water. Bring to a boil; skim off foam. Reduce heat to low; cover and simmer for about 50 minutes per pound.

2. Add vegetables to the pot. Cover and simmer for about 45 minutes or until vegetables are tender.

3. Arrange corned beef on a platter and surround with vegetables. Slice meat across the grain.

Beef and Barbecue Bean Stew

This is a quick and easy stew to make, and it's just the thing for fall or winter meals. Serve this easy stew with cornbread or corn muffins and a salad.

INGREDIENTS | SERVES 6

1 pound lean ground beef
½ cup chopped white onion
½ cup chopped green bell pepper
½ cup chopped celery
1 (28-ounce) can barbecue-flavored baked beans
1 small carrot, peeled and diced
1 (8-ounce) can tomato sauce
1 cup water
½ teaspoon garlic powder
1 (14.5-ounce) can diced tomatoes (undrained)
6 tablespoons sour cream

1. In a large saucepan or Dutch oven over medium-low heat, brown ground beef. Add onion, green pepper, and celery; continue to sauté, stirring frequently, until vegetables are tender, about 5–8 minutes.

2. Add beans, carrots, tomato sauce, water, garlic powder, and tomatoes. Reduce heat to low; cover and simmer for 45–60 minutes.

3. Add a dollop of sour cream to each serving.

Salisbury Steaks with Bacon

These hamburger steaks are delicious with mashed potatoes and a vegetable or side salad. Use store-bought or leftover beef gravy.

INGREDIENTS | SERVES 6

6 slices bacon, diced
2 pounds ground beef round
2 tablespoons minced yellow onion
1 tablespoon finely chopped green bell pepper
1 tablespoon finely chopped fresh flat-leaf parsley
1 teaspoon salt
¼ teaspoon ground black pepper
1½ cups beef gravy

1. Heat broiler. Lightly oil the rack of the broiler pan.

2. In a large bowl, combine bacon with ground sirloin, onion, bell pepper, parsley, salt, and pepper. Shape mixture into 6 oval patties about ¾" thick.

3. Place patties on prepared pan. Broil about 4" from the heat source for about 18 minutes. Turn and broil the other side for 10–15 minutes or until steaks are no longer pink inside.

4. Meanwhile, heat gravy to serving temperature in a small saucepan on medium. Serve steaks with hot beef gravy.

Country-Style Meatloaf

Serve this comfort-food classic with mashed potatoes and peas and carrots.

INGREDIENTS | SERVES 6

2 tablespoons butter

8 ounces fresh button or cremini mushrooms, sliced

1 medium yellow onion, peeled and chopped

3 medium ribs celery, chopped

2 medium carrots, peeled and shredded

2 tablespoons water or beef broth

2 pounds ground beef round

1 large egg, lightly beaten

½ cup fine dry bread crumbs, plain

1 teaspoon salt

1 teaspoon seasoned salt

¼ teaspoon dried thyme, crumbled

1 teaspoon dried parsley flakes

1 teaspoon Worcestershire sauce

⅓ cup ketchup or barbecue sauce

1. Preheat oven to 350°F. In a medium skillet, melt butter over medium heat; add mushrooms, onion, celery, carrots, and water or broth. Bring to a simmer and continue cooking for about 10 minutes until vegetables are just tender.

2. In a large bowl, combine ground beef, egg, bread crumbs, salt and seasoned salt, thyme, parsley, and Worcestershire sauce. Add mushroom mixture and mix gently to blend. Pack into a greased 9" × 5" loaf pan or shape into a loaf and place on a greased shallow baking pan.

3. Bake for 60–70 minutes until browned and cooked through. Spread ketchup or barbecue sauce over the top of meatloaf about the last 5 minutes of baking.

Spicy Beef Chili

This chili is made with ground beef and beans, along with a delicious combination of vegetables and spicy seasonings. Serve chili with crackers or freshly baked cornbread.

INGREDIENTS | SERVES 6

1 tablespoon vegetable oil

1 large sweet onion, peeled, quartered, and sliced

1 medium green bell pepper, seeded and chopped

1 pound ground beef round or sirloin

1 medium clove garlic, minced

1 (14.5-ounce) can diced tomatoes (undrained)

1 (8-ounce) can tomato sauce

1 (4-ounce) can diced mild green chilies

2 teaspoons finely chopped jalapeño pepper

1 tablespoon chili powder

1½ teaspoons salt

Dash ground cayenne pepper

1 small bay leaf

2 (15-ounce) cans red kidney beans, drained and rinsed

1. In a large skillet, heat oil over medium heat. Add onion, bell pepper, and ground beef. Sauté until beef is no longer pink and vegetables are tender.

2. Add garlic, tomatoes, tomato sauce, green chilies, jalapeño, chili powder, salt, cayenne, and bay leaf. Cover and simmer for 1½ hours. Add water as needed to keep from sticking.

3. Add beans to chili and heat through.

Cabbage Rolls

These are delicious with boiled potatoes.

INGREDIENTS | SERVES 4–6

1 large head green cabbage

1 pound lean ground beef

½ cup cooked long-grain white rice

1 small white onion, peeled and finely chopped

1 large egg, beaten

½ teaspoon salt

¼ teaspoon ground black pepper

½ teaspoon ground cinnamon, divided

1 (10.5-ounce) can condensed tomato soup, undiluted

2 (14.5-ounce) cans whole tomatoes

1. Cut the core out of cabbage and carefully cut off leaves, keeping them as large as possible. Blanch leaves in a pot of boiling water for about 5 minutes or until pliable. Drain and run cold water over leaves. Cut out large center veins of the largest leaves to make them easier to roll up.

2. Combine ground beef, rice, onion, egg, salt, and pepper in a medium bowl. Blend with your hands or a wooden spoon. Stir in ¼ teaspoon cinnamon.

3. Shape a few tablespoons of meat mixture into a round or cylindrical shape and place on a cabbage leaf. Roll up leaf, keeping filling enclosed. Secure roll with a toothpick and place in a large, heavy skillet or Dutch oven. Repeat with remaining meat mixture and cabbage leaves.

4. Combine tomato soup and tomatoes in a medium bowl with remaining ¼ teaspoon cinnamon. Stir to blend ingredients, breaking up tomatoes. Pour tomato mixture over cabbage rolls. Bring to a boil over medium-high heat. Reduce heat to low; cover and simmer for 1½ hours.

Barbecued Meatballs with Rice

These tangy meatballs are just wonderful cooked with a flavorful homemade barbecue sauce and served over hot rice.

INGREDIENTS | SERVES 8

1 pound ground beef round or sirloin
1 pound mild bulk pork sausage
⅓ cup minced white onion
2 large eggs, lightly beaten
½ cup fine dry bread crumbs
1 teaspoon salt
¼ teaspoon ground black pepper
½ teaspoon dried sage, crumbled
¼ teaspoon garlic powder
1½ cups ketchup
⅓ cup light brown sugar, packed
3 tablespoons apple cider vinegar
3 tablespoons soy sauce
2 cups hot cooked long-grain white rice

1. In a large bowl, combine ground beef, sausage, onion, eggs, bread crumbs, salt, pepper, sage, and garlic powder.

2. Shape meat into 1½" meatballs. Put half of the meatballs in a large, nonstick skillet over medium-low heat. Cook meatballs slowly, carefully turning to brown all sides. This will take about 12–18 minutes for each batch. Pour off excess fat.

3. In a small bowl, combine ketchup, brown sugar, vinegar, and soy sauce; mix until well blended. Transfer meatballs to a large, heavy saucepan or Dutch oven. Pour sauce over meatballs, mixing gently.

4. Cover and simmer for about 30–45 minutes, stirring occasionally to keep meatballs coated, until meatballs are cooked through. Serve meatballs over rice.

Beefy Macaroni Casserole

This is an easy and flavorful everyday family casserole. Serve with a tossed salad and crusty bread.

INGREDIENTS | SERVES 6

1½ pounds lean ground beef

1 cup chopped celery

1 cup chopped yellow onion

1 medium clove garlic, minced

1 cup small shell pasta or elbow macaroni

1 (14.5-ounce) can diced tomatoes (undrained)

1 teaspoon Worcestershire sauce

1 teaspoon salt

¼ teaspoon ground black pepper

1 teaspoon chili powder

2 cups shredded sharp Cheddar cheese, divided

1. In a large skillet over medium heat, cook ground beef, celery, onion, and garlic. When onion is tender and ground beef is no longer pink, about 6–8 minutes, drain off excess fat and transfer meat mixture to a large bowl.

2. Meanwhile, cook pasta in salted boiling water just until tender; drain and set aside.

3. Add tomatoes to meat mixture, along with Worcestershire sauce, salt, pepper, and chili powder. Stir in cooked pasta and 1½ cups shredded Cheddar cheese.

4. Transfer mixture to a baking dish sprayed lightly with nonstick cooking spray. Bake for 30 minutes until hot and bubbly. Top with remaining cheese and bake for about 5 minutes or until cheese is melted.

Ground Beef and Noodle Skillet

Another one-dish family meal, this beef-and-noodle skillet is very quick and easy.

INGREDIENTS | SERVES 4

1 pound lean ground beef

2 tablespoons butter

1 small yellow onion, peeled and chopped

2 medium cloves garlic, minced

8 ounces fresh button or cremini mushrooms, sliced

¼ cup dry red wine

1 tablespoon lemon juice

1 (10.5-ounce) can condensed beef broth

4 ounces uncooked wide noodles

Salt and ground black pepper

½ cup sour cream

Paprika

1. In a large skillet over medium-low heat, combine ground beef, butter, onion, garlic, and mushrooms. Cook, stirring and breaking up meat, until beef is no longer pink and vegetables are tender.

2. Add wine, lemon juice, and beef broth to beef mixture. Simmer for 10 minutes. Add noodles; cover and simmer for about 15 minutes or until noodles are tender. Check occasionally and stir to make sure mixture is not sticking to the pan; add a little water as needed. Season mixture with salt and pepper and stir in sour cream. Heat through.

3. Sprinkle with paprika just before serving.

Wine Substitutes

Some dishes are more dependent on wine for flavor, but it can be replaced in many recipes. Nonalcoholic wine, though it's a bit sweeter, can be used, or you can use a broth that will go with the recipe—beef broth in a beef or lamb dish or chicken broth in a veal, pork, or poultry dish. Other possibilities include soaking liquid from dried tomatoes or dried mushrooms and vegetable broth. For marinades, use 3 parts grape or apple juice and 1 part vinegar or lemon juice to take the place of wine, using red or white juice, depending on the color of the wine you are replacing.

Frito Pie

You can easily increase the number of servings in this recipe by adding another can of pinto beans or serving it over a large helping of Fritos. Choose mild, medium, or sharp Cheddar according to your preference.

INGREDIENTS | SERVES 12

2 pounds lean ground beef

2 tablespoons extra-virgin olive oil

1 large white onion, peeled and diced

2½ teaspoons garlic powder

3 tablespoons chili powder

4 teaspoons ground cumin

Salt and ground black pepper

2 (28-ounce) cans diced tomatoes (undrained)

1 (15-ounce) can pinto beans, drained and rinsed

1 (12-ounce) bag Fritos Original Corn Chips

4 cups shredded Cheddar cheese

Green onions, diced

1. Brown ground beef in a large nonstick skillet over medium heat, breaking apart meat as you do so. Drain off any fat rendered from meat.

2. Stir in oil, onion, garlic powder, chili powder, cumin, and salt and pepper to taste; sauté for 5 minutes or until onion is transparent. Transfer ground beef mixture to a 4- to 6-quart slow cooker.

3. Stir in tomatoes and pinto beans. Cover and cook on low for 5–6 hours. (When you taste chili for seasoning, keep in mind that it'll be served over salty corn chips.)

4. To serve, place a handful (1 ounce or more) of Fritos on each plate. Ladle chili over Fritos. Top with cheese. Sprinkle with diced green onion.

Veal Chops Marsala

These veal chops make a wonderful choice for a special weekend meal.
Serve with mashed potatoes and a vegetable side dish.

INGREDIENTS | SERVES 4

1 tablespoon butter

3 tablespoons olive oil, divided

4 ounces fresh cremini mushrooms, thinly sliced

4 green onions, thinly sliced

1 medium clove garlic, minced

2 tablespoons all-purpose flour

¼ cup dry Marsala wine

1½ cups beef broth

Ground black pepper

4 (1"-thick) veal chops

Salt

The Fluffiest Mashed Potatoes

Boil about 3 pounds of baking potatoes. When the potatoes are tender, drain well and put through a ricer. Mash the hot drained potatoes with about ⅓ cup whole milk or half-and-half, ¼ cup butter, and salt and pepper to taste.

1. Preheat oven to 375°F. In a medium, heavy saucepan over medium-low heat, melt butter with 2 tablespoons olive oil. Add mushrooms and sauté until just tender, about 5–8 minutes. Add green onions and garlic; sauté for 1 minute. Add flour and cook, stirring constantly, for about 30 seconds. Add Marsala wine and beef broth. Cook until thickened and slightly reduced, stirring frequently. Add a little pepper; set aside.

2. Season both sides of the veal chops with salt and pepper.

3. Heat remaining 1 tablespoon oil in a large ovenproof skillet over medium-high heat. Add veal chops; sear for about 3–4 minutes on each side. Pour sauce over chops and move the skillet to the oven. Bake for about 15–20 minutes until chops are cooked to desired doneness. Arrange veal on a serving plate and spoon sauce over chops.

Lemony Veal Cutlets with Mushrooms

This is a quick and easy dish to prepare, and it looks quite elegant. Try it with hot buttered noodles and a green vegetable, or you could serve the cutlets with hot cooked rice.

INGREDIENTS | SERVES 6

1½ pounds thin veal cutlets

Salt and ground black pepper

¼ cup all-purpose flour

2 tablespoons olive oil

4 tablespoons butter, divided

8 ounces fresh cremini mushrooms, sliced

1 medium clove garlic, minced

Zest and juice of 1 medium lemon

1 teaspoon chopped fresh rosemary

2 tablespoons chopped fresh flat-leaf parsley

2 tablespoons dry white wine

1. Sprinkle cutlets with salt and pepper. Dredge veal in flour to coat lightly.

2. In a large skillet over medium heat, combine olive oil and 2 tablespoons butter. Add several veal pieces and sauté, turning once, until browned. Remove browned veal from the skillet and repeat with remaining cutlets.

3. Add remaining 2 tablespoons of butter to the skillet. When butter has melted, add sliced mushrooms and sauté until tender and golden brown. Return veal cutlets to the skillet. Add minced garlic, lemon zest and juice, rosemary and parsley, and wine. Bring to a simmer. Cover and let simmer for about 3 minutes. Arrange veal cutlets on a serving plate and top with mushrooms and lemon sauce.

Fresh vs. Dry Herbs

Fresh herbs are often the best choice for flavor, but you'll still get great flavor with good dried herbs. Use about ⅓ the amount of herbs when substituting for fresh. Dried herbs do lose their strength over time, so it's a good idea to mark them with an expiration date when you first break the seal. As a general rule, dried herbs stored in an airtight container in a cool, dry place should retain their flavor for 1 year or longer, and ground spices should be good for about 2 years.

Savory Veal Stew with Vegetables

This mushroom-packed veal stew is delicious served over hot cooked rice. It's also great over mashed potatoes or polenta.

INGREDIENTS | SERVES 4

1½ pounds veal roast or stewing veal

2 tablespoons all-purpose flour

1½ teaspoons salt

¼ teaspoon ground black pepper

2 tablespoons olive oil, or more as needed

1 pound cremini mushrooms, sliced

1 cup water

12 small whole white onions, peeled

1 pound baby carrots

1½ cups frozen peas

2 cups hot cooked long-grain white rice

1. Cut veal into bite-sized cubes. Combine with flour, salt, and pepper in a food storage bag; toss to coat well.

2. In a large, heavy saucepan or Dutch oven, heat 2 table-spoons oil over medium heat. Cook veal in 2 batches, turning frequently until browned on all sides. As veal browns, transfer to a bowl.

3. Add mushrooms to pan drippings and cook until browned and tender. Add more oil to the skillet if needed. Return browned veal to the pan, then add water, onions, and carrots. Bring to a boil over high heat. Reduce heat to low; cover and simmer for about 1 hour or until veal is tender. Stir in peas and cook for 10–15 minutes or until peas are tender.

4. Arrange mounds of hot rice in individual shallow bowls or on plates. Spoon veal stew over and around rice.

Herb-Pecan Crusted Rack of Lamb

This is a delicious and elegant main dish for 2, but you can also double the recipe to serve 4 people. Rack of lamb pairs well with mashed potatoes and buttered green beans or wilted spinach.

INGREDIENTS | SERVES 2

1 rack of lamb (about 8 chops)
2 teaspoons olive oil
Salt and ground black pepper
1½ teaspoons dried rosemary, crumbled
1½ teaspoons dried oregano, crumbled
1 tablespoon chopped fresh flat-leaf parsley
⅓ cup finely chopped pecans
1 tablespoon Dijon mustard

1. Preheat oven to 400°F.

2. Wash lamb; pat dry and cut between ribs into 2 equal portions. Rub lamb with olive oil, salt, and pepper. Position lamb, meaty side up, in a roasting pan. Roast for 12 minutes. Remove from the oven and let cool for 10 minutes.

3. Combine rosemary, oregano, parsley, and pecans in a shallow bowl or plate. Rub mustard over lamb, then coat with pecan and herb mixture. Return to the oven and bake for about 10 minutes or to desired doneness.

Spring Lamb Stew with Okra

The flavors of okra and tomatoes complement each other and enhance this lamb stew beautifully. Serve with hot cooked rice and a green salad.

INGREDIENTS | SERVES 4

1 pound frozen sliced okra, thawed
¼ cup white wine vinegar
3 tablespoons olive oil
1½ pounds lean lamb, cut into small cubes
1 medium sweet onion, peeled and chopped
1 teaspoon salt
½ teaspoon ground black pepper
¼ teaspoon ground cumin
Dash garlic powder
1 (14.5-ounce) can diced tomatoes (undrained)
1 (8-ounce) can tomato sauce
2 tablespoons lemon juice

1. Place okra in a large bowl; pour vinegar over okra and let stand for about 25 minutes. Drain and rinse okra under cold water.

2. Meanwhile, heat olive oil in a large, heavy saucepan or Dutch oven over medium heat; add lamb and onion. Sauté, stirring frequently, until both are browned.

3. Sprinkle lamb mixture with salt and pepper. Add cumin, garlic powder, tomatoes, tomato sauce, lemon juice, and prepared okra. Reduce heat to low; cover and simmer for about 1 hour or until lamb is tender.

Garlic-Roasted Leg of Lamb

This is a wonderful roasted leg of lamb with garlic and herbs,
perfect for Sunday dinner or a family holiday meal.

INGREDIENTS | SERVES 6

1 (6-pound) bone-in leg of lamb
2 tablespoons lemon juice
2 medium cloves garlic, minced
1½ teaspoons dried rosemary, crumbled
1 teaspoon dried thyme, crumbled
1 teaspoon salt
¼ teaspoon ground black pepper
Lemon wedges

DIY Rack

If you don't have a rack for your roasting pan, try this quick alternative. Cut a few carrots in half lengthwise, and cut a few ribs of celery in half crosswise. Place the halved carrots and celery pieces in the roasting pan, flat side down. Place the roast on top of the vegetables. When the cooking is done, just throw away the vegetables.

1. Preheat oven to 325°F.

2. Rinse leg of lamb with cold water and then pat dry. Rub lamb all over with lemon juice.

3. Combine garlic, rosemary, thyme, salt, and pepper in a small bowl; rub all over lamb.

4. Place lamb, fat side up, on a rack in a roasting pan. Insert a meat thermometer into thickest part of the roast without touching bone or fat. Roast for 20–25 minutes per pound. The lamb should register 125°F–145°F, depending on what degree of doneness you like. Remove lamb from the oven and let stand for 10 minutes before carving.

5. Arrange slices of lamb on a serving platter with lemon wedges.

Orange and Thyme Lamb Chops

Orange and thyme add great flavor to these lamb chops. Serve with mashed or baked sweet potatoes and leafy greens.

INGREDIENTS | SERVES 4

4 shoulder lamb chops, about ¾" thick

½ teaspoon finely grated orange zest

¼ cup fresh orange juice

½ teaspoon dried thyme, crumbled

1 tablespoon olive oil

4 ounces fresh cremini mushrooms, sliced

Baked Sweet Potatoes

Baked sweet potatoes are easy and delicious, and they pair well with lamb. Brush each small to medium sweet potato with a little vegetable oil. Bake at 450°F until tender. With a sharp knife, cut slits in the tops lengthwise and crosswise; open up the sweet potatoes a bit and top with butter and a sprinkling of salt and paprika or cinnamon sugar.

1. Trim lamb chops. Combine orange peel, juice, and thyme in a small bowl. Pour over lamb chops and refrigerate for 4 hours. Turn a few times to keep lamb chops coated with orange mixture. Drain lamb chops, reserving orange marinade mixture.

2. In a large skillet over medium-high, heat 1 tablespoon olive oil; brown lamb chops quickly on both sides. Reduce heat to medium-low; add mushrooms and orange mixture. Cover and simmer for about 40 minutes until lamb is tender. Uncover and simmer for 5 minutes.

3. Arrange chops on a serving plate; spoon juices over them.

CHAPTER 7

Pork and Ham

Herb and Garlic Roasted Pork Loin and Potatoes

This is a wonderful meal and so easy to prepare. The potatoes are roasted right along with the pork. You can replace the potatoes with 1½ pounds fingerlings or new potatoes.

INGREDIENTS | SERVES 8

1 (4-pound) boneless pork loin roast
1 medium clove garlic, minced
1 teaspoon onion powder
2½ teaspoons dried thyme, divided
Salt and ground black pepper
8 medium Yukon gold potatoes
2 tablespoons olive oil
2 teaspoons minced fresh or freeze-dried chives
½ teaspoon garlic powder

1. Preheat oven to 325°F.

2. Rub pork roast all over with garlic, onion powder, and 1½ teaspoons thyme. Sprinkle with salt and pepper. Place in a shallow roasting pan and roast for 1 hour.

3. Meanwhile, peel and quarter potatoes or cut into wedges. Cook potatoes in boiling water for about 10 minutes. Drain and let cool slightly. In a large bowl, toss potatoes with olive oil, remaining thyme, chives, and garlic powder; sprinkle with salt and pepper.

4. Arrange potatoes around pork loin roast and return to the oven. Roast for about 1 hour longer or until pork registers 155°F–160°F. Remove from oven and loosely cover with foil. Let rest for 15 minutes before slicing.

5. Slice pork and arrange on a serving platter with potatoes.

Cajun-Seasoned Pork Tenderloin

This pork tenderloin is both easy and delicious, and it cooks up quickly. Serve it with creamy butter beans or Creamy Lima Bean and Corn Succotash (see recipe in Chapter 11), along with mashed potatoes or sweet potatoes.

INGREDIENTS | SERVES 4

2 pounds pork tenderloin

1¼ teaspoons salt

1 teaspoon garlic powder

½ teaspoon onion powder

½ teaspoon dried thyme, crumbled

½ teaspoon dried oregano, crumbled

½ teaspoon ground black pepper

¼ teaspoon ground cayenne pepper

"The Other White Meat"

According to the National Pork Board, lean and delicious pork tenderloin is actually lower in calories than boneless, skinless chicken breasts. Pork tenderloin makes a healthy alternative to beef and other cuts of pork. The National Pork Board website is a terrific resource where you'll find safety information, news, nutritional facts, and a great variety of recipes. Visit *www.pork.org.*

1. Cut pork tenderloin into 1" medallions (about 16). With the heel of your hand, gently flatten medallions slightly.

2. Combine salt, garlic powder, onion powder, thyme, oregano, pepper, and cayenne in a small bowl. Sprinkle over medallions, lightly rubbing spices into both sides.

3. Using a large stovetop grill pan or skillet, grill medallions over medium-high heat for about 2 minutes on each side to sear or make nice grill marks. Lower heat to medium and cook for about 12 minutes, turning occasionally, until cooked through. Pork should register about 155°F on an instant-read thermometer.

Stuffed Crown Roast of Pork with Apples

A tasty stuffing of apple and dried cranberry complements this impressive roast. You might have to order this cut from your butcher or grocer ahead of time, so keep that in mind if you're planning a special dinner.

INGREDIENTS | SERVES 8

4 cups bread cubes
2 tablespoons butter
½ cup minced yellow onion
¼ cup chopped celery
2 cups diced apple
¼ cup chopped dried cranberries or raisins
¼ cup light brown sugar, packed
¼ cup hot chicken broth or water
1 tablespoon lemon juice
1½ teaspoons salt
⅛ teaspoon ground black pepper
½ teaspoon dried sage, crumbled
¼ teaspoon dried thyme, crumbled
Dash ground marjoram
1 (7- to 9-pound) crown roast of pork

1. Preheat oven to 325°F.

2. Spread bread cubes on a large baking sheet; put in the oven to dry and toast lightly.

3. Heat butter in a large skillet over medium-low heat. When butter is hot, add onion, celery, apple, and cranberries or raisins. Cook mixture, stirring frequently, for about 8 minutes or until vegetables are tender.

4. Remove from heat and stir in brown sugar, broth or water, lemon juice, salt, pepper, sage, thyme, and marjoram. Stir in toasted bread cubes.

5. Place roast on a rack in a roasting pan. Scoop out any extra pork trimmings the butcher might have put in the center and carve out a little more so you'll have room for the stuffing.

6. Stuff the center of roast, piling stuffing in a mound. Cover stuffing with a piece of foil and wrap the ends of each bone with a small piece of foil.

7. Roast for 3–4 hours or until the temperature registers about 175°F on a meat thermometer or instant-read thermometer. Insert the thermometer into a meaty section, trying not to touch bone or fat.

8. Remove foil and decorate the tips of the bones with white paper frills if desired.

Roasted Pork Tenderloin with Rosemary

This is a delicious and light main dish made with only 4 ingredients, plus salt and pepper.

INGREDIENTS | SERVES 4

2 pounds pork tenderloin

2 medium cloves garlic, halved

1 tablespoon olive oil

3 tablespoons chopped fresh rosemary
or 3 teaspoons dried rosemary,
crumbled

Salt and ground black pepper

1. Preheat oven to 400°F. Line a large baking pan with foil; spray with nonstick cooking spray. Place the baking pan in the oven.

2. While pan is heating, trim pork, discarding excess fat. Using a sharp knife, butterfly pork tenderloin: Cut tenderloin nearly in half lengthwise. Open, turn over, and cut each thick side nearly in half lengthwise. Pound pork lightly with the palm of your hand to make meat an even thickness.

3. Rub butterflied pork tenderloin all over with garlic halves, then olive oil. Sprinkle rosemary on both sides. Sprinkle with salt and pepper.

4. Place pork on the hot baking pan; return to the oven. Roast for about 20 minutes or to about 155°F–160°F on a meat thermometer or instant-read thermometer. Remove from the oven and let stand for about 5 minutes. Slice and serve.

Chopped Pork Chili

Buy chopped pork from your favorite barbecue hut or make your own by slow smoking a pork shoulder roast, then deboning and chopping the meat.

INGREDIENTS | SERVES 6

2 pounds chopped barbecue pork

3 tablespoons chili powder

1 medium yellow onion, peeled and diced

1 medium green bell pepper, seeded and diced

2 large garlic cloves, minced

1 (10-ounce) can diced tomatoes and green chilies (undrained)

½ cup hickory-flavored barbecue sauce

1 (14-ounce) can tomato sauce

1 teaspoon Tabasco sauce

1 cup water

1 (16-ounce) can black-eyed peas, drained

Salt and ground black pepper

⅓ cup minced green onion

1. In a large soup pot, combine pork and chili powder; toss to mix. Let stand for 5 minutes.

2. Add onion, bell pepper, garlic, tomatoes and green chilies, barbecue sauce, tomato sauce, Tabasco, and water; mix well. Bring to a boil over high heat. Reduce heat to medium; simmer for 15 minutes.

3. Add peas; simmer for 15 minutes, adding small amounts of water if sauce becomes too dry.

4. Remove from heat. Add salt and pepper to taste. Stir in green onions; let stand for 5 minutes before serving.

A Matter of Convenience

Chili powder requires simmering time to dissolve and achieve full flavor, but that doesn't mean every batch of chili has to be a lengthy ordeal. Substituting cooked and shredded beef pot roast, cooked and cubed poultry, or cooked and chopped pork for raw meats can make chili preparations much easier. Allow 20–30 minutes of simmering time for the chili powder, tomatoes, and vegetables. You can add the meat or poultry at any point during the simmering process.

Oven-Barbecued Pork Chops

Make the barbecue sauce in the morning and let these chops marinate while you're at work, then pop them in the oven when you get home.

INGREDIENTS | SERVES 6

¾ cup ketchup

¾ cup apple cider vinegar

1½ cups water

1 medium yellow onion, peeled and finely chopped

1 medium clove garlic, minced

2 teaspoons salt

½ teaspoon ground black pepper

2 teaspoons Worcestershire sauce

3 tablespoons light brown sugar

¼ teaspoon ground cayenne pepper

6 (1"-thick) center-cut loin pork chops

1 medium yellow onion, peeled and sliced

Cooking Times for Pork

There's really no need to cook pork until well done. Better pork production makes trichinosis quite rare these days, and an internal temperature of 155°F–160°F will make pork perfectly safe. Use an instant-read thermometer to check pork chops, tenderloin, and other cuts, or a meat thermometer for pork roasts. Remember that the temperature will rise another 10°F or so during the 15 minutes you let it rest before carving.

1. In a medium saucepan, combine ketchup, vinegar, water, chopped onion, garlic, salt, pepper, Worcestershire sauce, brown sugar, and cayenne pepper. Bring to a boil. Reduce heat to low and simmer for about 15 minutes, stirring frequently. Let stand to cool slightly.

2. Rinse pork chops and pat dry. Place chops in a nonreactive bowl. Pour cooled sauce over chops, turning to coat thoroughly. Cover and refrigerate for at least 3 hours or all day.

3. Preheat oven to 350°F. Arrange pork chops in a shallow baking dish. Top with sliced onion, then pour sauce over all.

4. Bake for about 1–1½ hours or until chops are tender, basting occasionally.

Cornbread-Stuffed Pork Chops

This is great for a weekend meal or romantic dinner for two.

INGREDIENTS | SERVES 2

2 bone-in loin pork chops, about 1¼" thick
Salt and ground black pepper to taste
3 tablespoons butter
¼ cup finely chopped celery
¼ cup finely chopped yellow onion
1 tablespoon finely chopped red bell pepper
¼ cup frozen whole-kernel corn, thawed
1 cup fresh or packaged cornbread crumbs
¼ cup chopped pecans
¼ teaspoon dried thyme, crumbled
Dash dried sage, crumbled
3–4 tablespoons chicken broth

1. In a medium saucepan, heat butter over medium-low heat; add celery, onion, and red bell pepper. Sauté until tender. Add corn, cornbread crumbs, pecans, thyme, sage, and enough chicken broth to moisten.

2. Preheat oven to 350°F. Spoon stuffing into the pockets of the chops. Set remaining stuffing aside. In a large skillet over medium heat, brown pork chops, turning to brown both sides. If the skillet is not oven-safe, transfer to a baking dish. Push chops aside and spoon remaining stuffing in the middle of the skillet or baking dish. Position chops over stuffing. Cover and bake for 25–35 minutes or until pork chops are cooked through.

Pork Chops with Orange Sauce

Pork and oranges or juice are very good together. Serve the chops with hot cooked rice and green beans.

INGREDIENTS | SERVES 6

6 (1"-thick) pork chops
Salt
½ cup all-purpose flour
2 tablespoons olive oil
2 navel oranges
3 tablespoons light brown sugar
1½ tablespoons cornstarch
⅛ teaspoon ground allspice
1¾ cups water
3 tablespoons lemon juice
⅓ cup orange juice
¼ cup chopped dried cranberries

1. Trim pork chops, sprinkle both sides with salt, and then dredge in flour.

2. Heat oil in a large skillet over medium heat; brown pork chops on both sides. Section oranges and place a few sections on each chop.

3. In a medium saucepan, combine brown sugar with cornstarch and allspice; stir in water. Cook, stirring constantly, until thickened. Add lemon juice, orange juice, and cranberries. Pour sauce over chops. Reduce heat to low; cover and simmer for 30–45 minutes or until chops are tender.

Spicy Crab Cakes (Chapter 9)

Perfect Buttermilk Biscuits (Chapter 2)

Key Lime Pie (Chapter 13)

Pulled Pork Barbecue Sandwiches (Chapter 5)

Savory Collard Greens (Chapter 11)

Peach Cobbler (Chapter 15)

Kentucky Mint Julep (Chapter 16)

The Best Chocolate Chip Cookies (Chapter 14)

Corn Chowder (Chapter 4)

Fried Catfish (Chapter 9)

Crispy Fried Oysters (Chapter 9)

Creamy Macaroni and Cheese (Chapter 10)

Barbecued Chicken Wings (Chapter 2)

Chicken and Dumplings (Chapter 8)

Red Velvet Cake (Chapter 13)

Southern-Style Ice Tea (Chapter 16)

Cajun-Style Dirty Rice (Chapter 10)

Jambalaya (Chapter 9)

Fried Green Tomatoes (Chapter 11)

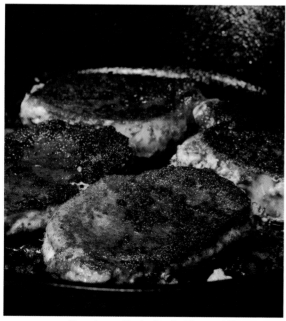

Southern-Style Pork Chops (Chapter 7)

Old-Fashioned Peanut Butter Cookies
(Chapter 14)

Brown Sugar Pecan Pie (Chapter 13)

Beignets (Chapter 3)

Cranberry Chutney (Chapter 12)

Southern-Style Pork Chops

To make this soul food dish healthier, bake the pork chops in a 375°F oven for 45 minutes instead.

INGREDIENTS | SERVES 6

6 (1"-thick) pork chops
2 teaspoons salt
2 teaspoons garlic powder
1½ teaspoons dry mustard
1 teaspoon smoked paprika
½ teaspoon ground black pepper
¼ teaspoon onion powder
½ teaspoon dried oregano, crumbled
½ cup all-purpose flour
½ cup vegetable oil

1. Rinse pork chops and pat dry. Combine salt, garlic powder, dry mustard, smoked paprika, pepper, onion powder, and oregano in a wide, shallow bowl. Place flour in another wide, shallow bowl.

2. Rub seasoning mix into each chop on both sides. Dredge pork chops in flour and shake off excess. Place chops on a wire rack for 30 minutes before cooking.

3. Add oil to a cast-iron skillet and place over medium heat. When oil is shimmering and hot, slide 3 or 4 pork chops into the skillet and cook on each side for 10–12 minutes. Place cooked pork chops on paper towels and keep warm. Repeat with the other pork chops. Serve while warm.

Slow-Cooker Spareribs

This main dish is designed to keep you out of the kitchen! Make these delicious ribs for visiting friends and relatives, parties, or potluck dinners. This recipe can easily be doubled for a crowd, and cooking instructions will remain the same.

INGREDIENTS | SERVES 4

4 pounds pork spareribs
Seasoned salt
Ground black pepper
1 large yellow onion, peeled, quartered, and sliced
1 (16-ounce) bottle barbecue sauce

1. Heat broiler. Line a broiler pan with foil and grease the broiler rack with oil. Sprinkle ribs with seasoned salt and pepper; cut into smaller portions of about 3 or 4 ribs each, slicing between ribs.

2. Place ribs on the prepared rack and broil about 4" from heat for 25 minutes. Turn ribs occasionally.

3. Transfer spareribs to a 4- to 6-quart slow cooker along with onion and barbecue sauce. Cover and cook on low setting for 6–8 hours until pork chops are tender.

Stovetop Spareribs

After first broiling the spareribs, you can simmer them on the stovetop over low heat, covered, for about 1½ hours. Or, cook them on the high setting in the slow cooker for 3–4 hours.

Barbecued Ribs with Spicy Sauce

These delicious ribs are oven-barbecued with a spicy homemade sauce.

INGREDIENTS | SERVES 6–8

6 pounds pork spareribs

1 teaspoon salt plus more to taste, divided

½ teaspoon ground black pepper plus more to taste, divided

2 medium yellow onions, peeled and thinly sliced

1 tablespoon apple cider vinegar

1 tablespoon Worcestershire sauce

1½ teaspoons paprika

¼ teaspoon ground cayenne pepper

1½ teaspoons chili powder

1 cup ketchup

1 cup water

Tender Spareribs

Here's a neat tip for the juiciest, most tender spareribs. Before cooking spareribs, remove the thin, cellophane-like skin from the back of the ribs. Put the ribs meaty side down, get your finger under the thin membrane, and then begin to pull it off. Repeat with the remaining skin, loosening as much as possible with your finger before pulling. The ribs will be more tender and easier to cut.

1. Preheat oven to 350°F. Line a large roasting pan with heavy-duty foil.

2. Cut racks of ribs into smaller portions of about 3 or 4 ribs each, slicing between the ribs. Sprinkle with salt and pepper to taste. Place ribs in the prepared pan. Cover with onions.

3. Combine vinegar, Worcestershire sauce, paprika, cayenne pepper, chili powder, ketchup, water, 1 teaspoon salt, and ½ teaspoon ground black pepper in a medium saucepan. Bring to a boil, stirring. Pour over ribs.

4. Cover the roasting pan with foil and bake for about 1½–2 hours or until very tender. Baste occasionally and turn spareribs a few times. Remove foil cover for the last 15 minutes of baking to let ribs brown.

Country-Style Pork Ribs with Apples

The sweet onions and apples are cooked slowly, but it's well worth it!

INGREDIENTS | SERVES 4

4 tablespoons butter, divided

1 large sweet onion, peeled and thinly sliced

3 large apples, peeled, cored, and thinly sliced

2 tablespoons honey

2 tablespoons light brown sugar

½ teaspoon ground cinnamon

½ cup all-purpose flour

1 teaspoon salt

¼ teaspoon ground black pepper

¼ teaspoon dried thyme, crumbled

6–8 boneless country-style pork ribs

2 tablespoons olive oil

¼ cup water or chicken broth

Best Apples for Eating and Cooking

Some of the best baking or cooking apples include Cortland, Gala, Golden Delicious, Northern Spy, Rome Beauty, Granny Smith, and Lady. The sweeter varieties include Golden Delicious and Lady apples, while the rest tend to be on the tart or tangy side. For eating, some of the best apples are Fuji, Red Delicious, Spartan, Winesap, and McIntosh.

1. In a large skillet or saucepan, melt 2 tablespoons butter. Add onion; sauté over medium-low heat until onion is tender, about 5–8 minutes. Add apple and remaining butter. Continue to cook, stirring frequently, until apples are tender. Add honey, brown sugar, and cinnamon. Continue cooking, stirring occasionally, until onions and apple are very tender and golden brown, about 10 minutes. Set aside and keep warm.

2. In a large food storage bag, combine flour with salt, pepper, and thyme. Add ribs a few at a time and shake well to coat with flour mixture.

3. Heat oil in a large, heavy skillet over medium heat. Add ribs and sear on all sides. Reduce heat to medium-low, add water or chicken broth, and cover the skillet. Cook for about 25 minutes until tender and cooked through.

4. Remove pork to a serving plate and serve with apples and onions.

Slow-Cooker Pork and Black Bean Stew

Serve with Southern Skillet Cornbread (see recipe in Chapter 2) and garnish with chopped tomatoes and sliced green onions.

INGREDIENTS | SERVES 8

1½ pounds lean pork tenderloin

½ cup all-purpose flour

1 teaspoon chili powder

½ teaspoon salt

¼ teaspoon ground black pepper

2 tablespoons olive oil

½–1 pound bulk pork sausage

1 large yellow onion, peeled and chopped

1 (10.5-ounce) can condensed chicken broth

4 medium cloves garlic, minced

1 tablespoon chopped fresh flat-leaf parsley

¼ teaspoon dried oregano, crumbled

2 (15-ounce) cans black beans, drained and rinsed

1 cup frozen whole-kernel corn, thawed

1 medium red bell pepper, seeded and chopped

2 large plum tomatoes, diced

1 teaspoon lemon juice

1. Rinse pork; pat dry, then cut into small cubes. Set aside. In a food storage bag, combine flour, chili powder, ½ teaspoon salt, and ¼ teaspoon pepper. Add pork cubes and toss to coat.

2. In a large skillet, heat olive oil over medium heat. Add coated pork to the skillet, along with any flour remaining in the bag. Brown pork cubes, stirring frequently. Transfer browned pork to a 4- to 6-quart slow cooker.

3. Add pork sausage and onions to the same skillet and cook over medium heat, stirring frequently, until browned. Add to the slow cooker along with condensed chicken broth and garlic. Cover and cook on low setting for 7–9 hours or on high setting for 3½–4½ hours.

4. Add parsley, oregano, black beans, corn, bell pepper, tomatoes, and lemon juice. Cover and cook on low for 1½–2 hours or on high setting for about 1 hour.

The Versatile Slow Cooker

Slow cookers come in several sizes and with many convenient features. The slow cooker is a wonderful way to cook tougher cuts of beef or pork for pot roasts or sandwiches, and slow-cooked stews are superb. You'll use it for keeping dips, meatballs, and other appetizers warm at parties. You can also use a slow cooker to make a wonderful moist dressing for poultry, and it keeps your oven free for other holiday dishes.

Ham with Cheese Grits

This delicious ham-and-grits meal is so easy to put together. Serve it with spinach or green beans for a complete dinner, or serve along with breads and other dishes as a brunch dish.

INGREDIENTS | SERVES 6

1½ cups whole milk

1⅔ cups chicken broth

½ teaspoon salt

½ cup water

3 tablespoons butter, divided

1 cup quick-cooking grits

12 thick-cut slices fully cooked ham (about 1 pound)

⅓ cup peach or apricot preserves

1 tablespoon apple cider vinegar

1 cup shredded sharp Cheddar cheese

What Are Grits?

Hominy is made from corn, and grits are ground from the hominy, using the same process used to make the finer masa harina flour. In fact, around Charleston, South Carolina, people call them "hominy grits." You can use quick grits, but whole-ground grits will have much better flavor if you can find them. Try your local natural foods store or an online source.

1. In a large saucepan, bring milk, chicken broth, salt, and water to a boil. Add 2 tablespoons butter and slowly whisk in grits. Reduce heat to low and cook, stirring frequently, for 15–20 minutes until creamy. Cover and remove from heat; set aside.

2. Melt remaining 1 tablespoon butter in a large skillet over medium-high heat. Cook ham slices in batches, cooking for about 1 minute on each side. Remove ham to a warm platter and cover with foil. Set aside.

3. Add preserves and vinegar to skillet with ham drippings. Stir to blend well. Cook until reduced and slightly thickened, stirring frequently. Pour over ham.

4. Add shredded cheese to hot grits; stir until cheese is melted.

5. Serve grits with sliced ham.

Creamy Ham with Cornbread Wedges

This is a great combination of flavors, similar to an "à la king" type of dish.
Bake fresh cornbread for this recipe, if you have the time.

INGREDIENTS | SERVES 8

4 ounces fresh button mushrooms, sliced

¼ cup butter

¼ cup all-purpose flour

1 cup chicken broth, warmed

1½ cups half-and-half

Salt and ground black pepper

1 cup diced cooked chicken

2 cups diced cooked ham

½ cup chopped green bell pepper

¼ cup chopped red bell pepper

8 wedges Southern Skillet Cornbread (see recipe in Chapter 2)

1. In a large skillet over medium-low heat, sauté mushrooms in butter until tender, about 5–8 minutes. Blend flour into mushroom mixture until well incorporated; cook for about 30 seconds.

2. Gradually add chicken broth, half-and-half, and salt and pepper to taste, stirring constantly. Cook until thickened and bubbly, stirring frequently. Add chicken, ham, and bell pepper to sauce mixture; combine thoroughly. Taste and adjust seasonings. Heat thoroughly.

3. Serve over split wedges or squares of warm cornbread.

Toasted Flour

Did you know you can eliminate the raw flour taste from sauces and gravies by toasting the flour? Spread the flour on a baking sheet and cook in a 300°F oven for about 25 minutes. The flour will be lightly browned and makes a more flavorful addition to a basic sauce or gravy. You might want to toast a cup or so to keep on hand.

Honey and Brown Sugar Glazed Ham

The honey and brown sugar make a flavorful glaze for this ham. You can also use maple syrup or sorghum in place of the honey.

INGREDIENTS | SERVES 10

1 (8-pound) fully cooked ham
Whole cloves
½ cup honey
½ cup light brown sugar, packed
½ cup apple juice or apple cider
1 tablespoon plus 1½ teaspoons Dijon mustard
Dash ground cinnamon
Dash ground ginger

1. Preheat oven to 325°F. Line a roasting pan with foil.

2. Place ham, fat side up, on the rack of the prepared pan. Score the fat in a diamond pattern and stud with cloves. Bake for about 18 minutes per pound or until the internal temperature reaches 145°F.

3. Meanwhile, in a medium saucepan, combine remaining ingredients; bring to a boil. Cook glaze for about 2 minutes. Spoon half of the glaze over ham about 20 minutes before ham is done. Spoon remaining glaze over ham about 10 minutes before done. Remove ham from the oven and let stand at room temperature for about 30 minutes before carving.

Glazed Cola Ham

This is a very popular way to cook ham. Serve it with pineapple slices, sweet potatoes, and green beans.

INGREDIENTS | SERVES 8

1 (7-pound) fully cooked ham
4 cups cola (not diet)
¾ cup light brown sugar, packed
2 teaspoons dry mustard
1½ tablespoons Dijon mustard

1. Preheat oven to 325°F.

2. Place ham, fat side down, in a roasting pan. Pour cola in the pan. Bake for about 18 minutes per pound to an internal temperature of about 145°F, basting with cola frequently.

3. Increase oven temperature to 350°F. Cut rind from ham. Combine brown sugar and mustards; spread mixture over ham. Place a rack in the roasting pan and place ham on it. Bake for 30–45 minutes, basting several times.

4. Remove ham from the oven and let stand at room temperature for about 30 minutes before carving.

Ham and Rice Casserole

This is a quick and easy dish to fix with leftover ham, and it's a delicious meal the whole family will enjoy.

INGREDIENTS | SERVES 6–8

2½ cups hot cooked long-grain white rice

2½ cups diced ham

2 cups frozen mixed vegetables, cooked and drained

¼ cup butter

1 cup sliced button or cremini mushrooms

¼ cup all-purpose flour

2 cups whole milk

1 cup shredded Cheddar cheese

Salt and ground black pepper

1 cup fresh bread crumbs

2 tablespoons melted butter

Make-Ahead Casserole

Like many casseroles, this one can be prepared in advance and frozen for up to 2 months. Just line your casserole dish with heavy-duty foil. Prepare the casserole ingredients as directed, adding the mixture to the foil-lined baking dish. Once the casserole is frozen, grasp the overhanging foil, lift out of the casserole dish, and then wrap completely with the foil. Label the casserole and include the current date. It will fit the same dish perfectly when you unwrap it and get ready to bake. You can thaw the casserole in the refrigerator, or if you don't thaw before cooking, double the baking time in a 350°F oven and check with a knife to make sure it's hot in the center.

1. Preheat oven to 325°F.

2. In a large bowl, combine rice, ham, and cooked mixed vegetables.

3. In a medium saucepan, melt ¼ cup butter over medium-low heat. Add mushrooms and sauté until tender and golden brown, about 6–8 minutes. Blend in flour, stirring until hot and bubbly. Gradually stir in milk. Cook sauce, stirring constantly, until mixture is thickened. Stir in cheese until melted and then add salt and pepper to taste.

4. Stir sauce into rice, ham, and vegetable mixture. Transfer to a 2½-quart baking dish. In a small bowl, toss bread crumbs with 2 tablespoons melted butter; sprinkle over the top of the casserole.

5. Bake for 30 minutes or until hot and bubbly. If bread crumbs aren't as brown as you like, turn on the broiler for about 2 minutes and broil just until browned.

Ham with Red-Eye Gravy

This is a traditional Southern recipe, and the ham is delicious with grits and eggs. The name "red-eye" purportedly comes from what looks like a red eye in the center of the gravy.

INGREDIENTS | SERVES 2

2 tablespoons butter
4 slices country ham, about ¼" thick
¾ cup ground coffee
¼ cup water

1. Melt butter in a medium skillet over medium-low to medium heat. Fry ham slices until browned on both sides. Remove ham to a platter; cut into serving-sized pieces and keep warm.

2. Add coffee and water to the same skillet. Bring to a boil and continue to boil for 2–3 minutes until reduced slightly, stirring constantly. Serve ham slices with gravy over the top.

Baked Ham and Pineapple Slices with Raisins

This is an easy and tasty dish to make with sliced leftover ham or packaged ham slices. Serve the ham and pineapple slices with sweet potatoes or mashed potatoes and a green vegetable.

INGREDIENTS | SERVES 4

8 slices cooked ham, about ½" thick
1 (8-ounce) can sliced pineapple, drained
½ cup raisins
1 cup pineapple juice
½ cup water
1½ tablespoons cornstarch
1 tablespoon cold water

1. Preheat oven to 350°F.

2. Arrange 4 slices of ham in a medium baking dish. Top with pineapple slices, then remaining 4 slices of ham.

3. In a small saucepan over medium-low heat, combine raisins, pineapple juice, and ½ cup water. Bring to a simmer; simmer for 10 minutes. Combine cornstarch with cold water; stir into hot mixture. Cook until thickened, stirring constantly.

4. Pour sauce over ham and bake for 20 minutes.

Ham Loaf with Mustard Glaze

*What a tasty way to prepare leftover ham! Serve this delicious loaf
with baked sweet potatoes and a creamy succotash.*

INGREDIENTS | SERVES 6

1½ pounds cooked ham, ground

1 large egg

¾ cup fine dry bread crumbs, plain

¼ cup finely chopped yellow onion

1 tablespoon chopped fresh flat-leaf parsley

¾ cup evaporated milk

1 tablespoon prepared yellow mustard

¾ cup light brown sugar, packed

1 teaspoon dry mustard

¼ cup apple cider vinegar

1 small tomato, sliced

1. Preheat oven to 350°F.

2. In a large bowl, combine ground ham, egg, bread crumbs, onion, parsley, evaporated milk, and prepared mustard. Blend well and shape into a loaf. Place in a greased 9" × 5" loaf pan. Bake loaf for 1 hour.

3. Meanwhile, in a small saucepan, combine brown sugar, dry mustard, and vinegar. Heat over medium-low heat, stirring until sugar is dissolved; set aside.

4. Pour over ham loaf and bake for about 20 minutes longer. Top with tomato slices before serving.

Black-Eyed Peas with Ham

This Southern classic is slow-cooked so the beans are extra creamy.

INGREDIENTS | SERVES 10

1 pound dried black-eyed peas

1 large yellow onion, peeled and diced

1 medium jalapeño pepper, seeded and diced

1 medium rib celery, diced

1 carrot, peeled and diced

6 cups ham stock or water

6 ounces diced ham

1 cup diced fresh tomato

1 tablespoon apple cider vinegar

1 tablespoon minced fresh thyme leaves

1 teaspoon ground cayenne pepper

½ teaspoon salt

½ teaspoon ground black pepper

1. The night before you want to serve this dish, place black-eyed peas in a 4- to 6-quart slow cooker. Fill it with water to cover peas. Cover and soak overnight.

2. The next day, drain black-eyed peas, then return them to the slow cooker and add remaining ingredients. Stir. Cook on low for 8–10 hours. Stir before serving.

CHAPTER 8

Chicken and Turkey

Southern Fried Chicken with Cream Gravy

This is truly one of the rock stars of Southern cooking, and it's a dish that people in the South like to talk about. This is a typical fried-chicken recipe, but there are many, many variations. You'll even find a few great cookbooks devoted to fried chicken from the South and other areas of the country.

INGREDIENTS | SERVES 4–6

4–5 pounds bone-in chicken pieces (breasts, thighs, wings, legs)

2–3 cups canola oil or shortening

2 large eggs

2 cups whole milk

2½ cups plus 2 tablespoons all-purpose flour, divided

2 tablespoons salt plus more to taste, divided

2 teaspoons ground black pepper plus more to taste, divided

½ teaspoon paprika

1 cup chicken broth

1 cup half-and-half or whole milk

Deep-Frying Safety

Use long tongs or a long-handled slotted spoon to turn and move the chicken, and you might want to wear gloves and an apron while working near the skillet to save your skin and clothing from grease spatters. Always keep the handle of the skillet or pan to the side where it won't get bumped. A Class ABC fire extinguisher is a good thing to have in the kitchen. In a pinch, slipping the lid on the skillet or dousing with baking soda will put out a grease fire, so keep a box of baking soda handy. Never use water on a grease fire, as it will only make it spread. Let the oil cool thoroughly before moving to another container.

1. Rinse chicken with cold water and trim excess loose skin and fat; pat dry and set aside.

2. Heat oil or melt shortening in a large, deep skillet with a heavy bottom and a cover. The oil is ready when it registers 350°F. Watch carefully for overheating.

3. Meanwhile, in a large bowl, whisk together eggs and milk. Combine 2½ cups flour, 2 tablespoons salt, 2 teaspoons pepper, and paprika in a large food storage bag. Dip a few chicken pieces in milk mixture, then drop into bag and shake gently to coat thoroughly.

4. Working with about 4 pieces of chicken at a time, place in hot oil. Cover and fry for 5 minutes. Uncover, fry for 5 more minutes on that side, then turn and fry the other side for about 10 minutes. Depending on thickness and whether meat is white or dark, the time could vary a bit. White meat generally takes less time. Check a few pieces of chicken by cutting into meat to see if juices run clear. Remove chicken to a plate lined with paper towels to drain; sprinkle with salt to taste and keep warm. Repeat with remaining chicken pieces.

5. Carefully pour all but 2 tablespoons of the oil into a metal bowl or another pan; set it aside to cool before discarding. Place the skillet over medium heat; stir in remaining 2 tablespoons flour, stirring up browned bits in the bottom of the skillet. Cook flour and oil for about 30 seconds, stirring constantly. Gradually stir in chicken broth and half-and-half. Cook gravy mixture, stirring constantly, until thickened and bubbly. Season gravy with salt and pepper to taste. If desired, strain before serving with fried chicken.

Fried Chicken Strips

These flavorful and spicy chicken strips are absolutely amazing with sweet-and-sour sauce. Time these carefully so they'll be cooked through but still juicy.

INGREDIENTS | SERVES 4–6

1–1½ pounds boneless, skinless chicken breasts

1½ cups low-fat buttermilk

1½ teaspoons salt, divided

3 teaspoons Creole or Cajun seasoning, divided

2 cups canola oil

2 cups all-purpose flour

½ teaspoon ground black pepper

1. Rinse chicken and pat dry with paper towels. Cut into strips about 1"–1½" in width.

2. In a large container or heavy-duty food storage bag, combine buttermilk, 1 teaspoon salt, and 2 teaspoons Creole or Cajun seasoning. Add chicken strips; seal the bag and refrigerate for 2–8 hours. When almost ready to cook, heat oil in a deep skillet over medium heat to about 350°F.

3. Meanwhile, combine flour, remaining Creole seasoning, ½ teaspoon salt, and pepper in a large food storage bag. Put chicken strips in the bag a few at a time and shake the bag gently to coat thoroughly.

4. Fry several chicken strips at a time, turning a few times with tongs, until deep golden brown, about 6–8 minutes for each batch.

Oven-Barbecued Chicken

This recipe can be made with chicken breasts, legs or leg quarters, thighs, or a combination of parts. Chicken breasts will generally take less time to cook than smaller pieces and dark meat, and time will vary depending on the size of the pieces.

INGREDIENTS | SERVES 6

5 pounds bone-in chicken pieces
1 cup ketchup
⅓ cup apple cider vinegar
Juice of 1 medium lemon
2 tablespoons grated yellow onion
2 tablespoons Worcestershire sauce
⅓ cup light brown sugar, packed
1½ teaspoons salt
½ teaspoon celery salt
2 teaspoons prepared yellow mustard
Dash garlic powder
1 teaspoon paprika

1. Preheat oven to 350°F.

2. Wash chicken pieces; pat dry with paper towels. Arrange in a large baking dish. Bake chicken for 45 minutes.

3. Meanwhile, in a medium saucepan, combine remaining ingredients. Cook sauce over low heat, stirring occasionally, for 10 minutes. Set aside.

4. Pour sauce over chicken, brushing and turning pieces to coat thoroughly. Bake for about 45–60 minutes longer or until juices run clear when chicken is pierced with a fork.

Chicken in Sweet Onion Sauce

Your family will love this rich, succulent one-pot meal. (You'll love it because it's quick and easy.) Serve with a tossed salad and dinner rolls.

INGREDIENTS | SERVES 6

1 tablespoon olive oil
1 tablespoon butter
2 large sweet onions, peeled and diced
8 ounces fresh cremini mushrooms, sliced
6 small (4-ounce) boneless, skinless chicken breast halves
1 (10.75-ounce) can condensed cream of mushroom soup
6 medium red potatoes, peeled and thinly sliced
1 pound baby carrots
2 tablespoons heavy cream

1. Heat oil and butter in a pressure cooker over medium heat. Add onion; sauté for 2 minutes. Stir in mushrooms; sauté for 3 minutes.

2. Add chicken, mushroom soup, and vegetables to pressure cooker. Lock the lid into place and bring to low pressure; maintain pressure for 8 minutes. Remove from heat and let the pressure release naturally.

3. Remove the lid and transfer chicken and vegetables to a serving platter; keep warm. Return the pan to medium heat and stir in cream. Simmer and then pour sauce over chicken and vegetables on the serving platter.

Chicken with Cajun Cream Sauce

Use a stovetop grill pan or skillet to make this tasty chicken recipe. This rich, spicy chicken and creamy sauce is delicious served over fresh fettuccine or linguine.

INGREDIENTS | SERVES 6

6 small (4-ounce) boneless, skinless chicken breast halves

2 teaspoons Creole seasoning

2 teaspoons olive oil

1 pound fettuccine or linguine

2½ cups heavy cream

1 tablespoon all-purpose flour

1 tablespoon butter, melted

½ teaspoon Worcestershire sauce

Tabasco sauce

Salt and ground black pepper

1 large tomato, seeded and diced

6 green onions, thinly sliced

Make Creole Seasoning at Home

Creole seasoning is easy to make, and you can control the heat level and adjust the other seasonings to suit your own taste and needs. Combine 1 tablespoon each of onion and garlic powder, 1 tablespoon dried oregano, 2 teaspoons dried thyme, 2 teaspoons black pepper, 1–2 teaspoons ground cayenne, 2 tablespoons paprika, and 1½ tablespoons salt. Blend the seasonings well and store in an airtight container or jar. This will make about ½ cup.

1. Trim chicken, rinse, and pat dry. Put chicken between pieces of plastic wrap and flatten slightly to an even thickness. Sprinkle chicken all over with Creole seasoning.

2. Heat oil in a large grill pan or skillet over medium-high heat. Sear chicken for about 2 minutes on each side. Reduce heat to medium and continue to cook, turning, for about 5 minutes.

3. Meanwhile, cook pasta according to package directions; set aside and keep warm.

4. In a medium saucepan over medium-high heat, bring cream to a boil. Reduce heat to medium-low; simmer for about 4 minutes. In a small bowl, blend flour with butter until smooth. Whisk flour mixture into cream. Add Worcestershire sauce and season to taste with Tabasco, salt, and pepper.

5. Arrange cooked pasta on serving plates. Slice chicken and arrange on pasta. Spoon a little sauce over each serving, then sprinkle with diced tomatoes and sliced green onions.

Creole Chicken and Rice

Serve with cornbread or baked corn tortillas. Have hot sauce at the table for those who wish to add it.

INGREDIENTS | SERVES 6

2 tablespoons vegetable oil

2 pounds boneless, skinless chicken breasts

1 medium white onion, peeled and diced

1 large green bell pepper, seeded and diced

4 medium cloves garlic, minced

1 teaspoon dried rosemary, crumbled

1 teaspoon dried thyme, crumbled

½ teaspoon paprika

¼ teaspoon crushed red pepper flakes

½ cup dry white wine

1 (28-ounce) can diced tomatoes (undrained)

1 (14.5-ounce) can chicken broth

2 cups frozen okra, thawed and sliced

1 cup frozen whole-kernel corn, thawed

2 large carrots, peeled and sliced

1 cup long-grain white rice, rinsed and drained

½ cup chopped fresh cilantro, packed

1 bay leaf

Salt and ground black pepper

1. Heat oil in a pressure cooker over medium-high heat. Cut chicken into bite-sized strips.

2. Add chicken along with onion and green pepper to oil; sauté for 3–5 minutes or until chicken is slightly browned and onion is soft.

3. Add garlic, rosemary, thyme, paprika, and crushed red pepper; sauté for 2 minutes.

4. Pour in wine; deglaze the pan, scraping up any bits stuck to the bottom of the pan.

5. Add remaining ingredients. Stir to mix. Lock the lid into place and bring to high pressure; maintain pressure for 7 minutes.

6. Remove from heat and allow the pressure to release naturally. Remove the lid. Remove and discard bay leaf. Fluff rice with a fork. Taste for seasoning and adjust if necessary. Serve.

Southern Chicken Stew

The sugar in this dish offsets the acidity of the tomatoes. If you're using apple juice instead of wine, you may want to wait until the dish is cooked to see if the sugar is needed.

INGREDIENTS | SERVES 8

3 tablespoons bacon fat

1 (3-pound) roasting chicken, cut into serving pieces

2 cups water

1 (28-ounce) can diced tomatoes (undrained)

2 large yellow onions, peeled and sliced

½ teaspoon sugar

½ cup dry white wine or apple juice

1 (10-ounce) package frozen lima beans, thawed

1 (10-ounce) package frozen whole-kernel corn, thawed

1 (10-ounce) package frozen okra, thawed and sliced

1 cup fine dry bread crumbs, toasted

3 tablespoons Worcestershire sauce

Salt and ground black pepper

Tabasco sauce

1. Heat bacon fat in a 6-quart Dutch oven over medium heat. Add chicken pieces and fry until lightly browned. Add water, tomatoes, onions, sugar, and wine or apple juice. Bring to a simmer; cover and simmer for 75 minutes or until chicken is cooked through. Use a slotted spoon to remove chicken and set it aside until it's cool enough to handle. Then, remove chicken from bones and discard skin and bones. Shred chicken meat and set aside.

2. Add lima beans, corn, and okra to the pot. Bring to a simmer and cook uncovered for 30 minutes. Stir in shredded chicken, bread crumbs, and Worcestershire sauce. Simmer for 10 minutes, stirring occasionally, to bring chicken to temperature and thicken stew. Taste for seasoning and add salt, pepper, and Tabasco sauce to taste.

Skillet Chicken Breasts with Mushrooms

Serve this dish with Savory Rice Pilaf with Green Onions (see recipe in Chapter 10).

INGREDIENTS | SERVES 6

6 small (4-ounce) boneless, skinless chicken breast halves

⅔ cup all-purpose flour

½ teaspoon salt

¼ teaspoon ground black pepper

¼ teaspoon paprika

2 tablespoons olive oil

1–2 tablespoons butter

8 ounces fresh cremini mushrooms, sliced

6 green onions, sliced

1 medium clove garlic, minced

Juice of 1 medium lemon (about 3 tablespoons)

¼ cup chicken broth

1 tablespoon chopped fresh flat-leaf parsley

1. Wash chicken and pat dry. Place a chicken breast half between 2 sheets of plastic wrap; pound gently until even in thickness. Repeat with remaining chicken.

2. In a food storage bag, combine flour, salt, pepper, and paprika. Add chicken pieces a few at a time and toss to coat thoroughly.

3. In a large skillet, heat olive oil and 1 tablespoon butter over medium heat. Sauté chicken for about 3–4 minutes on each side or until cooked through. Remove to a warm platter; cover with foil and keep warm.

4. Add mushrooms to the same skillet, along with remaining butter if needed. Sauté mushrooms for 3–4 minutes until tender and browned. Add green onions and garlic; sauté for about 1 minute. Add lemon juice and chicken broth; simmer for about 2 minutes. Add chicken to the skillet and return to a simmer. Simmer for about 1 minute.

5. Arrange chicken on a serving plate. Top with mushrooms and juices. Sprinkle with parsley.

Chicken and Dumplings

Every Southern cook has her own personal recipe for chicken and dumplings. Some prefer rolled dumplings, many pinch off pieces of dough, and some use a quick and easy biscuit mix dough.

INGREDIENTS | SERVES 6–8

1 whole chicken or chicken pieces, about 4½–5½ pounds

4 cups water

4 cups chicken broth

1 teaspoon salt, divided

¼ teaspoon ground black pepper

½ teaspoon dried thyme, crumbled

2 medium carrots, peeled and chopped

2 medium ribs celery, chopped

1 medium yellow onion, peeled and chopped

2 cups all-purpose flour

½ teaspoon baking soda

3 tablespoons shortening

¾ cup buttermilk

1 cup whole milk

4 tablespoons butter

3 tablespoons chopped parsley

Dropped Dumplings

Chicken and dumplings can be made without rolling the dough. Pat the dough down to a ¼" thickness. Pinch off 1" pieces and drop into the boiling broth. If you're short on time, try using thawed frozen biscuits in place of the homemade dough. Just pat them to flatten slightly, pinch off 1" pieces, and drop into the boiling broth.

1. Wash chicken and pat dry. Place chicken in a large stockpot; add water and chicken broth. Add ½ teaspoon salt, pepper, thyme, carrots, celery, and onion. Bring to a boil. Reduce heat to medium-low and simmer for about 60–75 minutes or until chicken is very tender.

2. Remove chicken to a large bowl and set aside to cool. Strain broth into another bowl, then pour back into the stockpot, discarding solids.

3. Combine flour, baking soda, and remaining ½ teaspoon salt in a medium bowl. With a pastry blender or 2 knives, cut shortening into dry ingredients until mixture resembles a coarse meal. Stir in buttermilk just until dough clumps together. Turn out onto a floured surface and knead about 5 times. Roll dough out to about ⅛" thickness. Use a sharp knife or a pizza cutter to cut dough into 3" × 1" strips or squares.

4. Meanwhile, bring chicken broth to a boil. Stir in milk and butter. Taste and add more salt and pepper if needed.

5. Drop dumplings a few at a time into boiling chicken broth. Reduce heat to medium-low and continue to simmer for about 10 minutes, stirring occasionally.

6. Meanwhile, remove cooled chicken meat from bones and cut into pieces. Add chicken pieces to simmering broth and heat through. Garnish with parsley before serving.

Chicken and Rice Bake

This dish is frequently made with cream of mushroom or cream of chicken soup, but a homemade sauce is so much better.

INGREDIENTS | SERVES 4–6

4 small (4-ounce) boneless, skinless chicken breast halves

1½ cups chicken broth

½ teaspoon seasoned salt

Ground black pepper

¼ cup butter

½ cup chopped celery

1 medium yellow onion, peeled and chopped

¼ cup all-purpose flour

1 cup whole milk

Salt

2½ cups cooked long-grain white rice

1 cup fresh bread crumbs

2 tablespoons melted butter

1. Rinse chicken and pat dry. Place chicken in a medium saucepan with chicken broth, seasoned salt, and a dash of pepper. Bring to a boil; reduce heat to medium-low, cover, and simmer for 20–30 minutes until cooked through. With a slotted spoon, remove chicken to a plate. Cover loosely with foil and let cool.

2. Preheat oven to 350°F.

3. Strain broth into a large cup or small bowl; set aside. In the same saucepan, melt ¼ cup butter. Over medium-low heat, sauté celery and onion until tender, about 5–8 minutes. Stir in flour until well blended. Gradually stir in reserved chicken broth and milk. Cook sauce, stirring constantly, until thickened and bubbly. Taste and add salt and pepper as needed.

4. Chop cooled chicken into bite-sized pieces. Add chicken to sauce along with cooked rice. Spoon chicken and rice mixture into a 2-quart casserole dish.

5. Toss bread crumbs with melted butter in a small bowl; sprinkle over the casserole. Bake for 30–40 minutes or until hot and bubbly and bread crumbs are lightly browned.

Chicken Noodle Casserole

This casserole makes a terrific family meal.

INGREDIENTS | SERVES 4

4 ounces medium egg noodles

¼ cup butter

8 ounces fresh cremini mushrooms, sliced

2 medium ribs celery, thinly sliced

1 medium yellow onion, peeled and chopped

¼ cup all-purpose flour

1 teaspoon salt

¼ teaspoon ground black pepper

½ teaspoon dried thyme, crumbled

1½ cups whole milk

½ cup chicken broth

2 cups diced cooked chicken

¼ cup dry white wine or chicken broth

¾ cup fine fresh bread crumbs

2 tablespoons melted butter

2 tablespoons chopped fresh flat-leaf parsley

Jazz Up Your Casserole

Try a different casserole topping on this family-favorite casserole. Sprinkle shredded cheese over the top just before the casserole is finished baking, or replace the bread crumbs with French fried onions, crushed chips, or chopped nuts. To dress up the casserole a little, add sliced tomatoes to the plate before serving, or garnish with stuffed olives, herbs, or hard-cooked eggs.

1. Cook noodles in boiling salted water, following package directions, until just tender. Drain and set aside.

2. Preheat oven to 400°F.

3. In a large saucepan over medium-low heat, melt ¼ cup butter. Add mushrooms, onion, and celery. Sauté for about 5 minutes or until vegetables are tender. Stir flour into mixture until well blended. Add salt, pepper, and thyme. Gradually stir in milk and chicken broth. Continue to cook, stirring constantly, until thickened and bubbly. Add diced chicken, wine or broth, and cooked noodles. Simmer for 1 minute.

4. Spoon chicken and noodle mixture into a 2-quart baking dish. Combine bread crumbs with melted butter and parsley in a small bowl; sprinkle over the casserole.

5. Bake for 20–25 minutes until hot and bubbly.

Southern Creamed Chicken with Biscuits

This dish is perfect for a party or family get-together. The creamed chicken is great on biscuits, but it's also wonderful over rice or baked puff pastry shells.

INGREDIENTS | SERVES 6–8

3 tablespoons butter

8 ounces fresh cremini mushrooms, sliced

3 tablespoons minced red bell pepper

¼ cup thinly sliced green onion

¼ cup all-purpose flour

1 teaspoon salt

⅛ teaspoon ground black pepper

2 cups chicken broth

2 tablespoons dry sherry

1½ cups half-and-half

3 cups diced cooked chicken

6–8 Perfect Buttermilk Biscuits (see recipe in Chapter 2)

1. In a large saucepan, melt butter over medium-low heat. Add mushrooms; sauté for about 3 minutes or until tender. Add red bell pepper and green onion and sauté for about 2 minutes. Blend in flour, salt, and pepper.

2. Gradually stir in chicken broth and sherry. Stir in half-and-half. Continue to cook over low heat, stirring constantly, until mixture is thickened and bubbly. Cook for about 1 minute longer. Add chicken and heat through.

3. Serve creamed chicken over hot split biscuits.

Replacement for Sherry

Sherry is a fortified Spanish wine, and it can add nice flavor to creamy sauces and soups, but you might not want to purchase a bottle for the small amount needed in a recipe. For dry to medium-dry sherry, substitute dry vermouth, sake, or dry white wine with a pinch of sugar. If you would like to avoid alcohol altogether, feel free to add more chicken broth to replace the sherry.

White Chicken Chili

Serve this dish with hot, fresh-baked Southern Skillet Cornbread (see recipe in Chapter 2) or corn muffins.

INGREDIENTS | SERVES 6

1½ pounds boneless, skinless chicken breasts

1 tablespoon vegetable oil

2 cups chopped yellow onion

4 medium cloves garlic, minced

1 medium jalapeño pepper, seeded and minced

2 teaspoons ground cumin

1 (4-ounce) can diced mild green chilies

2 (14.5-ounce) cans diced tomatoes (undrained)

2 (15-ounce) cans Great Northern beans, drained and rinsed

Juice of 1 small lime

2 cups fresh or frozen whole-kernel corn (thawed if frozen)

Salt and ground black pepper

2 tablespoons chopped fresh cilantro

½–¾ cup sour cream

¼ cup finely chopped green onion

1. Wash chicken and pat dry. Cut into 1" cubes. Set aside.

2. Heat vegetable oil in a large saucepan over medium-high heat. Add yellow onion and sauté until it begins to brown. Add garlic and sauté for about 30 seconds. Add cubed chicken; cook until chicken is browned on all sides. Add jalapeño, cumin, green chilies, and undrained tomatoes. Add beans to mixture. Reduce heat and simmer for 5 minutes.

3. Add lime juice and corn. Season mixture with salt and pepper. Cook for 5 minutes. Stir in cilantro.

4. Serve chili with a dollop of sour cream and a sprinkling of sliced green onion.

Savory Chicken Pot Pie

This pot pie is great topped with biscuits instead of the pie crust. Feel free to substitute frozen mixed vegetables or baby lima beans for the frozen peas.

INGREDIENTS | SERVES 6

4 pounds bone-in chicken pieces (breasts, thighs, wings, legs)

6 cups water

2 cups chicken broth

1 medium yellow onion, peeled and coarsely chopped

2 medium ribs celery, coarsely chopped

2 sprigs fresh flat-leaf parsley

1 bay leaf

½ teaspoon dried thyme, crumbled

2½ teaspoons salt, divided

¼ teaspoon ground black pepper, divided

6 medium carrots, peeled and sliced

¼ cup all-purpose flour

½ cup whole milk

1½ cups frozen peas, thawed

1 sheet pie crust pastry, unbaked

Food Processor Pie Crust

Put 1 cup all-purpose flour and ¼ teaspoon salt in the bowl of the food processor fitted with a metal blade. Cover and pulse a few times to combine. Add ¼ cup cold shortening; pulse 5 times. With the processor running, slowly add ¼ cup ice water to the mixture just until a ball of dough forms and begins to leave the sides of the processor. Chill for 30 minutes before rolling.

1. Wash chicken and pat dry. In a large stockpot or Dutch oven, combine chicken with water, broth, onion, celery, parsley, bay leaf, thyme, 1½ teaspoons salt, and ⅛ teaspoon pepper. Bring to a boil over high heat; reduce heat to medium-low, cover, and simmer for about 1½ hours or until chicken is very tender.

2. Remove chicken and strain broth into a bowl. Return 2 cups of strained broth to the pot. Refrigerate or freeze remaining broth for another use. Add carrots to the pot. Cover and simmer until carrots are tender.

3. Meanwhile, when chicken is cool enough to handle, remove meat from the bones and chop. Place chicken in a 2-quart baking dish.

4. In a cup or small bowl, combine flour, 1 teaspoon salt, ⅛ teaspoon pepper, and milk. Whisk until smooth. Stir flour mixture into the pot and then add peas. Bring to a boil, stirring constantly. Reduce heat to low and simmer until peas are tender.

5. Pour sauce and vegetables over chicken in the baking dish. Gently stir to combine ingredients.

6. Preheat oven to 425°F.

7. Prepare crust: Roll out dough to fit the baking dish with a ½" overhang. Fold the edge under, seal, and crimp the edges. With a sharp knife, cut several vents in the top so steam can escape.

8. Bake chicken pot pie for 20 minutes or until crust is browned and filling is hot and bubbly.

Roast Turkey with Currant Jelly Glaze

Serve with Home-Style Cornbread Dressing (see recipe in Chapter 10), if desired.

INGREDIENTS | SERVES 6–8

1 (12–14 pound) turkey
Vegetable oil
Salt and ground black pepper
2 tablespoons cold butter
½ cup red currant jelly
2 tablespoons dry red wine or water
¼ teaspoon coarsely ground black pepper
½ teaspoon ground cinnamon
¼ teaspoon ground allspice

1. Preheat oven to 325°F. Wash turkey inside and out. Remove giblets and neck and reserve for another use. Rub vegetable oil all over turkey. Sprinkle turkey inside and out with salt and pepper. Cut cold butter into pieces. With your fingers or the handle of a wooden spoon, loosen the skin over the breast of turkey and slide pieces of butter under the skin of turkey.

2. Place the turkey, breast side up, on a lightly oiled rack in a shallow roasting pan. Fold wings under turkey and secure drumsticks with twine if they are not already secured. Butter a piece of foil and place it, buttered side down, over breast of turkey. Roast turkey for 1 hour. Remove foil and roast until an instant-read thermometer registers 180°F when inserted deep into thigh. The total roasting time will be about 3–3½ hours.

3. Meanwhile, in a small saucepan, combine currant jelly, wine or water, pepper, cinnamon, and allspice. Bring to a boil, stirring constantly. Brush on turkey about 20 minutes before done. If turkey begins to brown too much, cover again with lightly buttered foil. Turn off oven when turkey is done and cover with foil. Let rest for about 20 minutes. Remove from oven and carve.

Turkey and Rice Casserole

This is a fantastic way to use leftover roast turkey, and it's easy to put together.

INGREDIENTS | SERVES 4

¼ cup butter

1 cup sliced button mushrooms

¼ cup thinly sliced green onion

¼ cup all-purpose flour

1¼ cups chicken broth

½ cup dry white wine

1 tablespoon chopped fresh flat-leaf parsley

¼ teaspoon poultry seasoning

1 cup shredded sharp Cheddar cheese, divided

2 cups cooked long-grain white rice

2 cups diced cooked turkey

Salt and ground black pepper

Paprika

Homemade Poultry Seasoning

You probably already have all the ingredients you need to make your own poultry seasoning. To make about 1 tablespoon of poultry seasoning, combine 1½ teaspoons crumbled dried sage, ½ teaspoon crumbled dried thyme, ½ teaspoon freshly ground black pepper, a dash of crumbled dried rosemary, and about ¼ teaspoon dried marjoram.

1. Preheat oven to 375°F. Spray a shallow 2- to 2½-quart baking dish with nonstick cooking spray.

2. In a large saucepan, melt butter over medium-low heat. Add mushrooms and sauté until tender, about 5–8 minutes. Add green onion and sauté for about 30 seconds. Stir in flour until well blended. Gradually stir in chicken broth and wine. Continue to cook, stirring constantly, until thickened and bubbly.

3. Stir in parsley, poultry seasoning, and half of the cheese. Continue to cook until cheese is melted, stirring constantly. Add rice and diced turkey. Season mixture with salt and pepper to taste.

4. Pour turkey and rice mixture into the prepared baking dish. Sprinkle remaining cheese over the top and sprinkle with paprika.

5. Bake for 25–30 minutes until hot and bubbly.

Turkey Cutlets with Creamy Mushroom Sauce

Turkey cutlets are low in fat, and they can be used in other recipes in place of chicken or veal. These cutlets are delicious with hot buttered pasta.

INGREDIENTS | SERVES 6

6 turkey cutlets, about 1½ pounds

⅔ cup plus 2 tablespoons all-purpose flour

1 teaspoon salt

¼ teaspoon ground black pepper

½ teaspoon paprika

1 tablespoon olive oil

2 tablespoons butter, divided

8 ounces fresh cremini mushrooms, sliced

1½ cups chicken broth

½ cup dry white wine

½ teaspoon dried rosemary, crumbled

1 tablespoon chopped fresh flat-leaf parsley

Dash garlic powder

2 tablespoons cold water

½–1 cup heavy cream

1. Put a turkey cutlet between 2 sheets of plastic wrap and flatten gently with a rolling pin, the smooth side of a meat mallet, or similar tool. Repeat with remaining cutlets. In a large food storage bag, combine ⅔ cup flour, salt, pepper, and paprika. Add cutlets a few at a time and coat well.

2. In a large skillet over medium heat, combine oil and 1 tablespoon butter. When the skillet is hot, add cutlets a few at a time. Sauté cutlets, turning to brown both sides, until cooked through, about 2 minutes per side. Remove to a warm plate and cover loosely with foil. Keep warm.

3. Add mushrooms and remaining 1 tablespoon butter to the skillet. Cook until tender, about 5–8 minutes. Gradually stir in chicken broth and wine. Add rosemary, parsley, and garlic powder. Simmer mixture over medium-high heat for several minutes until reduced by about ⅓. Reduce heat to medium-low.

4. Combine remaining 2 tablespoons flour with cold water in a cup. Whisk until smooth. Stir into sauce. Continue to cook until thickened, stirring constantly. Add about ½ cup of the cream. Taste and add more cream if desired. Heat through.

5. To serve, spoon sauce over the turkey cutlets.

Barbecue Turkey

Dark turkey meat stays moist, even after long slow-cooking times. Left to cook long enough, it becomes tender enough to use to make "pulled" turkey sandwiches that are especially good if you add coleslaw or shredded lettuce, bacon, and tomato. Or serve it over cooked rice or noodles.

INGREDIENTS | SERVES 4

½ cup ketchup

2 tablespoons light brown sugar

1 tablespoon quick-cooking tapioca

1 tablespoon apple cider vinegar

1 teaspoon Worcestershire sauce

1 teaspoon soy or steak sauce

¼ teaspoon ground cinnamon

⅛ teaspoon ground cloves

⅛ teaspoon crushed red pepper

2 turkey thighs, skin removed

1. Add ketchup, brown sugar, tapioca, vinegar, Worcestershire sauce, soy or steak sauce, cinnamon, cloves, and crushed red pepper to a 4- to 6-quart slow cooker; stir to combine.

2. Place turkey thighs in the slow cooker, meaty side down. Cover and cook on low for 8 hours or until turkey is tender and pulls away from the bone. Remove turkey; allow to cool enough to remove the meat from the bones. Skim off any fat from the top of the barbecue sauce in the slow cooker. Stir turkey into sauce and continue to cook long enough for it to come back to temperature.

Turkey Gumbo

Filé powder is ground dried sassafras leaves; it helps flavor and thicken the gumbo. For a more robust flavor, add cayenne pepper to taste when you add the black pepper or have hot sauce available at the table.

INGREDIENTS | SERVES 4

2 tablespoons olive or vegetable oil

½ pound andouille sausage or kielbasa, sliced

1 pound boneless, skinless turkey breast

1 large sweet onion, peeled and diced

4 medium cloves garlic, minced

1½ teaspoons dried thyme, crumbled

1 teaspoon filé powder

¼ teaspoon crushed red pepper

½ teaspoon ground black pepper

¼ teaspoon dried sage, crumbled

½ cup dry white wine

3 bay leaves

2 medium ribs celery, sliced

1 large green bell pepper, seeded and diced

1 (10-ounce) package frozen okra, thawed and sliced

½ cup minced fresh cilantro

1 (14.5-ounce) can diced tomatoes (undrained)

1 (14.5-ounce) can chicken broth

1. Heat oil in a pressure cooker over medium heat. Add sausage slices.

2. Cut turkey into bite-sized pieces and add to the pressure cooker along with onion.

3. Stir-fry for 5 minutes or until turkey begins to brown and onions are transparent.

4. Stir in garlic, thyme, filé powder, crushed red pepper, black pepper, and sage. Sauté for 1 minute and then deglaze the pan with wine, scraping the bottom of the pressure cooker to loosen anything stuck to the bottom of the pan. Stir in remaining ingredients.

5. Lock the lid into place and bring to low pressure; maintain pressure for 8 minutes. Remove from the heat and allow the pressure to release naturally.

6. Remove the lid. Remove and discard bay leaves. Taste for seasoning and adjust if necessary.

CHAPTER 9

Fish and Shellfish

Fried Catfish

Catfish is an absolutely delicious fish, especially when it's fried. Serve this wonderful Southern traditional favorite with Hush Puppies (see recipe in Chapter 2), Creamy Cabbage Slaw (see recipe in Chapter 4), and fries.

INGREDIENTS | SERVES 4

4 large catfish fillets (about 1 pound)
½ cup evaporated milk or whole milk
¾ cup yellow cornmeal
½ cup all-purpose flour
2½ teaspoons seasoned salt
½ teaspoon ground cayenne pepper
Canola oil
Lemon wedges

Seasoning a Cast-Iron Skillet

Some cast-iron cookware comes already seasoned, but if you need to season a pot or pan, it's easy. First, wash and dry the pot thoroughly. Coat the surface of the pot with oil, including the outside and handles. Place it in a 300°F oven with a baking sheet under it to catch dripping oil, and heat for 30 minutes. Let the cookware cool, then wipe with paper towels. After each use, wash with soapy water, dry thoroughly, then coat the inner surfaces with a little oil or melted shortening.

1. Rinse fish; pat dry with paper towels. Place catfish in a medium bowl with milk, turning to coat. Set aside.

2. In a wide, shallow dish, combine cornmeal, flour, seasoned salt, and cayenne pepper. Set aside.

3. Add oil to a deep, heavy skillet to a depth of about ¾–1". Heat oil to about 350°F.

4. Using tongs, lift a fish fillet out of milk, letting excess drip back into the bowl. Place fillet in cornmeal mixture, turning several times to coat thoroughly. Repeat with as many fillets as will easily fit in the pan. Place fillets in hot oil.

5. Fry fish for about 5–7 minutes, depending on size. If oil doesn't cover them, turn carefully with a wide spatula about halfway through cooking. Drain on paper towels. Repeat process until all fillets are fried.

6. Serve fried catfish with lemon wedges.

Baked Dijon Catfish with Crumb Coating

*The Dijon mustard gives this catfish a nice flavor boost, and it's
lower in fat than the more traditional fried catfish.*

INGREDIENTS | SERVES 4–6

1 tablespoon shortening or vegetable oil

4–6 large catfish fillets (about 1½ pounds)

3–4 tablespoons Dijon mustard

1 cup fine dry bread crumbs

½ teaspoon salt

¼ teaspoon ground black pepper

¼ teaspoon garlic powder

¼ teaspoon dried oregano, crumbled

1 teaspoon dried parsley flakes

Lemon wedges

Frozen vs. Fresh

It can be very difficult to find fresh fish in many parts of the country, but farm-raised catfish is probably found frozen in most areas. To thaw the fish, place it in a plastic food storage bag, then submerge the bag in cool water. To reduce any "frozen" taste, soak thawed fish fillets in milk before using them in a recipe.

1. Preheat oven to 450°F. Add oil or shortening to a shallow baking dish; place in the oven.

2. Rinse fish fillets; pat dry. Brush fish all over with Dijon mustard to coat well.

3. In a wide, shallow bowl, combine bread crumbs, salt, pepper, garlic powder, oregano, and parsley. With tongs or your hands, place fish in the bowl, turning to coat thoroughly.

4. Place coated fillets in the hot baking dish in a single layer. Bake for 6–10 minutes, depending on size, until fish flakes easily with a fork.

5. Serve catfish with lemon wedges.

Truly Blackened Catfish

This works best with small catfish fillets instead of large ones.
Ideally each fillet should be around 4 ounces.

INGREDIENTS | SERVES 4–6

1 cup butter
1 teaspoon ground black pepper
½ teaspoon dried thyme, crumbled
1 tablespoon spicy paprika
1 teaspoon garlic powder
1 teaspoon onion powder
½ teaspoon dried oregano, crumbled
2½ teaspoons salt
1 teaspoon chili powder
¼ teaspoon ground cayenne pepper
1½ pounds small catfish fillets

1. Melt butter in a shallow bowl. Combine spices and place on a plate. Dip fish in butter and then sprinkle or roll fish in spices.

2. Heat a charcoal or gas grill on medium-high. Place a cast-iron skillet over direct heat for 10 minutes. Let it sit until white ash forms in the bottom of the skillet.

3. Place fillets in the skillet. Pour 1 tablespoon of melted butter over each fillet. Be careful of flaming butter. Cook for 2 minutes before turning fillets and cooking for another 2 minutes. Serve with lemon wedges.

Broiled Red Snapper Fillets with Louisiana Seasonings

Red snapper is a big favorite of mine, and this is a super-easy way to cook it.

INGREDIENTS | SERVES 4

4 large red snapper fillets (about 1 pound)
¼ cup butter, melted
1 teaspoon salt
½ teaspoon ground black pepper
½ teaspoon garlic powder
½ teaspoon ground sweet paprika
Dash dried thyme, crumbled
Dash ground cayenne pepper
Sherry Cream Sauce (see recipe in Chapter 12)
1 small tomato, seeded and diced
2 or 3 green onions, thinly sliced

1. Preheat broiler. Lightly brush the rack of a broiler pan with a little vegetable oil.

2. Rinse snapper fillets; pat dry. Brush fillets all over with melted butter.

3. In a cup or small bowl, combine salt, pepper, garlic powder, paprika, thyme, and cayenne. Sprinkle over fish fillets.

4. Place fillets, skin side down, on the oiled rack of the broiler pan. Place about 5"–6" from the heat. Broil for 6–8 minutes or until fish flakes easily with a fork.

5. Serve with sauce and top with tomato and green onions.

Tuna Steaks with Peach Salsa

You can make this delicious tuna in a stovetop grill pan, or you can just as easily broil the steaks. Feel free to use salmon in place of the tuna. Start this recipe early, since the tuna should marinate for at least 1 hour.

INGREDIENTS | SERVES 4

4 (8-ounce) tuna steaks

¼ cup lime juice

2 tablespoons plus 2 teaspoons olive oil, divided

½ teaspoon ground ginger

¼ teaspoon salt

1 tablespoon honey

Dash hot sauce

1 medium clove garlic, minced

Peach Salsa (see recipe in Chapter 12)

Buying Fresh Tuna

Fresh tuna steaks are delicious grilled or broiled, but you should buy the freshest tuna you can find. The tastiest tuna will be a deep pink to red, and it will be somewhat shiny and moist looking, but not wet. Dullness, browning, or flaking all mean the tuna is older, while fresh tuna will smell a little like the ocean but should not have a strong fishy odor. You might want to avoid the strong-flavored brown streak that runs through whole tuna steaks, or you could cut it out before cooking.

1. Place tuna steaks in a large, heavy-duty food storage bag.

2. Combine lime juice, 2 tablespoons olive oil, ginger, salt, honey, hot sauce, and garlic in a small bowl. Pour marinade mixture over tuna steaks; seal the bag. Refrigerate for about 1–2 hours, turning frequently to keep tuna coated with marinade.

3. Brush a large grill pan with a remaining olive oil and heat over medium-high heat. Grill tuna steaks for about 4–6 minutes on each side or until the edges flake easily but steaks are still somewhat pink in the center.

4. Top tuna steaks with Peach Salsa before serving.

Halibut with Creamy Crawfish Sherry Sauce

This is a delicious way to prepare halibut, and it's an especially nice dish to make for a dinner with friends or family. Serve it with boiled new potatoes, fingerlings, or the Baby Dutch variety, along with spinach or other green vegetable.

INGREDIENTS | SERVES 6

6 (6-ounce) halibut fillets
Salt and ground black pepper
¼ cup butter, melted
1 large clove garlic, minced
1 tablespoon chopped fresh flat-leaf parsley
Sherry Cream Sauce (see recipe in Chapter 12)

Fish-Turning Trick

Turning fish can result in frustration and broken fillets. To make the procedure easier, place each of the fish fillets on a piece of nonstick or oiled foil that is double the width of the fish and about 2" longer. Put the foil and fish on the broiler rack or baking dish. When you're ready to turn the fish, carefully grasp each edge of the foil and flip the fish over to the other side of the foil.

1. Preheat broiler. Brush the rack of a broiler pan with a little vegetable oil.

2. Rinse fish fillets and pat dry. Sprinkle halibut all over with salt and pepper. Combine melted butter with garlic in a small saucepan; cook over medium-low heat for about 1 minute to meld the flavors. Stir in chopped parsley and brush mixture over halibut. Place fish on the broiler rack.

3. Broil about 5"–6" from the heat until fish flakes easily with a fork, about 5–8 minutes per side depending on thickness.

4. Transfer fish to plates and top each serving with sauce.

Louisiana Grouper

Grouper is a type of fish that is found all over the world. They use their famously large mouths to swallow their prey whole.

INGREDIENTS | SERVES 4

2 tablespoons peanut or vegetable oil

1 small yellow onion, peeled and diced

1 rib celery, diced

1 medium green bell pepper, seeded and diced

1 (14.5-ounce) can diced tomatoes (undrained)

¼ cup water

1 tablespoon tomato paste

1 teaspoon sugar

Pinch dried basil, crumbled

½ teaspoon chili powder

1½ pounds grouper fillets

Salt and ground black pepper

1. Heat oil in a pressure cooker over medium-high heat. Add onion, celery, and green pepper; sauté for 3 minutes. Stir in undrained tomatoes, water, tomato paste, sugar, basil, and chili powder.

2. Rinse fish and pat dry; cut into bite-sized pieces. Sprinkle with salt and pepper to taste. Gently stir fish pieces into sauce in the pressure cooker. Lock the lid into place and bring to high pressure; maintain pressure for 5 minutes. Quick-release the pressure.

Baked Tilapia with Pecan Topping

The pecans and Dijon topping are just amazing together. Serve the fish fillets with sliced tomatoes, hot cooked rice, and a green leafy vegetable.

INGREDIENTS | SERVES 4

1½ pounds tilapia fillets

⅔ cup mayonnaise

⅓ cup Dijon mustard

½ cup finely chopped pecans

2 tablespoons finely chopped green onion

1. Preheat oven to 350°F. Lightly butter a shallow baking pan.

2. Rinse tilapia fillets; pat dry. Arrange fillets in a single layer in the prepared pan.

3. In a small bowl, combine mayonnaise and Dijon mustard. Spread each fillet with mixture. Sprinkle each with pecans and green onion.

4. Bake for 12–16 minutes, depending on size, or until fish flakes easily with a fork.

Grilled Barbecue Salmon

Since salmon is a high-fat fish, it holds up incredibly well to grilling.

INGREDIENTS | SERVES 4

1 tablespoon vegetable oil
Salt and ground black pepper
4 (6- to 8-ounce) salmon steaks
¼ cup barbecue sauce

1. Brush a grill pan lightly with vegetable oil and place over medium-high heat.

2. Sprinkle salt and pepper over salmon. Brush one side of salmon lightly with barbecue sauce; place that side down in the warmed pan. Brush the other side with barbecue sauce.

3. Cook for 3 minutes on each side or until it is opaque about halfway up the side of fillet. Once salmon is opaque all the way through and flakes easily with a fork, brush it again with a light coating of barbecue sauce and serve while warm.

Salmon Croquettes with Corn

Salmon croquettes, also known as salmon patties, make a delicious weeknight meal. Serve them with rice, fries, or your favorite vegetables, along with Come Back Sauce (see recipe in Chapter 12) or ketchup.

INGREDIENTS | SERVES 4

1 (14.75-ounce) can salmon
1 cup canned or frozen whole-kernel corn
2 large eggs, slightly beaten
¼ cup ketchup
2 tablespoons finely chopped green onion
2 tablespoons finely chopped celery
¼ teaspoon salt
Dash ground black pepper
¾ cup fine dry bread crumbs
1–2 tablespoons vegetable oil

1. Drain salmon; flake, removing any large pieces of bone or skin.

2. In a medium bowl combine flaked salmon with corn, beaten eggs, ketchup, onion, celery, salt, pepper, and bread crumbs. Shape salmon mixture into 12 patties.

3. Heat vegetable oil in a heavy skillet on medium heat. Fry salmon croquettes for about 1½–2 minutes on each side or until browned and cooked through.

Oven-Fried Fish Fillets

These fillets are lower in fat than traditional fried fish. You can use catfish, orange roughy, haddock, tilapia, flounder, or your own favorite fish.

INGREDIENTS | SERVES 4

4 (4- to 6-ounce) fish fillets

½ cup whole milk

1 teaspoon seasoned salt

½ teaspoon salt

½ cup corn flake crumbs or fine dry bread crumbs

4 teaspoons butter, melted

Lemon wedges

1. Preheat oven to 475°F. Lightly oil a large, shallow baking pan.

2. Rinse fish and pat dry. If fillets are large, cut into serving-sized portions.

3. In a shallow bowl, combine milk, seasoned salt, and salt. Put corn flake crumbs or bread crumbs in another shallow bowl.

4. Dip fish fillets in milk, then place in corn flake crumbs, turning to coat thoroughly. Arrange in the prepared pan. Drizzle 1 teaspoon of melted butter over each fillet.

5. Bake for 12–15 minutes or until fish flakes easily with a fork. The baking time will vary depending on the thickness of fish. Serve with lemon wedges.

Jambalaya

This is a one-pot main dish that you can serve along with a tossed salad and garlic toast, crackers, or cornbread. Have hot sauce at the table for those who wish to add it.

INGREDIENTS | SERVES 8

2 tablespoons olive oil

½ pound smoked sausage, sliced

1 large yellow onion, peeled and diced

1 large red bell pepper, seeded and diced

2 medium ribs celery, finely diced

2 medium cloves garlic, minced

1 cup converted rice

½ pound boneless, skinless chicken thighs

1 (15-ounce) can diced tomatoes (undrained)

1 cup clam juice or fish stock

1 cup water or chicken broth

1 tablespoon Worcestershire sauce

½ teaspoon dried thyme, crumbled

½ teaspoon dried oregano, crumbled

½ teaspoon sugar

¼ teaspoon crushed red pepper

¼ teaspoon ground black pepper

½ pound medium shrimp, peeled and deveined

½ pound sea scallops, cut in half

Salt

1. Add oil, sausage, onion, bell pepper, and celery to a 4- to 5-quart slow cooker. Stir to coat vegetables in oil. Cover and cook on high for 45 minutes or until onion is transparent, stirring halfway through. Stir in garlic and rice.

2. Cut chicken into bite-sized pieces and stir into the other ingredients in the slow cooker. Cover and cook on high for 15 minutes.

3. Add tomatoes, clam juice or fish stock, water or chicken broth, Worcestershire sauce, thyme, oregano, sugar, crushed red pepper, and black pepper. Stir to mix. Reduce the heat setting to low, cover, and cook for 6 hours or until rice is tender.

4. Increase heat setting to high. Stir in shrimp and scallops. Cover and cook for 15 minutes or until shrimp are pink and scallops are opaque. Taste for seasoning and add salt if needed.

Spicy Shrimp and Grits

There are endless variations of the wildly popular shrimp and grits. This one adds the earthy flavor of mushrooms to the dish.

INGREDIENTS | SERVES 4–6

1½–2 pounds large to colossal shrimp

6 slices bacon, diced

2–3 teaspoons butter

8 ounces fresh button or cremini mushrooms, sliced

6 green onions, thinly sliced

1 (14.5-ounce) can diced tomatoes (undrained)

½ teaspoon Creole seasoning

Dash garlic powder

½ teaspoon salt plus more to taste, divided

¼ teaspoon ground black pepper plus more to taste, divided

Creamy Grits (see recipe in Chapter 10)

¼ cup chopped fresh flat-leaf parsley

1. Remove shells from shrimp, leaving tails on. To remove visible veins, cut about ⅛" into the upper curve of shrimp and rinse the vein out under cold water.

2. In a large, heavy skillet, cook diced bacon until fat is rendered. Add butter and mushrooms and cook over medium heat, stirring constantly until tender, about 5–8 minutes. Add shrimp. Cook shrimp and mushroom mixture for 1 minute, stirring constantly. Add green onions and cook for 1 minute longer. Add tomatoes, Creole seasoning, garlic powder, ½ teaspoon salt, and ¼ teaspoon black pepper. Bring to a boil over high heat; reduce heat to low and simmer for 2 minutes until slightly reduced. Add more salt or pepper as needed.

3. To serve, spoon shrimp over hot grits and sprinkle with parsley.

Shrimp Pilau

This Shrimp Pilau is a wonderful rice main dish, similar to jambalaya.

INGREDIENTS | SERVES 4

4 slices bacon, diced

3 tablespoons butter, divided

½ cup chopped celery

2 tablespoons chopped green bell pepper

2 green onions, thinly sliced

Dash dried thyme, crumbled

1 pound medium shrimp, peeled and deveined

1 tablespoon all-purpose flour

1 teaspoon Worcestershire sauce

2–4 tablespoons chicken broth, as needed

1 large tomato, diced

2 cups hot cooked long-grain white rice

Salt and ground black pepper

¼–½ teaspoon curry powder

1. Fry bacon in a large, heavy skillet or saucepan until crisp. Transfer to paper towels to drain.

2. Add 2 tablespoons butter to bacon drippings left in the skillet. Add celery, bell pepper, and green onions. Continue to cook vegetables until tender, about 5–8 minutes, stirring frequently. Add thyme.

3. In a medium bowl, toss shrimp with flour and Worcestershire sauce; add to vegetable mixture. Cook until shrimp is pink, stirring frequently and adding chicken broth to keep mixture from sticking. Stir in tomatoes and hot cooked rice and mix. Add salt and ground black pepper to taste along with curry powder and remaining butter. Heat through and toss with bacon just before serving.

History of Pilau

Pilau, also known as pilaf, is a versatile rice dish with chopped vegetables, along with meat, poultry, or seafood. The Southern rice crop and spice trade contributed to the popularity of rice pilau, particularly in Louisiana, Florida, and South Carolina. Many of these flavorful rice dishes are made with the addition of curry powder and other spices, depending on the region and preferences.

Shrimp Creole

This is a flavorful New Orleans–style shrimp Creole recipe with tomatoes, served over hot cooked rice.

INGREDIENTS | SERVES 6

2 pounds large shrimp

4–6 slices bacon

Vegetable oil

2 tablespoons all-purpose flour

1 cup chopped white onion

1 cup chopped celery

1 medium green bell pepper, seeded and thinly sliced

2 teaspoons Creole seasoning

2 (14.5-ounce) cans diced tomatoes (undrained)

½ cup chicken broth or shrimp stock

Worcestershire sauce

Tabasco sauce

3 cups hot cooked long-grain white rice

Make Your Own Shrimp Stock

Shrimp stock adds flavor to the recipe, and it is easy to make. Put shrimp shells from about 2 pounds of uncooked large to colossal shrimp into a large saucepan. Add 2 medium cut-up onions, ½ cup chopped celery, 2 cut-up lemons, 2 bay leaves, and 1 teaspoon dried thyme. Add a few sprigs of parsley and about 8 peppercorns, along with a few halved cloves of garlic, if desired. Bring the broth to a boil; reduce heat to medium and cook, uncovered, for about 25–30 minutes. Cool then strain through a fine-meshed sieve. Use what you need and freeze the remaining broth in small containers for up to 1 month.

1. Remove shells from shrimp, leaving tails on. Devein shrimp.

2. Cook bacon in a medium saucepan until crisp; remove to paper towels to drain. Crumble and set aside.

3. Pour bacon drippings into a cup; add enough oil to bacon drippings to make 2 tablespoons. Pour oil and drippings back into the pan. Stir in flour; continue to cook over medium heat, stirring constantly, until roux is medium to deep brown.

4. Add onion, celery, and bell pepper. Cook over medium heat until tender, about 5–8 minutes, stirring frequently. Add Creole seasoning, tomatoes, chicken broth or shrimp stock, and Worcestershire sauce and Tabasco sauce to taste. Simmer mixture for about 15–20 minutes or until thickened, stirring occasionally. Add shrimp and cook for 6–8 minutes until pink. For each serving, mound about ½ cup rice on a serving plate, then spoon shrimp and sauce over rice.

Cajun Shrimp

You can replace the beer with soda in this recipe.

INGREDIENTS | SERVES 4

1 pound large shrimp, peeled and deveined

¼ teaspoon ground cayenne pepper

1 teaspoon ground black pepper

1 teaspoon salt

1 teaspoon crushed red pepper

1 teaspoon dried thyme, crumbled

1 teaspoon dried oregano, crumbled

1 teaspoon ground marjoram

¼ cup butter

3 medium cloves garlic, minced

2 teaspoons Worcestershire sauce

1 cup beer, at room temperature

1. Rinse shrimp and shake them dry. Combine cayenne pepper, black pepper, salt, crushed red pepper, thyme, oregano, and marjoram in a small bowl.

2. Place a large skillet over medium-high heat. When it is hot, add butter and garlic and cook for 1 minute. Add seasoning mix, Worcestershire sauce, and beer.

3. Once sauce bubbles, add shrimp. Cook for 4–6 minutes, stirring so they cook evenly.

4. Once shrimp is pink and cooked through, remove from the pan and place in a serving bowl. Let liquid simmer for 10 minutes until it is a reduced sauce. Serve with white rice.

Spicy Crab Cakes

These delicious crab cakes can be served as a main dish or first course. Serve them with lemon wedges and Rémoulade Sauce or Come Back Sauce (see recipes in Chapter 12).

INGREDIENTS | SERVES 4

1 pound lump crabmeat
½ teaspoon lemon juice
1 large egg, beaten
¼ cup mayonnaise
1–1¼ cups fine, dry bread crumbs, divided
Few drops Tabasco sauce
1 teaspoon Old Bay Seasoning
¼ teaspoon Worcestershire sauce
Vegetable oil

Clarified Butter

Clarified butter will withstand a much higher heat than regular butter. To make it, put about 8 tablespoons butter in a saucepan and melt over medium-low heat. Continue heating over medium-low heat until it begins to bubble and the solids become golden. The butter can easily burn, so watch it carefully. Remove from heat and let the butter cool. With a spoon, skim off the foam from the top. Carefully pour or spoon the clear liquids (that is, your clarified butter) into a container with a lid, and discard the solids left in the saucepan. Clarified butter will keep for several months in the refrigerator.

1. Drain crabmeat and break up slightly, discarding any pieces of shell or cartilage. Sprinkle with lemon juice and set aside.

2. In a large bowl, whisk egg; stir in mayonnaise, ¾ cup bread crumbs, Old Bay Seasoning, Tabasco, and Worcestershire sauce. Gently fold crabmeat into mixture until well combined.

3. With your hands, shape mixture into patties, flattening slightly. Cover with plastic wrap and refrigerate for at least 30 minutes.

4. Heat about ½" oil in a large, heavy skillet over medium heat. Gently roll or press crab cakes into more bread crumbs. Fry patties for about 3 minutes on each side or until nicely browned. Drain on paper towels.

Crispy Fried Oysters

These are classic Southern-style fried oysters with that delicious crispy cornmeal coating. Serve hot with lemon wedges and tartar sauce or Come Back Sauce (see recipe in Chapter 12). These also make a great sandwich filling.

INGREDIENTS | SERVES 4

3 large eggs
24 large raw shucked oysters
3 cups yellow cornmeal
¼ cup all-purpose flour
1 teaspoon salt
1½ teaspoons Cajun seasoning
1½ teaspoons ground black pepper
Vegetable oil

1. Beat eggs in a medium mixing bowl. Add oysters and stir to coat thoroughly. Set aside.

2. Combine cornmeal, flour, salt, Cajun seasoning, and pepper in a large food storage bag. Working with a few at a time, let excess egg drip off of the oysters and put into the bag. Shake gently to coat oysters thoroughly.

3. Heat oil to 375°F in a deep fryer.

4. Fry oysters in batches for about 3 minutes or until golden brown. Remove to paper towels to drain.

Quick Seared Sea Scallops

These spicy seasoned scallops are flavorful and very easy to prepare. Here they are served with grits, but they would also be delicious with rice or potatoes.

INGREDIENTS | SERVES 4

1 pound sea scallops
Salt
2–3 tablespoons vegetable oil
1 tablespoon all-purpose flour
1 tablespoon Cajun seasoning
1½ teaspoons paprika
¼ teaspoon ground black pepper
¼ cup butter, melted
Fresh flat-leaf parsley, minced
Creamy Grits (see recipe in Chapter 10)

1. Cut very large scallops in half if desired. Pat scallops dry, then sprinkle lightly with salt.

2. Heat vegetable oil in a large, heavy skillet over medium heat.

3. In a shallow bowl, combine flour, Cajun seasoning, paprika, and pepper. Put melted butter in another shallow bowl. Press scallops into flour mixture, then turn to coat the other side. Quickly dip each side in butter.

4. Cook scallops in hot oil for about 3 minutes on each side or until browned and cooked through.

5. Sprinkle with parsley and serve over grits.

Slow-Cooker Étouffée

Serve étouffé over cooked rice.

INGREDIENTS | SERVES 6

2 tablespoons vegetable oil

1 large white onion, peeled and diced

6 green onions

2 medium ribs celery, finely diced

1 medium green bell pepper, seeded and diced

1 medium jalapeño pepper, seeded and diced

2 medium cloves garlic, minced

3 tablespoons tomato paste

3 (15-ounce) cans diced tomatoes, drained

½ teaspoon salt

½ teaspoon dried basil, crumbled

½ teaspoon dried oregano, crumbled

½ teaspoon dried thyme, crumbled

¼ teaspoon ground cayenne pepper

1 pound medium shrimp, peeled and deveined

1 pound sea scallops, quartered

2 teaspoons cornstarch

1 tablespoon cold water

Tabasco sauce

1. Add oil and white onion to a 4- to 6-quart slow cooker. Clean green onions and chop white parts and about 1" of greens. Add to the slow cooker along with celery, bell pepper, and jalapeño. Stir to coat vegetables in oil. Cover and cook on high for 30 minutes or until vegetables are soft.

2. Stir in garlic and tomato paste. Cover and cook on high for 15 minutes.

3. Stir in tomatoes, salt, basil, oregano, thyme, and cayenne pepper. Reduce the heat setting to low; cover and cook for 6 hours.

4. Stir in shrimp and scallops. Increase the heat setting to high, cover, and cook for 15 minutes.

5. Add cornstarch and water to a small bowl. Stir to mix. Remove any lumps. Uncover the slow cooker and stir in the cornstarch mixture. Cook and stir for 5 minutes or until mixture is thickened and the cornstarch flavor is cooked out. Stir in Tabasco sauce to taste.

Seafood and Chicken Gumbo

If you're using homemade chicken broth, you can skip steps 1 and 2; simply omit the oil and add the bacon, chicken, onion, and celery to the slow cooker and proceed to step 3.

INGREDIENTS | SERVES 4

1 tablespoon olive or vegetable oil

2 slices bacon, diced

4 large (4-ounce) chicken thighs, skin removed

1 large yellow onion, peeled and diced

2 medium ribs celery, diced

½ cup aromatic brown rice

1 (15-ounce) can diced tomatoes (undrained)

1 medium green bell pepper, seeded and diced

1 cup frozen okra, thawed

2 cups chicken broth

2 cups water

1 bay leaf

⅓ pound medium shrimp, peeled and deveined

⅓ pound sea scallops, quartered

⅓ pound cooked crabmeat

¼ teaspoon dried thyme, crumbled

1 teaspoon dried parsley flakes

2 teaspoons filé powder

Salt

1. Heat oil in a large nonstick skillet over medium-high heat. Add bacon and chicken; fry chicken for 3 minutes on each side. Use tongs to move chicken to a plate.

2. Add onion and celery to the skillet; sauté for 10 minutes or until onion is lightly browned.

3. Add rice to a 4- to 6-quart slow cooker and spread it over the bottom of the pot. Place chicken pieces over rice. Pour in sautéed onion and celery. Add tomatoes, bell pepper, okra, broth, water, and bay leaf. Cover and cook on low for 6 hours.

4. Add shrimp, scallops, crab, thyme, and parsley. Cover and cook on low for 15 minutes.

5. Turn off the heat. Stir in filé powder. Cover and let rest for 15 minutes or until shrimp are pink and scallops are opaque. Add salt to taste. Ladle into bowls and serve immediately.

Crawfish Stew

Every Cajun family has a favorite recipe for crawfish stew. Crawfish stew is not to be confused with étouffée, which has a more delicate sauce. Serve it over steamed rice.

INGREDIENTS | SERVES 4

1 cup vegetable oil

1 cup all-purpose flour

2 large yellow onions, peeled and diced

3 cups hot seafood broth or water, or more as needed

1 medium green bell pepper, seeded and diced

1 medium rib celery, diced

3 medium cloves garlic, minced

2 medium tomatoes, diced

1 tablespoon tomato paste

1 teaspoon Tabasco sauce

2 pounds peeled crawfish tails

¼ cup sliced green onion

¼ cup minced fresh flat-leaf parsley

Salt and ground black pepper

Ground cayenne pepper

1. In a large, heavy saucepan, combine oil and flour. Cook over medium-high heat, stirring constantly, until mixture reaches a deep brown color. Turn off heat; carefully add half of the yellow onions to roux; stir until onions have begun to caramelize. Whisk broth or water into roux a small amount at a time; whisk well to incorporate. If mixture seems too thick, add additional liquid.

2. Return to medium-high heat; add remaining yellow onion, bell pepper, celery, and garlic. Bring to a boil; stir in tomatoes, tomato paste, and Tabasco. Reduce heat to medium; cook, stirring occasionally, for 30 minutes.

3. Add crawfish tails; cook for 30–40 minutes.

4. Remove from heat; stir in green onion and parsley. Add salt, black pepper, and cayenne pepper to taste.

Les Écrevisses Est Arrivé! (Crawfish Have Arrived!)

Throughout Louisiana Cajun country, the arrival of crawfish in the springtime was heralded with signs outside markets and seafood stands. Crawfish is still a seasonal product, but with the advent of modern farm-raised crawfish, there are now two seasons: one in the fall and one in the springtime. In between, blanched, vacuum-sealed packs of peeled crawfish tails can be found at many supermarkets and fish markets. If you can't find crawfish, it's fine to substitute peeled shrimp.

Crawfish Pie

If you happen to have leftover crawfish étouffée, you can always use that as a crawfish pie filling.

INGREDIENTS | SERVES 6

3 tablespoons butter

2 tablespoons all-purpose flour

1 medium white onion, peeled and finely diced

1 cup shellfish broth or water, hot

½ small green bell pepper, seeded and finely diced

½ medium rib celery, finely diced

1 medium tomato, peeled, seeded, and chopped

1 teaspoon Tabasco sauce

Pinch ground cayenne pepper

1 pound crawfish tails, fresh or frozen and thawed

¼ cup heavy cream

Salt and ground black pepper

2 (9") pie crusts, unbaked

Crawfish Turnovers

In many Louisiana kitchens, crawfish pies are often prepared as crawfish-filled fried turnovers. To make this type of pie, skip the tomato in the baked pie filling recipe and remove the crawfish and vegetables from the sauce with a slotted spoon. Finely chop the filling in a food processor, then place spoonfuls on half of several small pie-crust circles. Fold the dough over, seal the edges well, and deep-fry until the pie crust is golden.

1. Preheat oven to 350°F. Grease a 9" pie pan with butter.

2. In a large, heavy saucepan, melt butter over medium-high heat. Add flour; stir until a paste forms. Cook, stirring constantly, until mixture turns light brown. Add half of the onions; stir until translucent. Carefully add hot broth or water; stir until roux dissolves and mixture is thickened. Reduce heat to medium; add remaining onion, bell pepper, celery, and tomato. Simmer for 10 minutes or until vegetables are tender, stirring often.

3. Add Tabasco, cayenne, and crawfish tails; simmer for 10 minutes.

4. Add cream, and salt and pepper to taste. Remove from heat; allow to cool to lukewarm. The mixture should be very thick.

5. Press 1 pie crust into prepared pan; spoon in crawfish mixture. Place remaining crust on a cutting surface; cut out circle, star, or diamond shapes to decorate and vent. The top crust should sit on top of the filling without touching the sides.

6. Bake for 40–45 minutes or until crust is browned. Let stand for 10 minutes before serving.

Shrimp Gumbo Pie

*If you like, you may add ½ cup frozen okra to this pie. The okra adds
an earthy flavor and will thicken the filling slightly.*

INGREDIENTS | SERVES 8

2 slices bacon, chopped

1 tablespoon butter

½ teaspoon salt

1 medium white onion, peeled and diced

1 medium rib celery, diced

½ medium green bell pepper, seeded and diced

1 medium clove garlic, minced

1 teaspoon Cajun seasoning

2 tablespoons all-purpose flour

½ cup seafood or chicken broth

1 (10-ounce) can diced tomatoes with green chilies (undrained)

1 pound medium shrimp, peeled and deveined

2 (9") pie crusts, unbaked

1 large egg, beaten

1. Preheat oven to 425°F.

2. In a large skillet, cook bacon over medium heat until crisp. Add butter and melt until it foams, then add salt, onion, celery, and bell pepper. Cook, stirring frequently, until vegetables are tender, about 8 minutes.

3. Add garlic and Cajun seasoning and cook until fragrant, about 30 seconds.

4. Sprinkle flour over the top of the vegetable mixture and mix until no raw flour remains. Stir in broth and diced tomatoes with green chilies. Bring to a simmer and cook until mixture thickens.

5. Add shrimp and cook for 2 minutes.

6. Press 1 pie crust into a 9" pie plate. Pour shrimp mixture into pie crust. Brush the edge of bottom pie crust with beaten egg so that the top crust will adhere. Top with remaining pie crust and trim dough to overlap 1" of the pan's edge. Tuck the edge of the top crust under the edge of the bottom crust. Crimp dough using your fingers or a fork. Brush entire top crust with beaten egg and cut 4 or 5 slits in the top to vent steam.

7. Place pie on a baking sheet and bake for 30 minutes. Reduce the heat to 350°F and bake for 30–40 minutes or until pie is bubbling and crust is golden brown. Cool for 30 minutes before slicing.

CHAPTER 10

Rice, Pasta, Grains, and Beans

Creamy Macaroni and Cheese

Who doesn't love macaroni and cheese? This is a wonderful creamy version, with a flavorful Cheddar sauce.

INGREDIENTS | SERVES 4–6

8 ounces elbow macaroni

¼ cup butter

¼ cup all-purpose flour

¼ teaspoon salt

⅛ teaspoon ground black pepper

2 cups whole milk

1 cup shredded sharp Cheddar cheese

½ cup fresh bread crumbs

1 tablespoon melted butter

Food for the Soul

In the South, macaroni and cheese is a beloved side dish. Many holiday dinners include a macaroni and cheese casserole, and it could be served in place of potatoes or rice at just about any family meal. Serve macaroni and cheese with meat or poultry, sliced tomatoes, and green beans for a very satisfying meal.

1. Cook macaroni according to package directions; drain and rinse under hot water.

2. Preheat oven to 375°F. Lightly butter a 2½-quart baking dish.

3. In a medium saucepan over medium-low heat, melt ¼ cup butter. Add flour, stirring until smooth and bubbly.

4. Stir in salt and pepper. Gradually add milk, stirring constantly. Continue to cook, stirring constantly, until sauce is thickened and bubbly. Stir in cheese until melted. Combine macaroni with cheese sauce; spoon into the prepared baking dish.

5. In a small bowl, drizzle 1 tablespoon melted butter over bread crumbs; toss to blend. Sprinkle over macaroni and cheese mixture.

6. Bake for 20–25 minutes or until macaroni and cheese is hot and bubbly and topping is lightly browned.

Cajun Chicken Pasta

This spicy, creamy pasta dish is super easy to pull together for a satisfying weeknight meal.

INGREDIENTS | SERVES 4

1 pound boneless, skinless chicken breasts, cut into strips

1 tablespoon Cajun seasoning

2 tablespoons butter

2 cups heavy cream

½ teaspoon dried basil, crumbled

½ teaspoon lemon pepper

½ teaspoon salt

¼ teaspoon ground black pepper

¼ teaspoon garlic powder

8 ounces linguine or fettuccine, cooked

½ cup grated Parmesan cheese

1. Place chicken and Cajun seasoning in a food storage bag. Rub and shake to coat chicken well.

2. In a large skillet over medium heat, melt butter and sauté chicken. Cook for about 7–9 minutes, then reduce heat to medium-low.

3. Add cream, basil, lemon pepper, salt, black pepper, and garlic powder. Stir for 5 minutes until sauce thickens.

4. Add pasta and toss to coat. Heat for another 5 minutes. Sprinkle with Parmesan cheese.

Jambalaya Pasta

Make this quick version of jambalaya for an easy and flavorful weeknight meal.

INGREDIENTS | SERVES 4

½ cup butter

2 teaspoons Cajun seasoning

1 pound boneless, skinless chicken breasts, cut into bite-sized pieces

½ cup clam juice

1 medium green bell pepper, seeded and sliced

1 medium red bell pepper, seeded and sliced

½ medium red onion, peeled and sliced

½ pound medium shrimp, peeled and deveined

½ cup diced tomatoes

1 pound linguine, cooked and kept warm

1. Melt butter in a large skillet over medium-high heat. Stir in Cajun seasoning. Add chicken and cook for 4 minutes until chicken is about halfway done.

2. Pour clam juice into the pan and add peppers and onions. Cook for 4 minutes until vegetables are heated through and chicken is almost done.

3. Stir in shrimp and continue to cook for 3 minutes until shrimp are almost done.

4. Add tomatoes and cook for 5 minutes until shrimp are pink and chicken is thoroughly cooked.

5. To serve, place warm pasta in a large bowl and top with jambalaya mixture.

Savory Rice Pilaf with Green Onions

The pecans jazz up the flavor of this lovely rice pilaf a bit, but it's also delicious without them.

INGREDIENTS | SERVES 4

2 tablespoons butter

1 tablespoon olive oil

1 cup thinly sliced button or cremini mushrooms

½ cup thinly sliced green onions

1 cup long-grain white rice

2 cups chicken broth

⅛ teaspoon ground black pepper

1 teaspoon lemon juice

½ cup pecan halves

2 tablespoons chopped fresh flat-leaf parsley

Dash Tabasco sauce

1. Combine butter and oil in a medium saucepan over medium heat. Add mushrooms and cook, stirring constantly, for 2 minutes. Add green onions and cook for about 1 minute. Add rice and cook for another 30 seconds. Add chicken broth, pepper, and lemon juice; bring to a boil over medium-high heat. Reduce heat to low; cover and cook for about 20 minutes until liquid has been absorbed and rice is tender. If necessary, add more chicken broth. Remove from heat and leave the lid on for about 10 minutes.

2. Meanwhile, toast nuts: Spread out pecans on a baking sheet and bake at 325°F for 8–10 minutes. Let cool, then chop.

3. Stir pecans into rice, along with chopped parsley and Tabasco. Taste and adjust seasonings.

Cajun-Style Dirty Rice

This flavorful recipe gets its name from the "dirty" appearance of the rice.

INGREDIENTS | SERVES 6

½–¾ pound chicken gizzards
3½ cups chicken broth, hot
½ pound lean ground pork
6 tablespoons butter, divided
½ cup chopped yellow onion
½ cup chopped green onion
¾ cup chopped celery
½ cup chopped red bell pepper
3 medium cloves garlic, minced
2 teaspoons Creole seasoning
½ teaspoon salt
¼ teaspoon ground black pepper
⅛ teaspoon ground cayenne pepper
1½ cups long-grain white rice
½ pound chicken livers, diced

1. Combine chicken gizzards and broth in a large saucepan. Bring to a boil over high heat; reduce heat to low and simmer for about 30 minutes. With a slotted spoon, remove gizzards and mince. Reserve broth.

2. Combine minced gizzards with pork in a large, heavy skillet over medium-high heat. Cook mixture, stirring and breaking up pork, until pork is no longer pink.

3. Reduce heat to medium; add 4 tablespoons butter, yellow onion, green onion, celery, and bell pepper to the skillet. Cook for about 5 minutes until tender. Add garlic, Creole seasoning, salt, black pepper, and cayenne and cook for about 30 seconds.

4. Add reserved broth and rice to the skillet. Increase heat to high and bring to a boil, stirring occasionally. Reduce heat to low; cover and simmer for 15 minutes or until rice is tender.

5. In a small skillet over medium heat; melt remaining 2 tablespoons butter. Cook diced chicken livers for about 3–4 minutes. Toss with rice. Cover and let rice sit for 10 minutes. Remove cover and fluff with a fork just before serving.

Home-Style Cornbread Dressing

This delicious dressing is an essential holiday side dish. Use homemade cornbread and homemade chicken broth with chunks of chicken for the tastiest dressing.

INGREDIENTS | SERVES 8

6 cups crumbled cornbread

3 cups fresh white bread crumbs

2 cups chopped yellow onion

2½ cups chopped celery

½ cup butter

3–4 cups chicken broth

2 cups diced cooked chicken

1 heaping tablespoon dried sage, crumbled

1½ teaspoons dried thyme, crumbled

1 teaspoon dried marjoram, crumbled

½ teaspoon dried rosemary, crumbled

1 teaspoon salt

½ teaspoon ground black pepper

2 large eggs, beaten

1. Preheat oven to 400°F. Grease a large, shallow baking or roasting pan measuring about 10" × 15".

2. In a large mixing bowl, combine cornbread and white bread crumbs.

3. In a medium saucepan over medium heat, sauté onion and celery in butter until tender, about 5 minutes. Do not brown.

4. Add sautéed vegetables to bread mixture. Stir in chicken broth until well moistened and then add chicken. Stir in sage, thyme, marjoram, rosemary, salt, pepper, and beaten egg, blending well.

5. Spread mixture in the prepared baking pan.

6. Bake for 20–30 minutes until heated through.

Dressing Safety

It's safer to bake dressing in a pan in the oven, but if you decide to stuff a turkey or chicken with the mixture, here are some safety tips. Stuff the bird just before roasting. If you stuff it in advance, bacteria might have an opportunity to move from the poultry to the stuffing. Make sure you stuff the bird loosely and that the stuffing is moist. The bird should register 180°F in the breast meat and 165°F in the center of the stuffing. Just before carving (about 20 minutes after the bird is removed from the oven), remove all of the stuffing to a separate bowl. Do not store the stuffing in the bird.

Creamy Grits

These savory grits go perfectly with shrimp, pork medallions, chops, or just about anything you might serve over rice or polenta. You can stir in a cup of shredded Cheddar or Havarti cheese, but these grits are delicious just as they are.

INGREDIENTS | SERVES 6

2 cups chicken broth

⅔ cup heavy cream

1 cup water

¼ cup butter

¼ teaspoon salt

¼ teaspoon ground black pepper

1 cup quick-cooking grits

1. In a medium saucepan, bring chicken broth, cream, and water to a boil.

2. Stir in butter, salt, and pepper. Whisk in grits gradually so mixture does not stop boiling. Lower heat to medium-low and simmer for 15–20 minutes, stirring frequently. Cover and remove from heat.

Grits Online

If you don't have grits in your area, here are a few online sources. The Peas & Corn Co. offers stone-ground flour, grits, and cornmeal, and they also have other hard-to-find Southern foods and utensils: *www.peasand cornco.com*. Hoppin' John's is the site of cookbook author John Martin Taylor. You'll find stone-ground grits and cornmeal, along with links to his cookbooks and other information: *www.hoppinjohns.com*. Bob's Red Mill has an online catalog with all of their grains, beans, nuts and seeds, flours and meals, seasonings, and baking aids: *www.bobsredmill.com*.

Garlic Cheese Grits Casserole

This is a garlicky version of a very popular Southern grits casserole—a classic comfort food.

INGREDIENTS | SERVES 8

2 cups whole milk
2 cups chicken broth
1 cup quick-cooking grits
¼ cup butter
3 medium cloves garlic, minced
1 teaspoon salt
½ teaspoon ground black pepper
2 cups shredded sharp Cheddar cheese
3 large eggs, beaten

1. Preheat oven to 350°F. Lightly butter a 2-quart casserole dish.

2. Bring milk and chicken broth to a rolling boil in a large saucepan over medium-high heat. Gradually whisk grits into boiling mixture. Boil for about 7–9 minutes, stirring until thick and grits are tender.

3. Meanwhile, melt butter with minced garlic in the microwave or in a small saucepan over low heat. Let stand for about 5 minutes. Strain butter into boiling grits mixture. Discard garlic.

4. Stir in salt, pepper, and shredded cheese. Stir in beaten eggs until well blended.

5. Spread cheese and grits mixture in the prepared casserole dish. Bake for 45–55 minutes until puffed up and browned.

Spicy Hoppin' John

You just cannot bring in the New Year without a dish of black-eyed peas for good luck, and hoppin' John is a tradition. To be extremely lucky in the New Year, serve this tasty dish with cooked greens or cabbage, along with rice and Southern Skillet Cornbread (see recipe in Chapter 2).

INGREDIENTS | SERVES 6

1 pound dried black-eyed peas

4 ounces salt pork or hog jowl, diced

1 cup chopped white onion

½ cup chopped celery

3 medium cloves garlic, minced

½ cup diced green bell pepper

1½ cups diced cooked ham

4 cups chicken broth or water, or more as needed

1 tablespoon Cajun seasoning

½ teaspoon salt

¼ teaspoon ground black pepper

Dash ground cayenne pepper

1. Soak peas in cold water overnight. Drain.

2. In a heavy skillet, sauté salt pork or hog jowl and onion until onion is browned.

3. In a large stockpot or Dutch oven, combine drained peas with sautéed salt pork and onion; add celery, garlic, bell pepper, and ham. Add water or broth and bring to a boil. Reduce heat to low, cover, and simmer for 1 hour.

4. Add Cajun seasoning, salt, black pepper, and cayenne pepper; cover and cook for about 30–60 minutes longer until peas are tender. Check occasionally and add more water if needed.

5. Taste and adjust seasonings if desired.

What's with the Name?

There are many theories on how the dish hoppin' John came by its name. According to one story, the ritual began on New Year's Day, when children would hop around the table before eating. Another claims guests were invited to eat with the phrase "Hop in, John." Whatever its origin, it was an important dish in the early South, and it's still an important dish, especially on January 1.

Louisiana Red Beans and Rice

A classic Louisiana favorite, red beans and rice is pure comfort food to many.
This recipe is simple, but it's a flavorful version of the dish.

INGREDIENTS | SERVES 8

1 pound small dried red beans
1 cup chopped white onion
½ cup chopped green bell pepper
3 medium ribs celery, chopped
3 medium cloves garlic, minced
1 meaty ham bone or large smoked ham hock
1 pound smoked sausage, sliced
1 bay leaf
½ teaspoon dried thyme, crumbled
Few drops Tabasco sauce
Few dashes Worcestershire sauce
1 teaspoon Creole seasoning
Salt
2 cups hot cooked long-grain white rice

1. Wash beans and discard any stones and shriveled or bad beans. Cover with water and let soak overnight. Drain well.

2. In a large stockpot or Dutch oven, cover beans with just enough fresh water to cover. Bring to a boil over high heat, then reduce heat to medium-low. Cook for about 45–60 minutes until beans are tender.

3. Add onion, bell pepper, celery, and garlic. Add ham bone or hock and sausage, along with bay leaf and thyme. Add enough water to cover all ingredients. Bring to a boil over medium-high heat; reduce heat to low, cover, and simmer until vegetables are tender, about 20 minutes.

4. Add Tabasco sauce, Worcestershire sauce, Creole seasoning, and salt. Continue cooking for another 15 minutes. Remove ham bone or hock and chop meat; return chopped meat to beans. If desired, mash a few cups of the beans to make mixture thicker.

5. Serve red beans with hot cooked rice.

Down-Home Pinto Beans

Serve these delicious Southern-style pinto beans with hot, buttered cornbread.

INGREDIENTS | SERVES 6–8

1 pound dried pinto beans

6 ounces thick-sliced bacon, fatback, or hog jowl

1½ cups chopped sweet onion

2 medium cloves garlic, minced

1 teaspoon salt

½ teaspoon crushed red pepper

¼ teaspoon ground black pepper

1. Sort beans and remove any small stones and damaged beans. Put in a large bowl and cover with about 1½ quarts of cold water. Soak overnight. Refrigerate after about 8–10 hours if not cooking until later in the day.

2. Drain and rinse beans; transfer to a large stockpot or Dutch oven. Add diced bacon, fatback, salt pork, or hog jowl, onion, and garlic. Bring to a simmer. Reduce heat to low, cover, and cook for about 1½–2 hours or until beans are tender.

3. Add salt, crushed red pepper, and black pepper to beans. Continue to cook, uncovered, for about 20 minutes or until beans are tender and juices are creamy.

Barbecue Baked Beans

These easy and delicious beans make a wonderful side dish to take to a cookout or potluck dinner or to serve with any family meal.

INGREDIENTS | SERVES 8

1 tablespoon vegetable oil
1 pound lean ground beef
½ cup chopped green bell pepper
1 cup chopped sweet onion
1 cup chopped celery
1 (15-ounce) can tomato sauce
¾ cup water
2 medium cloves garlic, minced
¼ cup apple cider vinegar
2 teaspoons dry mustard
1 teaspoon dried thyme, crumbled
3 tablespoons light brown sugar
Salt and ground black pepper
2 (28-ounce) cans pork and beans

1. Preheat oven to 375°F.

2. In a large skillet over medium heat, heat vegetable oil. Add ground beef, onion, bell pepper, and celery; sauté until beef is no longer pink and vegetables are tender.

3. Add tomato sauce, water, garlic, vinegar, mustard, thyme, and brown sugar to the skillet. Stir to combine. Bring to a boil; reduce heat and simmer for 5 minutes. Add salt and ground black pepper to taste.

4. Add beans to beef and vegetable mixture. Transfer to a 2-quart baking dish. Bake for 30 minutes until hot and bubbly.

CHAPTER 11

Vegetables

Creamy Lima Bean and Corn Succotash

Succotash is a popular Southern vegetable combination. The dish is perfect with just about anything.

INGREDIENTS | SERVES 6

1 (1-pound) bag frozen baby lima beans, thawed

½ teaspoon salt plus more to taste, divided

2 cups frozen whole-kernel corn, thawed

¼ cup butter

¾–1 cup heavy cream

Ground black pepper

1. Put baby lima beans in a large saucepan with ½ teaspoon salt. Cover with water and bring to a boil over high heat. Reduce heat to medium; cover and simmer for 10 minutes.

2. Add corn and more water to cover. Increase heat and bring to a boil; reduce to a simmer, cover, and cook for 5–8 minutes or until beans and corn are tender.

3. Drain well. Stir in butter and add heavy cream to reach the desired consistency. Add salt and pepper to taste.

Green Bean Casserole

This casserole is a standard on many holiday dinner tables, and it's delicious.

INGREDIENTS | SERVES 6

5 tablespoons butter

½ cup chopped yellow onion

½ cup chopped button or cremini mushrooms

6 tablespoons all-purpose flour

2½ cups whole milk

Salt and ground black pepper

3 (14.5-ounce) cans French-style green beans, drained

1 (8-ounce) can sliced water chestnuts, drained

1 cup shredded sharp Cheddar cheese

1 (2.8-ounce) container French-fried onion rings, crumbled

1. Preheat oven to 350°F. Lightly grease a 2½-quart baking dish.

2. In a large, heavy saucepan, melt butter over medium-low heat. Add onion and mushrooms and sauté until tender. Stir in flour until blended. Gradually stir in milk. Continue cooking, stirring constantly, until thickened and bubbly. Add salt and pepper to taste.

3. Combine drained green beans and water chestnuts with sauce. Stir in cheese. Transfer mixture to the prepared baking dish. Top with crumbled French-fried onion rings.

4. Bake for 30 minutes until hot and bubbly.

Grandma's Green Beans

This recipe is easy to double if you need extra servings for a church social or buffet. Serve these green beans with meatloaf or any grilled meat.

INGREDIENTS | SERVES 6

1 (1-pound) bag frozen green beans, thawed

6 medium red potatoes, peeled and diced

1 medium sweet onion, peeled and diced

1 teaspoon sugar

Salt and ground black pepper

6 slices bacon

1. Add green beans, potatoes, onion, and sugar to a 4- to 6-quart slow cooker. Season with salt and pepper to taste.

2. Dice bacon and add ⅔ of it to the slow cooker. Stir to mix well. Sprinkle remaining bacon pieces over the top of bean mixture. Cover and cook on low for 4 hours or until potatoes are cooked through. Taste for seasoning and add additional salt and pepper if needed.

Fresh Green Beans

You can substitute 1–1½ pounds washed, trimmed, and cut fresh green beans for the frozen. Increase the cooking time to 6 hours if you do.

Summer Squash Casserole

Use fresh yellow crookneck squash for this dish. Zucchini also works well—or use a combination.

INGREDIENTS | SERVES 4

2 pounds yellow summer squash

3 tablespoons butter

½ cup chopped sweet onion

4 ounces fresh button or cremini mushrooms, chopped

3½ tablespoons all-purpose flour

1½ cups whole milk

1½ cups shredded mild Cheddar cheese

2 tablespoons chopped fresh flat-leaf parsley

½ teaspoon salt

¼ teaspoon seasoned salt

¼ teaspoon ground black pepper

½ cup sour cream

¾ cup fine dry bread crumbs

1 tablespoon melted butter

1. Cut squash into slices about ¼" thick. Add to a large saucepan and cover with water. Bring to a boil over high heat. Reduce heat to medium; cover and simmer for 10–15 minutes until tender. Drain and set aside.

2. Preheat oven to 350°F. Lightly grease a 2-quart baking dish.

3. In a large saucepan, melt 3 tablespoons butter over medium-low heat. Add onion and mushrooms; sauté until tender. Add flour and stir until well incorporated. Gradually stir in milk. Continue cooking, stirring constantly, until thickened and bubbly. Stir in cheese, parsley, salt, seasoned salt, and pepper. Remove from heat. Taste and adjust seasonings. Stir in sour cream.

4. Combine squash and sauce. Pour mixture into the prepared dish. Toss bread crumbs with 1 tablespoon melted butter; sprinkle over squash mixture. Bake for 30 minutes or until browned and bubbly.

Easy Fried Corn

Fresh corn, also known as green corn, isn't really fried; it is cooked in a skillet. It's a great Southern dish.

INGREDIENTS | SERVES 4

6 ears fresh corn
2 tablespoons butter or bacon drippings
½ teaspoon salt
¼ teaspoon ground black pepper
Dash sugar

Cutting Corn from the Cob

First, place the cob over a shallow bowl, holding the top to keep it upright. With the sharp side of the knife, position it as close to the cob as you can. Cut straight down to cut the kernels from the cob. Using the blunt side of the knife, scrape the juices left on the cob.

1. Slice corn kernels from each cob into a bowl. Scrape the cob to get any remaining corn and milky liquid.

2. Add butter or bacon drippings to a large, heavy skillet over medium-low heat. Add corn; cook, stirring frequently, for 15–20 minutes, taking care not to let it burn. Sprinkle with salt, pepper, and sugar and stir. Serve hot.

Creamed Corn

This recipe is definitely not for somebody on a low-fat or low-carb diet. The cream cheese helps make the rich sauce for the corn. In fact, because of the cream cheese there will be enough sauce that if you need extra servings for a carry-in buffet, you can double the amount of corn you use and still have enough sauce.

INGREDIENTS | SERVES 8

4 cups frozen whole-kernel corn, thawed
8 ounces cream cheese
½ cup butter
½ cup whole milk
1 tablespoon sugar
Salt and ground black pepper

1. Add corn to a 4- to 6-quart slow cooker. Cube cream cheese and slice butter; add to the slow cooker along with milk and sugar. Season with salt and pepper to taste. Stir to combine.

2. Cover and cook on low for 2 hours. Stir corn mixture, cover, and cook for about 2 more hours, watching it carefully and switching the slow cooker to the warm setting as soon as cream sauce is thickened. (The corn can scorch and change flavor if the heat is left too high for too long.) Keep warm until ready to serve.

Savory Collard Greens

Greens have long been a favorite in Southern kitchens, and collard greens are wonderful. Serve this dish with plenty of Tabasco sauce at the table.

INGREDIENTS | SERVES 6

2 or 3 meaty ham hocks

3 pounds collard greens

1 teaspoon seasoned salt

1½ teaspoons salt

Dash ground black pepper

Dash ground cayenne pepper

Dash garlic powder

Washing Collard Greens

Collard greens can be quite gritty. To clean them, strip the thick stalks out of the collard leaves or use a knife and cut them out. Smaller leaves should not need to be stripped. Wash the leaves separately and rinse. You can tell they're clean when you no longer feel any grit in the bottom of the sink.

1. In a large stockpot over high heat, bring about 4–5 quarts of water to a boil with ham hocks. Reduce heat to a simmer and continue cooking for about 1–1½ hours or until ham hock meat is tender. Add more water as needed.

2. Stack several collard green leaves together. Roll them, then cut into ½" slices.

3. Working with batches, add sliced collard leaves to the pot of simmering water with ham hocks. (You'll probably have to let some of the greens wilt down before adding more.) Add seasoned salt, salt, black pepper, cayenne, and garlic powder. Bring to a boil. Reduce heat to medium and simmer for about 45 minutes, stirring occasionally. Remove ham hocks. If you like, remove meat from hocks and return it to the pot.

4. Taste and adjust seasonings.

Spinach Casserole with Eggs and Cheese

Hard-cooked eggs are a popular addition to Southern casseroles.

INGREDIENTS | SERVES 6

4–6 slices bacon

1½ pounds spinach, cleaned and chopped

1 teaspoon salt, divided

¼ teaspoon ground black pepper, divided

2 medium tomatoes, sliced

3 large hard-cooked eggs, peeled and sliced

¼ cup butter

¼ cup all-purpose flour

Dash paprika

2 cups whole milk

1½ cups shredded mild Cheddar cheese

Spinach—Nutritious and Delicious!

This leafy green vegetable is a rich source of vitamins A and C, as well as potassium and other nutrients. Try cooking spinach in 1–2 teaspoons bacon drippings with a little salt, pepper, and freshly cooked and crumbled bacon. More delicious flavors for spinach include hard-cooked eggs, freshly grated nutmeg, and, of course, butter.

1. Cook bacon in a medium skillet over medium heat until crisp; drain on paper towels. Crumble and set aside.

2. Preheat oven to 350°F. Lightly butter a 9" × 13" baking dish.

3. Place spinach in the prepared dish; season with ½ teaspoon salt and ⅛ teaspoon pepper. Arrange tomatoes and eggs over spinach.

4. In a medium saucepan over medium-low heat, melt butter. Add flour and stir until smooth and bubbly. Add paprika and remaining salt and pepper. Gradually stir in milk. Cook, stirring constantly, until sauce is thickened and bubbly. Add cheese; stir until melted. Pour sauce over spinach and eggs. Top with crumbled bacon. Bake for 30 minutes.

Spicy Fried Eggplant Strips

Eggplant is surprisingly popular in the South, especially when it's fried.

INGREDIENTS | SERVES 6

1 medium eggplant

1 teaspoon salt

1 cup all-purpose flour, or more as needed

1 teaspoon baking powder

2 teaspoons Creole seasoning

½ teaspoon onion powder

¼ teaspoon garlic powder

Dash ground cayenne pepper

2 large eggs, beaten

⅔ cup whole milk, or more as needed

1 tablespoon canola oil

Vegetable oil

Choosing Eggplant

Eggplant is highly perishable, so you want to choose the freshest possible. Fresh eggplants have a thinner skin and will not taste as bitter. An eggplant should feel heavy for its size. Lift a few of similar size, and then choose the one that feels heaviest. The eggplant should spring back when gently pressed, and the skin should be smooth and free of blemishes or soft spots. If you can't use the eggplant the day you buy it, store it for up to 2 days in a cool, dry place.

1. Peel eggplant and cut into strips ½" in width and 3" in length. Place eggplant strips in a medium bowl; cover with water and sprinkle with salt. Let eggplant strips soak for 45–60 minutes. Drain; pat dry with paper towels.

2. In another medium bowl, combine flour, baking powder, Creole seasoning, onion powder, garlic powder, and cayenne pepper. Add beaten eggs, milk, and canola oil; blend until smooth. The batter should be thin enough to drip a bit but thick enough to coat eggplant. Add a little more milk if too thick or more flour if too thin.

3. Heat oil to 375°F in a deep fryer. Dip eggplant strips in batter; let excess batter drip back into the bowl. Fry eggplant in small batches in hot oil for 3 minutes, turning to cook both sides, until golden brown.

Okra, Corn, and Tomato Stew

*For best flavor, make this dish during the summer with corn cut
from the cob and just-picked tomatoes and okra.*

INGREDIENTS | SERVES 4

3 tablespoons oil or butter

1 medium yellow onion, peeled and finely diced

1 small green bell pepper, seeded and finely diced

1 medium rib celery, finely diced

2 medium cloves garlic, minced

2 cups sliced okra

2 cups diced ripe tomatoes

2 cups fresh corn kernels

1 cup water or chicken broth

¼ teaspoon ground cayenne pepper

1 green onion, sliced

2 tablespoons minced fresh flat-leaf parsley

Salt and ground black pepper

1. In a large, deep skillet or Dutch oven, heat oil or butter over medium-high heat. Add yellow onion, bell pepper, celery, and garlic; sauté for 5 minutes.

2. Add okra; cook, stirring constantly, for 3 minutes or until okra begins to release thick liquid.

3. Add tomatoes, corn, and water or broth; bring to a boil. Reduce heat to medium-low. Simmer, stirring often and adding more liquid if needed, for 20 minutes or until corn is tender.

4. Stir in cayenne, green onion, and parsley. Add salt and pepper to taste; remove from heat.

Sautéed Okra and Tomatoes

Okra cooked with tomatoes is a classic Southern dish, and by pan-frying the okra first before mixing in the tomatoes, you prevent them from becoming sticky.

INGREDIENTS | SERVES 6–8

1 pound fresh okra, cut into ¼" slices

3 tablespoons vegetable oil

1 small yellow onion, peeled and chopped

3 large tomatoes, seeded and chopped

2 medium cloves garlic, minced

1 tablespoon apple cider vinegar

Salt and ground black pepper

1. Pat okra slices dry with a paper towel to prevent oil splatters. Place a medium skillet over medium-high heat. Once it is heated, add oil, onion, and okra. Cook, stirring often, until onion is golden brown and okra is crispy on the cut sides.

2. Add tomatoes and garlic, stirring continually for 2–3 minutes or just until tomatoes are cooked through. Pour into a bowl and sprinkle with vinegar. Stir to combine and add salt and pepper to taste.

Easy Skillet-Glazed Sweet Potatoes

Your family will love these skillet sweet potatoes, and the recipe is so simple. These make a great side dish with ham, pork, or lamb.

INGREDIENTS | SERVES 6

4 or 5 medium sweet potatoes

¾ cup light brown sugar, packed

½ cup water

¼ teaspoon salt

2 tablespoons butter

Cook Sweet Potatoes Before Peeling

Sweet potatoes should be boiled in their jackets so they retain their great nutrients. Boiled sweet potatoes are very easy to peel. Just pick them out of the water with a slotted spoon and dip in cold water. The skins will slip off easily.

1. Boil unpeeled sweet potatoes until tender. Let cool slightly, then peel and slice into ½"-thick rounds.

2. In a large, heavy skillet, combine brown sugar, water, salt, and butter. Heat on medium until mixture begins to simmer; reduce heat to low and simmer for 5 minutes.

3. Add sliced sweet potatoes and simmer for 10 minutes, turning often to keep them coated with sugar mixture.

4. Spoon into a serving dish and serve hot.

Sweet Potato Casserole

This delicious casserole is the perfect complement to a holiday ham or roast turkey.

INGREDIENTS | SERVES 8

4 or 5 medium sweet potatoes (about 3 pounds)

2 large eggs, slightly beaten

2 tablespoons butter, melted

3 tablespoons light brown sugar

1 teaspoon salt

½ teaspoon ground cinnamon

¼ teaspoon ground ginger

⅛ teaspoon freshly grated nutmeg

Dash ground black pepper

½ cup chopped pecans

1. Scrub sweet potatoes and place in a large stockpot. Cover with water. Bring to a boil over high heat; reduce heat to medium-low, cover, and simmer for about 30 minutes until tender. Set aside to let sweet potatoes cool slightly.

2. Slip sweet potatoes out of the skins and place in a medium bowl. If you have a ricer, cut them into smaller pieces and put them through the ricer, then mash until smooth. If you don't have a ricer, just mash with a potato masher. Add beaten eggs, butter, brown sugar, salt, cinnamon, ginger, nutmeg, and pepper. Whisk or beat until smooth.

3. Preheat oven to 350°F. Lightly butter a 7" × 11" baking dish.

4. Turn sweet potato mixture into the prepared baking dish. Sprinkle pecans over the top. Bake for 35–45 minutes or until puffy and hot. Serve hot.

Creamy Potato Scallop

This luscious potato casserole is a nice departure from the everyday boiled or mashed potatoes.

INGREDIENTS | SERVES 6

2 pounds red or round white potatoes

1 teaspoon salt

¼ teaspoon ground black pepper

2 tablespoons all-purpose flour

¼ cup chopped yellow onion

2 cups shredded sharp Cheddar cheese

2 tablespoons butter, cut into small pieces

2 cups whole milk

Potato Types

Before you choose potatoes for a recipe, be sure you know the difference between the various types. Waxy potatoes are low-starch potatoes, and they hold up better for dishes such as potato salads and scalloped potatoes. Starchy potatoes make great mashed potatoes, French fries, and baked potatoes. If you aren't sure what kind you have, test by slicing. If the knife is coated with a creamy white film or if the potato lightly clings to the knife, the potato is starchy. If it doesn't, it's a waxy potato. If it has only a little creamy film, it's probably a good all-purpose potato, and it should work well in most dishes.

1. Preheat oven to 350°F. Lightly butter a 2-quart baking dish.

2. Peel potatoes and slice into about ¼"-thick rounds. You should have about 4 cups. Arrange half of the potatoes in the prepared baking dish.

3. Sprinkle with half of the salt, pepper, flour, onion, and cheese. Dot the layer all over with half of the small pieces of butter. Repeat layer; dot with remaining butter and add milk to cover potatoes. Cover with foil.

4. Bake the casserole for about 30–40 minutes or until potatoes are tender. Remove the foil the last 10 minutes of baking or put under the broiler for 1–2 minutes after baking to brown the top.

Judy's Hash Brown Casserole

This popular country-style hash-brown side dish is easy and it makes a great brunch dish. It also works as a hearty dinner side dish.

INGREDIENTS | SERVES 8

1 (30-ounce) package frozen country-style hash browns

1 (10.75-ounce) can condensed cream of chicken or cream of celery soup

1 cup sour cream

½ cup plus 2 tablespoons melted butter, divided

2 cups shredded sharp Cheddar cheese

1 cup minced yellow onion

½ teaspoon salt

¼ teaspoon ground black pepper

1 cup fresh bread crumbs

1. Thaw hash browns quickly on the defrost setting in the microwave or leave in the refrigerator overnight.

2. Preheat oven to 350°F. Lightly butter a 9" × 13" baking dish.

3. In a large bowl, combine thawed hash browns with condensed soup, sour cream, ½ cup butter, cheese, onion, salt, and pepper. Stir to blend ingredients thoroughly.

4. Spread in the prepared baking dish. In a small bowl, combine bread crumbs with remaining melted butter. Sprinkle over potato mixture. Bake for 45 minutes or until lightly browned and bubbly.

Crispy Fried Okra

Okra, fried with a crispy cornmeal coating, is a Southern favorite.
If you've never tried okra, this is the recipe to try.

INGREDIENTS | SERVES 6

1 pound fresh okra
2 large eggs, beaten
Several drops hot pepper sauce
1 cup yellow cornmeal
½ cup all-purpose flour
½ teaspoon salt
¼ teaspoon ground black pepper
Dash ground cayenne pepper
Vegetable oil

1. Wash okra; cut off tips and stem ends. Cut okra pods crosswise into ½" slices.

2. Beat eggs in a shallow bowl with hot sauce.

3. Combine cornmeal, flour, salt, black pepper, and cayenne in a large food storage bag or shallow bowl.

4. Heat oil to 375°F in a deep fryer.

5. Add okra to beaten eggs; stir to coat well. Drop several pieces of okra into cornmeal mixture and shake gently to coat well. Repeat with remaining okra.

6. Fry okra in hot oil in batches until browned, about 4–6 minutes for each batch. Turn as needed to brown all sides. Drain on paper towels and keep warm.

Quick and Easy Broiled Tomatoes

This is a perfect side to a backyard barbecue or a quick summer meal with grilled chicken or shrimp.

INGREDIENTS | SERVES 6

4 medium tomatoes
2 tablespoons Dijon mustard
Salt and ground black pepper
6 tablespoons butter, melted
½ cup seasoned fine dry bread crumbs
½ cup grated Parmesan cheese

1. Preheat broiler. Lightly oil the rack of a broiler pan.

2. Cut tomatoes in half and arrange on the prepared rack; spread cut side with mustard and sprinkle with salt and pepper. Combine melted butter with bread crumbs and Parmesan cheese in a small bowl; spoon over tomato halves.

3. Place tomatoes under the broiler, about 6" from the heat source, and broil until crumbs are browned and tomatoes are tender.

Baked Vidalia Onions

This is wonderful way to enjoy sweet onions. Feel free to substitute any large sweet onions in season.

INGREDIENTS | SERVES 6

6 large Vidalia onions
6 tablespoons cold butter, cut into pieces
1½ teaspoons salt
¼ teaspoon ground black pepper
1–1½ cups grated Parmesan cheese

1. Preheat oven to 350°F. Lightly butter 6 large squares of foil (large enough to wrap each onion).

2. Peel onions, leaving the roots intact. Cut each into eighths, cutting just to, but not through, the roots.

3. Place each onion on a piece of foil. Divide cold butter equally among onions, pressing it into the centers. Sprinkle with salt and pepper, and sprinkle each with 3–4 tablespoons of cheese.

4. Wrap each onion in foil and arrange in a 9" × 13" baking dish. Bake wrapped onions for about 45–60 minutes or until onions are tender.

Fried Green Tomatoes

There are many ways to make these, but a cornmeal mixture provides the right amount of crunch.
Serve these as a side dish or combine with a sauce or sliced cheese and serve as a first course.

INGREDIENTS | SERVES 4

4 large, firm green tomatoes
Salt and ground black pepper
¾ cup all-purpose flour, divided
2 large eggs, beaten
1 cup yellow cornmeal
Dash ground cayenne pepper
⅓ cup vegetable oil, or more as needed

Fried Green Tomatoes Appetizer

Fried green tomatoes are not only a great side dish; they also make a flavorful and interesting first course or appetizer. Stack a few with a couple rounds of goat cheese and Rémoulade Sauce, or serve on a bed of spinach with Sherry Cream Sauce (see recipes in Chapter 12). They would also be fabulous topped with a couple of cooked medium-sized shrimp, or with sliced mozzarella cheese or freshly grated Parmesan cheese with a little basil-seasoned tomato sauce.

1. Slice tomatoes into rounds about ¼"–½" thick. Sprinkle tomatoes with salt and black pepper on both sides. Dip in ¼ cup flour to lightly coat.

2. In a shallow bowl, whisk eggs. In another shallow bowl, combine cornmeal, remaining ½ cup flour, and cayenne pepper.

3. Heat about ⅓ cup oil in a large, heavy skillet over medium heat. The bottom of the skillet should be completely covered with oil to a depth of about ⅛"–¼".

4. Dip floured green tomato slices in beaten egg, then dredge in cornmeal mixture to coat thoroughly. Fry in batches until browned, then turn to brown the other side. They'll take about 3 minutes on each side.

Broccoli with Cheese Sauce

This broccoli dish is delicious and uncomplicated, and the cheese sauce is wonderful with cauliflower as well.

INGREDIENTS | SERVES 8

1½ pounds fresh broccoli
3 tablespoons butter
1 tablespoon grated sweet onion
3 tablespoons all-purpose flour
Dash garlic powder
Dash paprika
⅛ teaspoon ground black pepper
1½ cups whole milk
1 cup shredded sharp Cheddar cheese

1. Trim broccoli, discarding large leaves and tough ends of lower stalks. Wash well, drain, and cut stalks and florets into bite-sized pieces.

2. Place a steamer in a large saucepan over about 1" water. Add broccoli to steamer and steam broccoli over medium-high heat for about 5–7 minutes or to desired doneness.

3. Meanwhile, in a large saucepan over medium heat, melt butter; add onion and sauté until soft. Stir in flour, garlic powder, paprika, and pepper until well blended. Gradually stir in milk. Continue cooking, stirring constantly, until sauce is thickened and bubbly. Stir in cheese until melted; remove from heat.

4. Serve broccoli with cheese sauce.

Baked Cabbage

Use a mixture of red and green bell pepper. You can add a little yellow if you have it.

INGREDIENTS | SERVES 6–8

1 medium head green cabbage

¼ cup butter

¼ cup chopped green bell pepper

¼ cup chopped red bell pepper

¼ cup finely chopped yellow onion

¼ cup finely chopped celery

¼ cup all-purpose flour

2 cups whole milk

½ teaspoon salt

¼ teaspoon ground black pepper

⅓ cup mayonnaise

1 cup shredded mild Cheddar cheese

Tips for Reducing the Odor of Cooked Cabbage

The odor of cooking cabbage can make the whole house smell bad. One remedy is to add a few thick chunks of crusty bread to the cooking liquid. The bread will absorb some of the odors. The best solution is to cook it quickly, because the odor is released as the sulfur-containing compounds are cooked.

1. Preheat oven to 375°F. Lightly butter a 9" × 13" baking dish.

2. Cut cabbage into 8 wedges; place in a large stockpot or Dutch oven with 1 cup lightly salted water. Cover and bring to a boil over high heat; cook for 10 minutes. Drain well and place wedges in the prepared baking dish.

3. Heat butter in a large saucepan or skillet over medium heat. Add bell pepper, onion, and celery; sauté for about 4–5 minutes or until tender. Add flour; stir to blend. Continue cooking, stirring constantly, for about 30 seconds. Gradually stir in milk. Cook sauce mixture over medium heat until thickened and bubbly, stirring constantly. Stir in salt and pepper. Pour over cabbage in the baking dish.

4. Bake for 20 minutes. In a small bowl, combine mayonnaise and cheese; spoon over cabbage wedges and bake until cheese is melted, about 10 minutes more.

Asparagus Cheddar Casserole

If your family likes asparagus, this delicious casserole will become a holiday dinner tradition.

INGREDIENTS | SERVES 8

6 tablespoons butter

2 tablespoons grated yellow onion

¼ cup chopped red or green bell pepper

6 tablespoons all-purpose flour

2 cups whole milk

2½ teaspoons salt

½ teaspoon ground black pepper

6 cups cooked asparagus

5 large hard-cooked eggs, peeled and sliced

1½ cups shredded mild Cheddar cheese

¾ cup fine dry bread crumbs

3 tablespoons melted butter

1. Preheat oven to 350°F. Butter a 9" × 13" baking dish.

2. Melt 6 tablespoons butter in a medium saucepan over medium-low heat. Add onion and bell pepper; sauté until tender. Stir in flour until well blended. Gradually add milk, stirring constantly over medium-low heat until thickened and bubbly. Stir in salt and pepper.

3. Arrange about half of the asparagus in the prepared baking dish; top with half of the sliced eggs and half of the cheese. Repeat layers.

4. Pour hot sauce over the casserole. In a small bowl, toss bread crumbs with melted butter; sprinkle over the casserole.

5. Bake for 25–30 minutes until hot and bubbly.

Buttered Beets

This down-on-the-farm comfort food side dish goes well with just about any entrée.

INGREDIENTS | SERVES 8

4 large golden or red beets

1 cup water

½ cup butter, melted

Salt and ground black pepper

The-Night-Before Buttered Beets

You can fix the unpeeled beets ahead of time. Let the cooked beets cool, then put them in a resealable plastic bag and refrigerate. When you're ready to use them, peel and slice the beets, then microwave covered at 70 percent power for 3 minutes or until heated through.

1. Scrub beets and trim both ends. Place beets on a rack in a pressure cooker. Pour in water. Lock the lid into place and bring to high pressure; maintain pressure for 25 minutes.

2. Remove the pressure cooker from the heat, quick-release the pressure, and remove the lid. Transfer beets to a cutting board. Test for doneness. If beets aren't cooked, simmer or cook, covered, in the microwave for a few extra minutes.

3. When beets are cool enough to handle, use a paring knife to remove the peel and slice beets. Reheat beets in a medium saucepan with melted butter. Season with salt and pepper to taste.

Braised Lima Beans with Bacon

For a tomato-based dish, add 1 or 2 peeled and diced plum tomatoes (and their juice) when you add the lima beans and add an additional ¼ teaspoon freshly ground black pepper.

INGREDIENTS | SERVES 4

4 slices bacon, diced

1 small yellow onion, peeled and diced

1 medium clove garlic, minced

1 (1-pound) bag frozen lima beans, thawed

¼ cup water

¼ teaspoon ground black pepper

2 tablespoons minced fresh flat-leaf parsley

1. Add bacon to a pressure cooker and fry over medium-high heat until almost crisp. Add onion and sauté for 3 minutes or until soft.

2. Stir in garlic; sauté for 30 seconds. Stir in lima beans, water, and pepper.

3. Lock the lid into place and bring to high pressure; maintain pressure for 10 minutes. Remove the pressure cooker from the heat and allow the pressure to release naturally for 10 minutes.

4. Quick-release any remaining pressure and remove the lid. Stir in parsley. Transfer to a serving bowl and serve.

CHAPTER 12

Sauces, Pickles, and Preserves

Creamy Sausage Gravy

Serve this delicious old-fashioned Southern gravy with biscuits or grits.

INGREDIENTS | SERVES 8

1 pound bulk pork sausage

2 tablespoons shortening, bacon drippings, or lard

6 tablespoons all-purpose flour

3–3½ cups whole milk

Salt and ground black pepper

Dash ground cayenne pepper

Variations

Jazz up this recipe with your favorite flavors. Try Creole- or Cajun-style seasoning, chopped fresh parsley, garlic powder, fine-chopped onion, or a little dried basil or thyme.

1. In a heavy skillet, cook sausage, breaking it up with a spatula, until no longer pink. Use a slotted spoon to transfer sausage to a plate.

2. Add shortening, bacon drippings, or lard to the skillet drippings and heat on medium-low. Add flour, stirring until well blended and bubbly, about 30 seconds. Gradually stir in 3 cups of milk, stirring and cooking until thickened and bubbly. Add more milk depending on how thick you like your gravy. Stir in sausage and season to taste with salt, black pepper, and cayenne pepper.

Giblet Gravy

This delicious gravy is absolutely essential with a holiday turkey dinner.

INGREDIENTS | SERVES 8

Giblets and neck from 1 whole turkey

5 cups chicken broth

Roast turkey drippings

3 tablespoons all-purpose flour

Salt and ground black pepper

Lump-Free Gravy

A wire whisk is a must-have for a smooth sauce or gravy, and this tool comes in many shapes and sizes. If you use nonstick pans, make sure you have a coated whisk; for whisking in a sauté pan or roasting pan, a flat whisk works well. For separated or lumpy sauces, an immersion blender can be a lifesaver. Just be careful when you're working with hot sauce or gravy.

1. Put turkey giblets and neck in a medium saucepan; add 4 cups chicken broth and bring to a boil. Skim off foam. Reduce heat to low; cover and simmer for 1½ hours.

2. Remove giblets and neck from cooking liquid and add more broth to make 3 cups.

3. Remove meat from the neck of turkey and mince along with liver and heart. Discard gristle and excess fat.

4. Put juices from cooked turkey in a medium saucepan over medium-low heat, or remove turkey to a platter and heat roasting pan on the stovetop over medium-low heat. Stir flour into juices until well blended. Gradually add chicken and giblet broth, stirring constantly, along with minced giblets and neck. Cook until thickened and bubbly, stirring constantly. Add salt and pepper to taste.

Jezebel Sauce

This tasty sauce is delicious served with ham, pork, beef, or corned beef, or pour it over a block of cream cheese for a flavorful holiday spread.

INGREDIENTS | MAKES ABOUT 3 CUPS

1 (10-ounce) jar pineapple preserves

1 (10-ounce) jar apple jelly

¼–½ cup prepared horseradish

2 tablespoons dry mustard

1 teaspoon ground black pepper

1. Combine all ingredients in a medium bowl or food processor. Whisk or process until smooth and well blended.

2. Cover and refrigerate for at least 2 hours before serving.

Rémoulade Sauce

This sauce is delicious with just about any fish or seafood, and it's great with cold beef or corned beef or as a dip for fried vegetables.

INGREDIENTS | MAKES 1 CUP

1 cup mayonnaise

1½ teaspoons Dijon mustard

2 teaspoons chopped sweet pickle

1 teaspoon chopped capers

2 teaspoons finely chopped fresh flat-leaf parsley

½ teaspoon dried chervil, crumbled

½ teaspoon dried tarragon, crumbled

Dash Tabasco sauce

½ teaspoon salt

Dash ground white pepper

1. In a medium bowl, combine all ingredients and blend well.

2. Cover and refrigerate to chill thoroughly before serving.

Cajun Roux

This recipe makes enough roux to thicken a large pot of gumbo. Leftovers can be refrigerated for 1 week or frozen for 3 months.

INGREDIENTS | MAKES 3 CUPS

1 cup vegetable oil or peanut oil

1¼ cups all-purpose flour

1 medium yellow onion, peeled and chopped

1 small green bell pepper, seeded and chopped

3 medium ribs celery, chopped

2 medium carrots, peeled and chopped

1. Heat oil in a medium skillet over medium heat. Stir oil with a whisk while slowly adding flour. Once all of the flour is added, whisk continuously for about 25 minutes until roux looks just darker than peanut butter. Use the whisk to scrape the edges of the skillet while cooking to prevent any of the roux from burning.

2. Turn off the heat and stir in onion, bell pepper, celery, and carrots. The roux will finish cooking and get darker from the residual heat of the hot skillet and the sugars in the vegetables.

Quick Mayonnaise Mustard Sauce

This is a simple sauce, and quick to prepare. Serve with Fried Chicken Strips (see recipe in Chapter 8), Cheddar Sausage Balls (see recipe in Chapter 2), or other similar appetizers.

INGREDIENTS | MAKES 1 CUP

1 cup mayonnaise

2 teaspoons prepared yellow mustard

1½ teaspoons Dijon mustard

¼ teaspoon dried dill

1. In a small bowl, combine all ingredients.

2. Cover and chill until serving time.

Come Back Sauce

Serve this flavorful Southern sauce with fried fish or seafood, Salmon Croquettes with Corn (see recipe in Chapter 9), Fried Chicken Strips (see recipe in Chapter 8), appetizer wings, or use in place of mayonnaise on a sandwich. It also makes a nice salad dressing.

INGREDIENTS | MAKES 1 CUP

1 cup mayonnaise
¼ cup chili sauce
¼ cup ketchup
2 teaspoons prepared yellow mustard
½ cup olive oil
2 teaspoons Worcestershire sauce
1 teaspoon ground black pepper
1 tablespoon grated sweet onion
2 medium cloves garlic, minced
2 tablespoons lemon juice
Few drops hot sauce

1. Put all ingredients in a large jar; screw on the top and shake until well blended.

2. Refrigerate for at least 4 hours before using to let the flavors blend.

Peach Salsa

This delicious salsa is the perfect accompaniment for grilled chicken, pork, or fish. You can replace the peaches with diced mango or pineapple, or use a combination of fruit. If you want to tame the heat of the salsa, substitute a milder chili pepper for the minced jalapeño.

INGREDIENTS | SERVES 6

3 medium peaches, peeled, pitted, and diced
2 medium plum tomatoes, seeded and diced
½ cup diced red onion
2 tablespoons diced red bell pepper
¼ cup peeled, seeded, and diced cucumber
2 teaspoons minced jalapeño pepper
Juice of 1 medium lime
1 tablespoon chopped fresh cilantro
Ground black pepper

1. In a medium serving bowl, combine peaches, tomatoes, and remaining ingredients. Stir to blend ingredients. Add pepper to taste.

2. Cover and let salsa sit at room temperature for about 30 minutes to let the flavors blend.

Roasted Corn Salsa

This is a great salsa to make in the summer, when corn on the cob is bursting with sweetness. You can serve it with chips or put it on tacos, but it's also hearty enough to be a side dish.

INGREDIENTS | MAKES 3½ CUPS

3 ears fresh corn

2 tablespoons butter

4 green onions, thinly sliced

2 medium cloves garlic, minced

1½ teaspoons salt, divided

1½ teaspoons ground cumin, divided

1 teaspoon chili powder, divided

½ teaspoon ground black pepper, divided

2 medium plum tomatoes, seeded and finely diced

2 medium jalapeño peppers, with seeds, finely diced

1. Shuck corn and shave corn kernels from the cob. Heat a large, dry cast-iron skillet over medium-high heat and pan-roast corn kernels, stirring occasionally, until golden brown, about 8–9 minutes. Transfer to a medium bowl.

2. In the same skillet over medium heat, melt butter. Add green onions, garlic, 1 teaspoon salt, ½ teaspoon cumin, ½ teaspoon chili powder, and ¼ teaspoon pepper. Cook until tender, about 3 minutes.

3. Remove pan from heat and stir in corn, tomatoes, jalapeños, and remaining salt, cumin, chili powder, and pepper.

4. Transfer to a medium bowl. Serve warm or chill in the refrigerator.

Tequila Hot Sauce

This simple, boozy sauce is especially delicious on grilled fish. This sauce will become more flavorful the longer it sits. Also, the higher quality the tequila you use, the better the sauce will be.

INGREDIENTS | MAKES 1 PINT

¼ teaspoon whole allspice
¼ teaspoon black peppercorns
¼ teaspoon cumin seed
1 (1-pint) bottle tequila blanco
5 fresh red Thai chilies, lightly smashed with the side of a knife, or dried chilies

1. Toast allspice, peppercorns, and cumin in a small skillet over medium heat until fragrant, about 2–3 minutes. Remove from heat and set aside.

2. Pour out about 1" of tequila from the bottle to make room for the other ingredients.

3. Add spices and chilies to the tequila bottle.

4. Screw the top back on the bottle. Let sauce sit for 1 week before using. Sauce will keep in the refrigerator for up to 3 weeks.

Sherry Cream Sauce

*Try a little of this versatile sauce on a fish fillet or broiled shrimp.
You can vary the sauce with seafood or mushrooms.*

INGREDIENTS | MAKES 1½ CUPS

3 tablespoons butter
1 medium clove garlic, minced
2 tablespoons grated sweet onion
2 cups heavy cream
¼ cup dry sherry
Salt and ground black pepper
Paprika

1. Melt butter in a medium saucepan over medium-low heat. Add garlic and onion. Cook for about 1 minute until onion is tender, stirring constantly.

2. Stir in cream and sherry. Simmer for about 10 minutes to reduce by about ¼. Add salt, pepper, and paprika to taste.

Barbecue Sauce with Bourbon

Here's a delicious bourbon barbecue sauce to use on beef, chicken, or pork—you can also serve it on the side.

INGREDIENTS | MAKES ABOUT 3 CUPS

3 tablespoons butter
¼ cup canola oil
1½ cups chopped sweet onion
1 medium clove garlic, minced
½ cup good-quality bourbon
¾ cup ketchup
½ cup orange juice
½ cup apple cider vinegar
½ cup light brown sugar
¼ cup light molasses
1 tablespoon Worcestershire sauce
¼ teaspoon ground black pepper
½ teaspoon salt

1. In a medium saucepan, combine butter and oil over medium-low heat; add onion and garlic. Cook, stirring occasionally, until onion is tender.

2. Add remaining ingredients, stirring to blend. Reduce heat to low; cook for about 30–45 minutes, stirring frequently, until reduced and thickened.

3. Cover tightly and store in the refrigerator for up to 10 days.

Wine Vinegar–Based Barbecue Sauce

This sauce is thinner and more like a mop sauce than a traditional thick barbecue sauce. You can use it as a basting sauce for grilled tender cuts of meat. It's even good mixed into a glass of tomato juice or in tomato soup.

INGREDIENTS | MAKES 2½ QUARTS

½ cup light brown sugar, packed
½ cup Worcestershire sauce
½ cup Dijon mustard
1⅓ cup ketchup
⅛ teaspoon ground black pepper
1 tablespoon crushed red pepper
4 cups red wine vinegar
2⅔ cups water
1⅓ cups dry white wine
½ teaspoon salt

1. Add all ingredients to a 4- to 6-quart slow cooker. Stir to mix. Cover and, stirring every 15 minutes, cook on high for 1 hour or until mixture has come to a simmer.

2. Reduce heat to low and cook for 1 additional hour, covered. Ladle cooled sauce into glass jars, cover, and store in the refrigerator. Keeps for about 6 months.

South Carolina Barbecue Sauce for Pork

*There are probably as many variations on this sauce, also called
"bone sucker sauce," as there are South Carolinians.*

INGREDIENTS | MAKES 2 CUPS

3 tablespoons bacon fat

1 large yellow onion, peeled and minced

2 medium cloves garlic, minced

1 cup Dijon mustard

1 teaspoon salt

½ teaspoon ground black pepper

½ cup white wine vinegar

½ cup light molasses or honey

1. Heat bacon fat in a large, heavy saucepan. Sauté the onion and garlic over low heat for about 6 minutes until onion is softened.

2. Add remaining ingredients and bring to a boil. Chill overnight in the refrigerator before using.

Bread and Butter Pickles

These sweet-tart pickles are perfect for sandwiches and burgers. You can skip the canning steps to make refrigerator pickles that will last 2 weeks.

INGREDIENTS | MAKES ABOUT 4 PINTS

2 pounds cucumbers, thinly sliced (unpeeled)

6 cups thinly sliced yellow onion

1 medium green bell pepper, seeded and thinly sliced

1 medium red bell pepper, seeded and thinly sliced

4 small cloves garlic, peeled

⅓ cup kosher salt

Ice

5 cups sugar

1½ teaspoons ground turmeric

1½ teaspoons celery seed

2 tablespoons mustard seed

3 cups distilled white vinegar (5 percent acidity)

Water Bath Canning

Canned, high-acid foods need to be covered with water then boiled to kill harmful molds, yeasts, and some bacteria. A water bath canner should be tall enough to allow at least 1" of water over the jars and 1" of headspace. Preheat the water to 180°F before putting jars of hot-packed food into the water (to 140°F for raw-packed foods). Cover and bring to a boil over high heat, and then adjust the heat to maintain a gentle boil for 15–25 minutes, depending on altitude. Place jars on a protected surface, not touching, to cool.

1. In a large nonreactive pot, combine cucumbers, onions, bell peppers, and whole garlic cloves. Sprinkle cucumber mixture with salt and cover with ice; mix well to combine ingredients. Let stand for 3–4 hours.

2. Drain cucumber mixture well. Combine remaining ingredients in a large bowl; pour over cucumber mixture. Bring to a boil; remove from heat.

3. Transfer to hot, sterilized 1-pint canning jars. Clean the jar rims of any spills and then seal and process the jarred pickles in a boiling water bath for 15–25 minutes in a water bath canner or large stockpot with a lid. (Boil for 15 minutes for altitudes under 1,000'; 20 minutes for altitudes of 1,000'–6,000'; 25 minutes for altitudes over 6,000'.)

4. Remove the jars from the canner and place them on a protected surface at least 1" apart. Cool to room temperature. Check to make sure all the jars are sealed and then store the pickles in a cool, dark place for 1–2 weeks before using.

Green Tomato Chow-Chow

This is a wonderful way to use the last of your garden's green tomatoes.

INGREDIENTS | MAKES ABOUT 16 PINTS

16 cups chopped green tomatoes

1 large head green cabbage, cored and chopped

6 large yellow onions, peeled and chopped

6 medium green bell peppers, seeded and chopped

6 medium red bell peppers, seeded and chopped

½ cup kosher salt

15 cups distilled white vinegar (5 percent acidity)

5 cups sugar

3 tablespoons dry mustard

2 teaspoons ground ginger

1 tablespoon ground turmeric

¼ cup mustard seed

3 tablespoons celery seed

2 tablespoons pickling spice

1. Combine green tomatoes, cabbage, onions, and bell peppers in a large nonreactive pot. Stir in salt and let stand for at least 8 hours at room temperature. Drain well.

2. In another large nonreactive pot, combine vinegar, sugar, dry mustard, ginger, and turmeric. Wrap mustard, celery seed, and pickling spices in a square of cheese-cloth or put in a cheesecloth bag and tie securely; add to pot. Bring mixture to a boil over high heat. Reduce heat to medium-low and simmer for 30 minutes.

3. Drain salted vegetables and add to vinegar mixture; return to a simmer and simmer for 30 minutes. Discard the bag with the spices.

4. Spoon chow-chow into hot, sterilized 1-pint canning jars, clean spills from the rims with dampened paper towels, and screw on the lids. Process the jars in a boiling water bath for 15–25 minutes in a water bath canner or large stockpot with a lid. (Boil for 15 minutes for altitudes under 1,000'; 20 minutes for altitudes of 1,000'–6,000'; 25 minutes for altitudes over 6,000'.)

5. Remove the jars from the canner. Let cool to room temperature on a protected surface with the jars at least 1" apart. Store in a cool, dry place.

Sweet Onion Relish

Use sweet onions like Vidalia, Candy, First Edition, Maui, or Walla Walla for this relish.

INGREDIENTS | MAKES 4 CUPS

4 medium sweet onions, peeled and thinly sliced

¾ cup golden raisins

1 cup honey

1 tablespoon apple cider vinegar

⅛ teaspoon salt

1. Add onions to a pressure cooker and pour in enough water to cover. Bring to a boil over high heat; drain immediately and discard water.

2. Return onions to the pressure cooker; stir in raisins, honey, vinegar, and salt until honey is evenly distributed throughout onion slices.

3. Lock the lid, bring to high pressure, and cook for 5 minutes. Reduce heat and maintain low pressure for 10 minutes. Remove from heat and allow the pressure to release naturally.

4. Remove the lid and stir the relish. If relish needs thickening, return the pan to medium-high heat and bring to a gentle boil for 5 minutes. The relish can be served warm or stored in a covered container in the refrigerator for up to 4 weeks.

Cranberry Chutney

This chutney is delicious, and it will take you right through the holiday season if you freeze it in containers or jars. Take it out when you need it for a meal of turkey, chicken, pork, or ham.

INGREDIENTS | MAKES 4 CUPS

1 large orange
¼ cup fresh orange juice
¾ pound fresh cranberries
1¾ cups sugar
1 large Golden Delicious or Cortland apple
½ cup golden raisins
1 tablespoon apple cider vinegar
½ teaspoon ground ginger
½ teaspoon ground cinnamon
¼ teaspoon ground cloves

1. Remove peel and tough white membrane from orange; cut into small pieces. Combine with orange juice, cranberries, and sugar in a large saucepan.

2. Peel apple, remove core, and chop. Add to cranberry mixture along with remaining ingredients.

3. Bring mixture to a boil; reduce heat and simmer, stirring occasionally, for 6–8 minutes until cranberries are popping. Chill until serving time.

Freezer Peach Jam

This is an easy and tasty peach jam made for the freezer.

INGREDIENTS | MAKES 8 PINTS

4 cups peeled and crushed fresh peaches
¼ cup lemon juice
1 (1.75-ounce) package powdered fruit pectin
1 cup light corn syrup
5½ cups sugar

1. Add peaches to a large kettle; with a wooden spoon, stir in lemon juice. Stir in pectin. Let mixture stand for 20 minutes.

2. Add corn syrup and stir to blend; add sugar and blend well. Cook mixture over low heat to about 100°F. It should be warm to the touch. Do not allow mixture to get very hot. Pour jam into jars, leaving ½" headspace. Cover immediately and let stand until the consistency is that of jelly. Freezer jams can be stored for up to 1 year in the freezer, and they will keep for several weeks in the refrigerator.

Corn Relish

This old-time recipe makes a delicious condiment for pork, ham, or grilled poultry.

INGREDIENTS | MAKES 6 PINTS

4 cups fresh corn kernels

3 cups chopped green bell pepper

1 cup chopped red bell pepper

2 cups seeded and chopped cucumber (unpeeled)

4 cups chopped tomato

4 cups distilled white vinegar (5 percent acidity)

2 cups sugar

¼ cup kosher salt

1 tablespoon ground turmeric

1 tablespoon mustard seed

1. Combine all ingredients in a large nonreactive pot. Bring to a boil over high heat. Reduce heat to medium-low and simmer for 25 minutes or until vegetables are tender.

2. Spoon relish into hot, sterilized 1-pint canning jars; wipe the mouths of the jars with a wet paper towel and screw on the lids.

3. In a water bath canner or large stockpot with a lid, process the jarred relish in boiling water for 15–25 minutes. (Boil for 15 minutes for altitudes under 1,000'; 20 minutes for altitudes of 1,000'–6,000'; 25 minutes for altitudes over 6,000'.)

4. Remove the jars from the canner. Let cool to room temperature on a protected surface with the jars at least 1" apart. Store in a cool, dry place.

Traditional Apple Butter

To ensure that the peels haven't been waxed, buy your apples directly from an orchard or at a farmers' market. (The natural pectin in the peels helps thicken the butter.) Don't forget to pick up some freshly pressed cider while you're there.

INGREDIENTS | MAKES ABOUT 3 CUPS

4 pounds Jonathan, McIntosh, or Rome Beauty apples, cored and quartered

Zest and juice of 1 medium lemon

1⅓ cups light brown sugar, packed

1 cup apple cider

1 (6") cinnamon stick

1. Add apples to a 4- to 6-quart slow cooker. Stir in lemon zest and juice, brown sugar, and cider. Add cinnamon stick. Cover and cook on low for 10 hours or until apples are soft and tender.

2. Uncover and, stirring occasionally, cook on high for 8–10 hours or until mixture has reduced to about 3 cups.

3. Remove and discard cinnamon stick. Use a spatula to press apple butter through a large-meshed strainer to remove the peel. Ladle warm apple butter into hot, sterilized canning jars. Screw the 2-piece lids onto the jars. Allow to stand at room temperature for 8 hours; refrigerate for up to 6 months.

CHAPTER 13

Cakes and Pies

Pineapple Upside-Down Cake

Feel free to use a seasoned cast-iron skillet instead of the cake pan.

INGREDIENTS | SERVES 8

3 tablespoons plus ½ cup butter, divided

¾ cup light brown sugar, packed

6 slices pineapple

6 maraschino cherries

12 pecan halves

½ cup sugar

1 large egg

1 teaspoon vanilla extract

1½ cups all-purpose flour

1½ teaspoons baking powder

½ teaspoon salt

½ cup whole milk

Check Your Oven Temperature

Did you know that ovens can vary greatly in temperature? It isn't unusual for an oven to be up to 50°F off, and possibly more. Cakes are particularly picky when it comes to temperature, and oven thermometers are relatively inexpensive. Check the oven regularly to make sure it's heating correctly. Remember to position racks in the center of the oven before you heat, and decrease the temperature by 25°F if you're using a glass baking pan.

1. Preheat oven to 375°F. Melt 3 tablespoons butter in a 9" square cake pan or 10" cast-iron skillet. Sprinkle evenly with brown sugar. Arrange pineapple slices, maraschino cherries, and pecan halves decoratively over sugar and butter. Set aside.

2. In a large bowl, cream remaining ½ cup butter with sugar; beat until light. Beat in egg and vanilla. Sift together flour, baking powder, and salt into a medium bowl. Add dry ingredients to batter, alternating with milk and ending with dry ingredients. Beat until smooth. Pour batter over arranged pineapple layer.

3. Bake for 35 minutes or until cake springs back when lightly touched. Let cake cool in the pan on a wire rack for about 5 minutes. Put a serving plate over the top of the pan and flip it to invert cake onto the plate. Serve warm.

Lemon-Glazed Pound Cake

Try this cake with fresh blueberries or strawberries and whipped cream.

INGREDIENTS | SERVES 10–12

1¼ cups butter, softened

3¾ cups sugar, divided

5 large eggs

1 teaspoon lemon or vanilla extract

3 cups all-purpose flour

2½ teaspoons baking powder

¼ teaspoon salt

1 cup whole milk

½ cup water

1 tablespoon lemon zest

½ cup lemon juice

Measuring Flour

Too much flour could make your cake too dry, and not enough flour can cause the cake to fall. Unless the flour must be sifted before measuring, stir it with a spoon before measuring so it isn't packed. Spoon the flour into a measuring cup until it is mounded, then use the back side of a knife or spreading spatula to level it off. If you've been scooping your flour right out of the bag or canister with the measuring cup, you should notice a nice improvement in the things you bake!

1. Preheat oven to 300°F. Grease and flour a 10" tube pan.

2. In a large mixing bowl with an electric mixer, beat butter until light. Beat in 3 cups sugar until fluffy. Add eggs 1 at a time, beating well after each addition. Beat in lemon or vanilla extract.

3. Combine flour, baking powder, and salt in a medium bowl. With mixer on low speed, gradually beat dry ingredients into egg mixture, alternating with milk, just until blended. Do not overmix.

4. Spoon batter into the prepared tube pan. Set on a rack in the center of the oven and bake for 1 hour and 30 minutes or until a wooden toothpick or cake tester comes out clean when inserted in the center of the cake.

5. Cool cake in the pan on a wire rack. Remove from the pan and set on the rack. In a small bowl, combine remaining ¾ cup sugar with water, lemon zest, and lemon juice. Brush glaze over top and sides of warm cake. Let cake cool completely.

Coca-Cola Cake and Frosting

This is absolutely delicious! The cola is a surprise ingredient that makes a flavorful cake and creamy frosting. Generic or other brands of cola can be used in this cake.

INGREDIENTS | SERVES 10–12

2 cups all-purpose flour

1½ teaspoons baking powder

¼ teaspoon salt

2 cups granulated sugar

1½ cups softened butter, divided

6 tablespoons unsweetened cocoa powder, divided

1 cup plus 5–7 tablespoons cola, divided

1½ cups miniature marshmallows

2 teaspoons vanilla extract

½ cup buttermilk

2 large eggs, beaten

2 teaspoons baking soda

1 pound powdered sugar

1 cup chopped pecans

1. Preheat oven to 350°F. Grease and flour a 9" × 13" baking pan.

2. Combine flour, baking powder, salt, and granulated sugar into a large mixing bowl. Set aside.

3. In a large saucepan, combine 1 cup butter, 3 tablespoons cocoa powder, and 1 cup cola. Bring mixture to a boil over high heat; remove from heat and add marshmallows and vanilla. Stir until marshmallows are melted. Pour chocolate mixture over dry ingredients in the mixing bowl; blend well. Add buttermilk, beaten eggs, and baking soda. Beat well.

4. Pour batter into the prepared pan. Bake for 30–35 minutes or until cake springs back when lightly touched. Cool in pan on a wire rack.

5. Make the frosting: In a medium bowl, blend remaining butter and cocoa powder with powdered sugar and 5 tablespoons cola. Beat, adding more cola as needed to make a smooth and creamy frosting. Spread over cooled cake and top with chopped pecans.

Kentucky Jam Cake

This is a delicious spice cake made with the addition of blackberry jam and a wonderful date filling. A caramel frosting is traditional, but a cream cheese frosting is just as delicious!

INGREDIENTS | SERVES 12

3 cups all-purpose flour
1 teaspoon baking soda
½ teaspoon salt
1 teaspoon ground cinnamon
1 teaspoon ground allspice
½ teaspoon ground cloves
1 cup butter, softened
1½ cups granulated sugar
6 large eggs
1 cup seedless blackberry jam
1 cup buttermilk
1 cup finely chopped pecans
1 pound chopped dates
2 tablespoons light brown sugar
1 teaspoon vanilla extract
1½–2½ cups water
Caramel Frosting (see recipe in this chapter)

Even Layers

A thick cake batter can result in uneven baked layers. Lopsided cakes are hard to deal with, but you can prevent them. When the batter is put in the pan, hold the pan on both sides, then gently spin or gently shake back and forth from side to side. The force of the spin or shaking should level out the batter.

1. Preheat oven to 325°F. Generously grease the bottoms and sides of 3 (9") layer cake pans. Dust pans with flour.

2. Stir flour before measuring. Combine flour, baking soda, salt, cinnamon, allspice, and cloves in a medium bowl.

3. In a large mixing bowl, cream together butter and sugar until light and fluffy. Add eggs 1 at a time, beating well after each addition. Beat in jam. Gradually add dry ingredients, alternating with buttermilk; beat until smooth. Stir in chopped pecans. Using a small measuring cup or spoon, evenly distribute batter among the prepared pans. Bake for 30–35 minutes or until cake springs back when lightly touched.

4. While cake cooks, make date filling: In a small saucepan, combine chopped dates, brown sugar, and vanilla. Add 1½ cups water and bring to a boil over high heat. Reduce heat to medium-low and simmer until dates are very soft and thick. Add more water as necessary. If desired, push mixture through a sieve. Cover and let cool completely.

5. Cool cake in pans on wire racks for 15 minutes. Carefully invert onto the racks to cool completely. Spread date filling on the tops of 2 of the cake layers and stack them. Top with the final cake layer and frost the top and sides of the cake with Caramel Frosting.

Texas Sheet Cake

This version of the classic Texas sheet cake has a mocha cake and a creamy chocolate frosting.

INGREDIENTS | SERVES 12

2 cups all-purpose flour

1 teaspoon baking soda

⅛ teaspoon salt

2 cups granulated sugar

1 cup plus 6 tablespoons butter, divided

1 cup brewed black coffee

½ cup unsweetened cocoa powder, divided

½ cup buttermilk

2 large eggs

2 teaspoons vanilla extract, divided

⅓ cup whole milk

3¾ cups powdered sugar, sifted

¾ cup finely chopped pecans

1. Sift together flour, baking soda, salt, and granulated sugar into a large mixing bowl; set aside.

2. Preheat oven to 350°F. Grease and flour a 10" × 15" jelly-roll pan.

3. In a small saucepan over medium heat, combine 1 cup butter, coffee, and ¼ cup cocoa. Heat mixture, stirring constantly, until butter is melted and mixture just begins to bubble. Pour over dry ingredients in the mixing bowl and blend well.

4. In another bowl combine buttermilk, eggs, and 1 teaspoon vanilla. Stir buttermilk mixture into chocolate batter. Pour into the prepared pan.

5. Bake for about 25 minutes. The cake should spring back when lightly touched.

6. Meanwhile, make the chocolate pecan frosting: Combine milk and remaining butter and cocoa in a medium saucepan; bring to a boil over medium-high heat, stirring constantly. Gradually stir in powdered sugar. Add pecans and remaining vanilla. Mix to blend thoroughly. Spread frosting over the hot cake in the pan.

Red Velvet Cake

Cream cheese frosting is traditional for this beautiful cake, but Cooked Vanilla Frosting (see recipe in this chapter) is another option.

INGREDIENTS | SERVES 10

¾ cup butter, softened

1½ cups sugar

2 large eggs

1½ teaspoons vanilla extract

2 tablespoons unsweetened cocoa powder

2 tablespoons red gel food coloring

2 tablespoons water

2½ cups all-purpose flour

1 teaspoon salt

1 cup buttermilk

1 tablespoon apple cider vinegar

1 teaspoon baking soda

Cream Cheese Frosting (see recipe in this chapter)

The Legend of Red Velvet Cake

Details are somewhat sketchy, but the story has been around since the 1940s. The story claims that the elegant Waldorf Astoria restaurant granted a woman's request for the recipe for this delicious cake, and then sent her a bill for $100. With revenge in mind, the angry woman purportedly began circulating the tale along with the recipe. The delicious moist red chocolate cake is also known as the Waldorf Astoria Cake.

1. Preheat oven to 350°F. Generously grease and flour 3 (8") layer cake pans or 2 (9") layer cake pans.

2. In a large mixing bowl, cream together butter and sugar until light and fluffy; beat in eggs 1 at a time, beating well after each addition. Beat in vanilla.

3. In a small bowl, combine cocoa, food coloring, and water; blend well. Beat cocoa mixture into creamed mixture.

4. Combine flour and salt in a small bowl; gradually beat it into creamed mixture, alternating with buttermilk. Combine vinegar and soda in a cup and beat into batter.

5. Spoon batter evenly into prepared layer cake pans. Bake for 22–30 minutes until cake bounces back when lightly touched. Cool cake in pans on wire racks.

6. Remove cakes from the pans. Spread frosting over the top of each layer. Stack the cake layers and frost the sides, spreading the frosting evenly over the entire cake.

Caramel Frosting

This is a delicious cooked frosting for a spice or caramel cake.

INGREDIENTS | FROSTS 2 OR 3 LAYERS

3 cups light brown sugar, packed

2 tablespoons light corn syrup

3 tablespoons butter

Dash salt

½ cup heavy cream or evaporated milk

1 teaspoon vanilla extract

1. Combine all ingredients in a large saucepan; bring to a boil over medium-high heat. Reduce heat to medium-low; cover and cook for 3 minutes. Uncover and position a candy thermometer in mixture. Continue to cook until the thermometer registers 236°F or until a small amount of the mixture forms a soft ball when dropped into cold water, about 10–15 minutes.

2. Remove from heat and let cool for 5 minutes. Beat until thick. If frosting is too thick or becomes too thick while spreading, add a little very hot water to it. If necessary, dip the spatula in hot water to smooth the frosting.

Cooked Vanilla Frosting

This is an old-fashioned frosting, thickened with flour. The flour actually makes this frosting taste less sweet, but it's just as delicious.

INGREDIENTS | FROSTS 2 OR 3 LAYERS

1 cup whole milk, or more as needed

⅓ cup all-purpose flour

1 cup butter, softened

1 cup sugar

1½ teaspoons vanilla extract

1. In a large saucepan, whisk together 1 cup milk and flour. Cook over medium heat, stirring constantly, until thickened. Transfer to the refrigerator to cool quickly.

2. In a medium mixing bowl, combine butter, sugar, and vanilla. Beat until light. Add flour and milk mixture a little at a time. Beat well, adding a little more milk if needed for spreading consistency.

Cream Cheese Frosting

This delicious cream cheese frosting is absolutely perfect on a spice cake, carrot cake, or a chocolate cake, along with many others.

INGREDIENTS | FROSTS 2 OR 3 LAYERS

½ cup butter, softened

8 ounces cream cheese, softened

Dash salt

4 cups powdered sugar

2 teaspoons vanilla extract

1. In a large mixing bowl, combine all ingredients. Beat well with an electric mixer until smooth and fluffy.

2. Chocolate Cream Cheese Frosting: Add 3 ounces unsweetened melted chocolate and an additional 1 teaspoon vanilla; beat until smooth, adding a little heavy cream as needed for consistency.

Cake Frosting Rules

Your cake should be completely cooled before frosting, unless the recipe states otherwise. If your cake has loose crumbs, take a pastry brush and brush it as free of the crumbs as possible. If your cake filling is different from the frosting, don't spread the filling all the way to the edge. If your cake layers are a bit uneven, you can easily frost to hide the imperfections! It's best to frost the cake on the serving plate because transferring the frosted cake might be difficult.

Praline Cheesecake with Pecan Crust

This wonderful cheesecake is guaranteed to become a family favorite!

INGREDIENTS | SERVES 12

1¼ cups graham cracker crumbs

5 tablespoons butter, melted

1 cup, packed, plus 5 tablespoons light brown sugar, divided

¼ cup finely chopped pecans

3 (8-ounce) packages cream cheese, softened

3 large eggs

2½ teaspoons vanilla extract, divided

1 cup heavy whipping cream

½ cup dark corn syrup

2 tablespoons cornstarch

Frozen Cheesecake

Cheesecakes with a high fat content can be frozen with good results. A dense cheesecake with at least 1½ pounds of cream cheese will freeze well. If you're freezing a whole cheesecake, you might want to wait to add the topping until just before serving. Make sure the cheesecake is thoroughly cooled, and then wrap it as airtight as possible in plastic wrap, then in foil. Freeze for up to 1 month. Store it on a freezer shelf where it won't be bumped or damaged.

1. Preheat oven to 450°F. Combine graham cracker crumbs, melted butter, 3 tablespoons brown sugar, and chopped pecans in a medium bowl. Press into the bottom of a 9" springform pan.

2. In a mixing bowl, beat cream cheese until light. Beat in 1 cup brown sugar and blend well. Beat in eggs and 1½ teaspoons vanilla until blended. Blend in cream. Pour batter into prepared crust.

3. Bake for 10 minutes. Reduce heat to 250°F; continue to bake for 65–75 minutes or until center is set. The edges will be firm and center will remain somewhat jiggly.

4. Let cool for 12 minutes, then carefully remove the sides of the pan. Cool completely.

5. In a small saucepan, combine corn syrup, cornstarch, and remaining 2 tablespoons brown sugar. Cook over low heat until thickened, stirring constantly; stir in remaining vanilla and remove from heat. Pour over cooled cheesecake. Refrigerate leftovers.

Flaky Butter Pie Crust

This makes enough pastry to line a 9" pie plate for a single-crust pie.

INGREDIENTS | MAKES 1 CRUST

1 cup all-purpose flour

⅔ cup cake flour

1 tablespoon powdered sugar

½ teaspoon salt

¼ cup cold butter, cut into small pieces

5 tablespoons cold shortening, cut into small pieces

¼ cup ice-cold water

Pie Crust Add-Ins

You can make some easy additions to jazz up a pie crust. Spices can be added, such as ground allspice, cinnamon, nutmeg, or ginger. Try lemon oil or chili oil, depending on whether the pie is sweet or savory. Fennel seed, celery seed, coarse black pepper, and caraway seed make nice additions to savory crusts, as does a little crumbled bacon.

1. In the bowl of a food processor fitted with a metal blade, combine all-purpose flour, cake flour, sugar, and salt. Pulse a few times to combine ingredients.

2. Sprinkle pieces of butter over flour mixture; stir into flour mixture lightly, then pulse about 6 times. Sprinkle shortening pieces over mixture, stir in lightly, and then pulse 6–8 times. Sprinkle with half of ice water; pulse 5 times. Sprinkle with remaining water; pulse about 6 times or until pastry dough begins to form large clumps. Empty into a large bowl and knead 2 or 3 times, just until dough holds together to form a ball. Chill for about 20 minutes.

3. Roll out dough on a floured surface, then fit it into pie plate. Crimp the edge all around and cut away excess dough.

4. Fill pie shell and bake according to recipe instructions. If pie shell must be baked first, prick it all over with a fork and bake at 450°F for about 10 minutes or until lightly browned.

Key Lime Pie

Feel free to use a purchased graham cracker crust for this recipe.

INGREDIENTS | SERVES 8

2 cups graham cracker crumbs

½ cup butter, melted

⅓ cup sugar

5 large egg yolks

1 (14-ounce) can sweetened condensed milk

½ cup heavy whipping cream

½ cup Key lime juice

1 teaspoon Key lime zest, plus extra for garnish

Whipped cream or whipped topping

1 small Key lime, thinly sliced

1. Preheat oven to 325°F. In a small bowl, combine graham cracker crumbs, butter, and sugar. Press over the bottom and up the sides of a 9" pie plate.

2. Using a mixer on low speed, beat egg yolks with sweetened condensed milk in a medium bowl. Blend in cream, Key lime juice, and 1 teaspoon zest. Pour into pie crust.

3. Bake for about 20 minutes or until firm. Let pie cool for 15 minutes. Refrigerate for about 2 hours or until completely set.

4. Before serving, top the whole pie with whipped cream or top individual servings with a dollop of whipped cream; garnish with lime zest and lime slices.

Meringue Topping

Use some of the leftover egg whites to make a meringue for this pie. In a medium bowl, beat 3 or 4 egg whites until soft peaks begin to form. Combine 6 tablespoons sugar and about 1 teaspoon cornstarch, and then gradually beat the sugar mixture into the egg whites, along with a dash of salt. Continue beating until stiff peaks form, and test by rubbing a little of the meringue between your fingers. The sugar should be completely dissolved so that you don't feel any grittiness. Spread the meringue over the hot pie filling, spreading to the crust edge to seal and prevent the meringue from shrinking, then bake for about 12–15 minutes at 350°F.

Peanut Butter Silk Pie

This peanut butter pie recipe was inspired by a restaurant pie. Top it with shaved chocolate and peanuts if you like.

INGREDIENTS | SERVES 8–10

1¼ cups graham cracker crumbs

1¼ cups granulated sugar, divided

5 tablespoons butter, melted

2 ounces bittersweet chocolate

⅓ cup evaporated milk

1 tablespoon light corn syrup

½ cup plus 1 heaping tablespoon smooth peanut butter, divided

8 ounces cream cheese, softened

1 cup powdered sugar

1 teaspoon vanilla extract

½ cup whole milk

3 cups whipped cream or whipped topping

1. In a medium bowl, combine graham cracker crumbs, ¼ cup granulated sugar, and melted butter. Pat into a 9" pie pan. Chill in the refrigerator for 25 minutes.

2. In a small saucepan, combine remaining 1 cup granulated sugar, bittersweet chocolate, evaporated milk, and corn syrup. Cook fudge mixture over medium heat, stirring occasionally, to about 236°F on a candy thermometer or to the soft ball stage. Remove from heat and stir in 1 heaping tablespoon peanut butter. Beat for a few minutes; pour into pie crust. Chill thoroughly.

3. In a medium mixing bowl, beat cream cheese with remaining ½ cup peanut butter, powdered sugar, vanilla, and milk. Fold in whipped topping. Spoon over chilled fudge layer. Chill before cutting.

Mississippi Mud Pie

This easy chocolate pie is supposed to resemble the muddy bottom of the Mississippi River. It's delicious with ice cream or whipped topping.

INGREDIENTS | SERVES 8

½ cup butter
2 ounces unsweetened chocolate
3 large eggs
3 tablespoons light corn syrup
1⅓ cups sugar
1 teaspoon vanilla extract
1 (9") graham cracker pie shell

1. Preheat oven to 350°F.

2. In a small saucepan, combine butter and chocolate over low heat, stirring frequently until melted and well blended.

3. In a medium mixing bowl, beat eggs; stir in corn syrup, sugar, and vanilla. Add melted chocolate mixture to beaten mixture, stirring well. Pour mixture into pie shell.

4. Bake for 35–40 minutes or until the top is slightly crunchy and filling is set.

Chocolate Chip Pie with Bourbon Whipped Cream

This is a wonderful Kentucky-style pie, with lots of nuts and a healthy dash of bourbon.

INGREDIENTS | SERVES 8–10

1 cup semisweet chocolate chips

1 cup chopped pecans or walnuts

1 (9") pie shell, unbaked

2 large eggs

½ cup granulated sugar

½ cup light brown sugar, packed

½ cup butter, melted

½ cup all-purpose flour

Dash salt

1½ teaspoons vanilla extract, divided

1 cup heavy whipping cream, chilled

2 tablespoons powdered sugar

1 tablespoon good-quality Kentucky bourbon

Whipped Cream Secrets

First of all, use real heavy cream. Have everything chilled, including the beaters and bowl. Beat just until the cream holds soft peaks when the beaters are lifted. Add sugar or flavorings just when the cream begins to form soft peaks. If you've made the whipped cream a few hours in advance, put it in a sieve and position the sieve over a bowl; cover with plastic wrap and refrigerate. Any liquid that might have separated will run into the bowl. Whisk the separated liquids back in just before using.

1. Preheat oven to 325°F. Sprinkle chocolate chips and chopped nuts over the bottom of unbaked pie shell; set aside.

2. In a small mixing bowl, whisk eggs. Whisk in granulated and brown sugar, melted butter, flour, salt, and 1 teaspoon vanilla. Pour batter into the pie shell over chocolate chips and nuts.

3. Bake for 35–40 minutes or until set. Remove to a wire rack and let cool.

4. Beat chilled whipping cream in a medium bowl until thickened; add powdered sugar and remaining vanilla and beat until soft peaks form. Beat in bourbon. Cover and refrigerate until serving time. Serve pie with dollops of bourbon whipped cream on top.

Sweet Potato Pie

This is a delicious sweet potato pie, made with just the right combination of spices and sugar.

INGREDIENTS | SERVES 8

2 cups mashed sweet potatoes (about 1 large or 2 medium sweet potatoes)
½ cup butter, softened
¾ cup granulated sugar
¼ cup light brown sugar, packed
½ cup whole milk or half-and-half
2 large eggs
½ teaspoon ground cinnamon
½ teaspoon ground nutmeg
1 teaspoon vanilla extract
1 (9") pie shell, unbaked

1. Preheat oven to 350°F.

2. In a large mixing bowl, beat mashed sweet potato with butter, sugars, milk, eggs, cinnamon, nutmeg, and vanilla. Beat until smooth and well blended. Pour filling into unbaked pie shell.

3. Bake for 55–60 minutes or until a knife inserted near the center comes out clean. Cool on a wire rack. The pie will settle as it cools.

Salted Peanut Pie

The salty and sweet flavor of this pie makes it almost addictive. If you prefer, you can use unsalted peanuts.

INGREDIENTS | SERVES 8

6 tablespoons butter, melted
¼ cup creamy peanut butter
¾ cup light brown sugar, packed
½ cup light corn syrup
1 teaspoon vanilla extract
3 large eggs
1 cup salted peanuts
1 (9") pie shell, unbaked

1. Preheat oven to 350°F.

2. In a large bowl, whisk together the butter, peanut butter, sugar, corn syrup, vanilla, and eggs until well combined.

3. Spread peanuts evenly over the bottom of pastry crust, then pour egg mixture over the top. Tap pie gently on the counter to release any air bubbles.

4. Place pie on a baking sheet and bake for 50–60 minutes or until filling is puffed all over and set. Let cool to room temperature before serving.

Brown Sugar Pecan Pie

This is a delicious pecan pie, perfect for the holiday season.
Serve with whipped cream or vanilla ice cream.

INGREDIENTS | SERVES 8

1 Flaky Butter Pie Crust (see recipe in this chapter), unbaked

3 large eggs, beaten

1 cup light corn syrup

⅛ teaspoon salt

1 teaspoon vanilla extract

1 cup light brown sugar, packed

2 tablespoons butter, melted

1¼ cups pecan halves

Perfect Pie Crust Tip

Set a baking sheet in the oven while it's heating, and then set the filled pie right on the hot metal of the baking sheet. The bottom of the crust will bake more quickly on the metal, and it will be flakier.

1. Prepare pastry and fit into a 9" pie plate. Preheat oven to 400°F.

2. In a medium mixing bowl, beat eggs. Whisk in corn syrup, salt, vanilla, brown sugar, and melted butter, blending well. Stir in pecans. Pour pecan mixture into unbaked pie shell.

3. Bake for 10 minutes. Reduce heat to 350°F and continue baking for 25–30 minutes longer. If crust becomes too dark, cover the edge with a protective pie shield or fashion a ring of foil to lightly cover the pastry edge. When pie is finished, the edge of the filling should be slightly puffed and firm, and the center should move only slightly.

Peach Pie

Fresh peaches are always best, but frozen can be used if peaches are not in season. Be sure to thaw and drain frozen peaches before use to keep the pie from becoming watery.

INGREDIENTS | SERVES 8

1 cup sugar

¼ cup cornstarch

¼ teaspoon ground cinnamon

½ teaspoon vanilla extract

10 medium peaches, peeled and sliced ¼" thick

2 Flaky Butter Pie Crusts (see recipe in this chapter), unbaked

2 tablespoons butter, cut into pieces

1 egg, beaten

Best Peaches for Baking

When selecting peaches for baking consider two things: First, freestone peaches are easier to pit than clingstone, meaning there will be less loss of flesh. Second, yellow peaches tend to have a more robust flavor, making them best for pies. White peaches are better in open-faced tarts where they can be the star.

1. Preheat oven to 425°F. In a large bowl, combine sugar, cornstarch, cinnamon, vanilla, and peaches; turn peaches gently to coat. Let stand for 10 minutes.

2. Line a 9" pie plate with 1 pie crust. Fill crust with peach mixture and dot the top with butter. Brush the edge of the bottom pie crust with beaten egg so that the top crust will adhere.

3. Top with remaining crust and trim dough to 1" of the pan's edge. Tuck the edge of the top crust under the edge of the bottom crust. Crimp dough using your fingers or a fork. Brush the entire top crust with beaten egg and cut 4 or 5 slits in the top to vent steam.

4. Place pie on a baking sheet and bake for 30 minutes. Reduce the heat to 350°F and bake for 30–40 minutes or until pie filling is bubbling and juices are thick. Let cool for 1 hour before slicing.

Spiced Apple Crumb Pie

This is a cross between an apple pie and a spiced apple crisp.

INGREDIENTS | SERVES 8

5–6 cups thinly sliced apples

2 tablespoons lemon juice

¾ cup granulated sugar, divided

½ cup light brown sugar, packed, divided

¼ cup melted butter

½ cup plus 3 tablespoons all-purpose flour, divided

2 teaspoons ground cinnamon

⅛ teaspoon ground nutmeg

6 tablespoons cold butter, cut into pieces

¼ cup quick-cooking rolled oats

¼ cup chopped pecans

1 (9") deep-dish pie shell, baked

1. Preheat oven to 375°F.

2. Toss apples with lemon juice in a large bowl. Add ½ cup granulated sugar and ¼ cup brown sugar, along with melted butter, 3 tablespoons flour, cinnamon, and nutmeg. Stir to blend ingredients; set aside.

3. In a medium bowl, combine remaining flour, granulated sugar, and brown sugar, along with cold butter, rolled oats, and pecans. Mix with a pastry blender or fork.

4. Pour apple mixture into prepared pie pastry. Sprinkle evenly with crumb mixture.

5. Bake for 30–35 minutes, then check for browning. Make a foil ring to set on the crust edge to keep it from browning further or use a pie shield ring. Continue baking for about 15–25 minutes longer until apples are tender. Cool before cutting.

Old-Fashioned Chess Pie

This is an old-time Southern pie. The meringue topping makes this a special version.

INGREDIENTS | SERVES 8

1 cup plus 6 tablespoons granulated sugar, divided
1 cup light brown sugar, packed
½ cup whole milk
¼ cup sifted all-purpose flour
½ cup butter, softened
4 large eggs, divided
2 teaspoons vanilla extract, divided
1½ teaspoon salt
1 (9") pie shell, unbaked

Sky-High Meringue

One way to make a meringue even higher without having it bead up is to add ½ teaspoon baking powder to the sugar. Beading can be caused by sugar that doesn't dissolve fully, by humidity, or by meringue that is overcooked or cooked too long at a low temperature. There's no way to fix a beaded meringue, but you can try cooking your next meringue at a higher temperature for a shorter time.

1. In a medium saucepan, combine 1 cup granulated sugar, brown sugar, milk, flour, and butter. Cook over medium-low heat, stirring until sugar is dissolved. Set aside and let cool.

2. Preheat oven to 350°F.

3. In a medium bowl, beat 3 egg yolks and 1 whole egg, reserving the whites; add 1 teaspoon vanilla and salt. Combine egg mixture with cooled mixture and blend well. Pour filling into unbaked pie shell.

4. Bake for 30–35 minutes until crust is browned. Lower temperature to 250°F and continue baking until pie is firm around the edges and set in the center but slightly jiggly, about 10–15 minutes longer. Remove pie from the oven.

5. Increase oven temperature to 375°F.

6. In a medium bowl, beat 3 remaining egg whites until they begin to form soft peaks. Gradually beat in remaining sugar and salt. Beat in remaining vanilla. Spread meringue over top of the hot pie, making sure to spread it all the way to the edge of the crust to seal in the filling with the meringue. Put pie back in the oven and bake for 10–12 minutes longer until meringue is nicely browned.

Shoofly Pie

Shoofly is a Southern tradition that has a moist, yet somewhat cakey, texture. If you like a robust molasses flavor, replace the corn syrup with molasses.

INGREDIENTS | SERVES 8

1¼ cups all-purpose flour

¾ cup light brown sugar, packed

1 teaspoon ground cinnamon

¼ teaspoon salt

6 tablespoons butter, cut into ½" pieces and chilled

1 cup boiling water

¾ cup light molasses

¼ cup light corn syrup

1 teaspoon baking soda

1 large egg, lightly beaten

1 (9") pie shell, unbaked

1. Preheat oven to 400°F.

2. In a large bowl, combine flour, brown sugar, cinnamon, and salt. Mix well. Add butter and, with your fingers or a fork, rub it in until mixture becomes crumbly. Cover and chill until ready to use.

3. In a medium bowl, whisk together boiling water, molasses, and corn syrup until well blended. Whisk in baking soda and egg until well mixed. Pour molasses mixture into pie shell and top with crumb mixture.

4. Place pie pan on a baking sheet and bake for 10 minutes. Reduce heat to 350°F and bake for 35–45 minutes or until pie is golden brown and puffed. Let cool completely before serving.

Cookies and Candy

Pecan Sandies

This is a delicious little Southern cookie, loaded with chopped pecans and coated with powdered sugar. These are beautiful cookies to pack in small tins and give to friends and relatives.

INGREDIENTS | MAKES 4 DOZEN

1 cup butter, softened

⅓ cup plus ½ cup powdered sugar, divided

1½ teaspoons vanilla extract

¼ teaspoon salt

2 cups all-purpose flour

1 cup chopped pecans

Toasted Nuts

For a nuttier pecan flavor, toast the chopped pecans before you start the cookies. Spread the chopped pecans out on a baking sheet and toast in a 325°F oven for about 8 minutes or until the pecans are lightly browned and aromatic.

1. In a large mixing bowl, combine butter and ⅓ cup powdered sugar; beat until light. Beat in vanilla. Gradually add salt and flour; blend well. Blend in chopped pecans. Chill dough for about 30 minutes.

2. Preheat oven to 325°F.

3. Shape cookie dough into small balls and place about 1" apart on an ungreased baking sheet. Bake for 18–20 minutes or until just browned on the bottoms. Let cool completely.

4. Sift remaining ½ cup powdered sugar into a large food storage bag. Add a few cookies at a time and gently turn the bag to coat cookies.

Old-Fashioned Peanut Butter Cookies

These peanut butter cookies are just like the ones Mom made, with the little crisscross fork marks. Add fine-chopped roasted peanuts to the dough if you'd like a crunchier cookie, or dip them in a little melted chocolate for a special occasion.

INGREDIENTS | MAKES 5 DOZEN

1 cup granulated sugar

1 cup light brown sugar, packed

1 cup butter, softened

1 cup smooth peanut butter

2 large eggs

1 teaspoon vanilla extract

1 teaspoon baking soda

1 teaspoon baking powder

2½ cups all-purpose flour

½ teaspoon salt

Cookies When You Want Them

Cookie dough can be frozen, so make some extra and freeze half of the dough. Freeze this peanut butter cookie dough into a disk or cylinder shape, then wrap well, first in plastic wrap, then in foil. Freeze for up to 1 year, and make sure you label the package. When you're ready to bake the cookies, let thaw until the dough can be shaped into balls, and then shape as instructed. If you have time and the freezer space, go ahead and bake the cookies and then freeze them in airtight containers for up to 1 year.

1. In a large bowl, cream granulated sugar and brown sugar with butter and peanut butter until light. Beat in eggs and vanilla extract. Sift dry ingredients together into a small bowl; blend into creamed mixture until well blended. Cover and chill dough for about 30–45 minutes.

2. Preheat oven to 350°F. Lightly grease a baking sheet.

3. Shape dough into small balls and place about 1½" apart on the prepared baking sheet. Dip the tines of a fork in flour, then press each cookie, dipping again and pressing again to flatten slightly and form crisscross marks.

4. Bake for about 10–12 minutes until just browned on the bottoms.

Molasses Cookies

Do not use any other type of molasses for this recipe except unsulfured, preferably Grandma's Molasses brand. The molasses can give a bitter flavor to the cookies if it isn't the right kind.

INGREDIENTS | MAKES 72

2¼ cups all-purpose flour

2 teaspoons baking soda

1 teaspoon ground cinnamon

¾ teaspoon ground ginger

½ teaspoon ground allspice

½ teaspoon ground cloves

¼ teaspoon ground cayenne or chipotle pepper

½ teaspoon salt

½ cup vegetable shortening, at room temperature

½ cup butter, at room temperature

1 cup dark brown sugar, packed

1 large egg

½ cup unsulfured molasses

1 cup granulated sugar

1. Preheat oven to 375°F. Whisk together flour, baking soda, cinnamon, ginger, allspice, cloves, cayenne pepper, and salt in a medium bowl.

2. In a large mixing bowl, beat together shortening, butter, and brown sugar until creamy. Add egg and molasses; beat well. Stir in flour mixture.

3. Roll cookie dough into 1" balls. Place granulated sugar in a shallow bowl. Dip the top of each ball in sugar; place on an ungreased baking sheet, sugar side up.

4. Bake for 10–12 minutes. Let cool on wire racks.

Pecan Praline Cookies

These yummy, buttery, brown-sugar pecan cookies are a favorite for holiday baking. For variety, make half of them with the powdered sugar coating and then roll the other half in cinnamon sugar.

INGREDIENTS | MAKES 5–6 DOZEN

1½ cups butter, softened
¾ cup light brown sugar, packed
2 teaspoons vanilla extract
3 cups sifted all-purpose flour
2 cups finely chopped pecans
Sifted powdered sugar or cinnamon sugar

1. Preheat oven to 325°F. Lightly grease a baking sheet.

2. In a mixing bowl, cream together butter and brown sugar until light. Stir in vanilla, then stir in flour. Using your hands, mix in chopped pecans. The dough will be crumbly.

3. Shape dough into small balls about 1" in diameter. Place on prepared baking sheet.

4. Bake for 15–20 minutes until cookies are firm and lightly browned on bottoms. Let cool slightly, then gently roll in powdered sugar or cinnamon sugar.

The Best Chocolate Chip Cookies

This is a delicious buttery version of the classic favorite.

INGREDIENTS | MAKES 4 DOZEN

1 cup butter, softened
¾ cup granulated sugar
1 cup light brown sugar, packed
2 large eggs
1½ teaspoons vanilla extract
1 teaspoon baking soda
1 tablespoon very warm water
3 cups all-purpose flour
1 teaspoon salt
2 cups semisweet chocolate chunks
1 cup chopped pecans

1. Preheat oven to 350°F.

2. In a large mixing bowl, cream butter with sugars. Beat in eggs and vanilla.

3. Combine baking soda and water in a cup; blend into batter. Gradually blend in flour and salt. Stir in chocolate chunks and chopped pecans.

4. Drop by teaspoonfuls onto ungreased baking sheets. Bake for about 12 minutes or until cookies are set and edges are browned.

Chocolate-Dipped Shortbread Cookies

These cookies are easy, and they look like you bought them at a bakery.

INGREDIENTS | MAKES 5 DOZEN

1¼ cups softened butter, divided
2 cups all-purpose flour
⅔ cup cornstarch
½ cup light brown sugar, packed
⅔ cup ground almonds
2 teaspoons vanilla extract
½ teaspoon almond extract
8 ounces semisweet chocolate
1 cup chopped blanched almonds

Prevent Seizing

A few drops of water, if not part of the recipe, can cause chocolate to seize or become a clump of chocolate you can't do a thing with. Keep any bowls or utensils thoroughly dry when working with melted chocolate.

1. Preheat oven to 350°F.

2. In a food processor fitted with a metal blade, combine 1 cup butter, flour, cornstarch, sugar, ground almonds, and vanilla and almond extracts. Pulse until dough begins to clump.

3. Shape dough into 2 cylinders. Divide 1 cylinder into 4 equal portions. Pinch and press each portion into a 14" rope about ¾" in diameter. Gently roll on a smooth surface to smooth out wrinkles and cracks. Cut each rope into 2" lengths and place on ungreased baking sheets. Bake for 18–20 minutes or until golden brown on the bottom. Cool cookies on wire racks.

4. In a double boiler over hot water, combine semisweet chocolate with remaining butter. Heat over low heat, stirring constantly, until chocolate is melted. Dip about ⅓ of each cookie in chocolate, then press into chopped almonds. Place on a wire rack over waxed paper to catch the drips. Let cool.

Pecan Dainties

These tiny meringues are fantastic served with coffee or coffee ice cream. For an extra-special treat, dip the bottoms in melted bittersweet chocolate and let set.

INGREDIENTS | MAKES 36

1 egg white, at room temperature
Pinch salt
1 cup light brown sugar, packed
1½ cups pecan halves

1. Preheat oven to 250°F. Line a baking sheet with parchment paper and spray with nonstick spray.

2. Beat egg white and salt in a medium bowl until soft peaks form. Add sugar gradually; beat until stiff and glossy. Gently fold in pecans.

3. Drop by teaspoonfuls on prepared baking sheet; bake for 30 minutes.

4. Remove from the baking sheet immediately and cool on wire racks.

Mom's Blond Brownies

Kids and adults alike love these buttery blondies.

INGREDIENTS | MAKES 16–24

1 cup all-purpose flour
½ teaspoon baking powder
¼ teaspoon baking soda
⅛ teaspoon salt
½ cup butter, softened
1 cup light brown sugar, packed
1 large egg
1 teaspoon vanilla extract
1 cup semisweet chocolate chips
½–1 cup chopped walnuts or pecans

1. Preheat oven to 350°F, or 325°F if using a glass baking pan. Grease and flour an 11" × 7" baking pan.

2. In a small bowl, combine flour, baking powder, baking soda, and salt; set aside.

3. In a medium mixing bowl, cream together butter and brown sugar until light. Beat in egg and vanilla. Stir in dry ingredients until well blended. Fold in chocolate chips and chopped nuts.

4. Bake for about 25 minutes or until brownies are set and edges are browned. Be careful not to overbake.

Key Lime Bars

The addition of rose water to these tangy bars takes them from average to incredible; it adds a delicate flavor that is hard to describe. Rose water is available at many health food stores, Middle Eastern markets, or online.

INGREDIENTS | MAKES 2 DOZEN

Crust
1½ cups all-purpose flour
½ cup powdered sugar
¾ cup butter, at room temperature
½ teaspoon vanilla extract
1 teaspoon rose water

Filling
4 large eggs
1½ cups granulated sugar
½ cup Key lime juice
1 tablespoon all-purpose flour
1 tablespoon lime zest
Powdered sugar

Key Limes

Key limes are a particularly tangy, small lime that grows in Key West, Florida. The juice is often available year-round in your grocery store next to the lemon and lime juices. It is a little more expensive than regular lime juice, but the taste is worth it. Fresh Key limes are sometimes available during the summer months.

1. Preheat oven to 350°F. Butter a 9" × 13" baking pan.

2. Make the crust: In a medium bowl, combine flour and powdered sugar. Add butter, vanilla, and rose water; cut in butter with your fingers until it looks like coarse crumbs. Gently but firmly press mixture into bottom of pan

3. Bake crust for 20 minutes or until golden brown.

4. Make the filling: Whisk together eggs, granulated sugar, lime juice, flour, and lime zest in a small bowl; blend well. Pour into crust

5. Bake for 20 minutes more or until mixture is set. Let cool. Sift powdered sugar over the top before serving.

Hello Dolly Bars

These are very popular bars in the South, and they're truly delicious.
They're super easy to make for the holidays.

INGREDIENTS | MAKES 16–24

½ cup butter

1½ cups graham cracker crumbs

1 cup semisweet chocolate chips

1 cup sweetened coconut flakes

1 cup chopped pecan

1 (14-ounce) can sweetened condensed milk

1. Preheat oven to 350°F.

2. Melt butter and pour into a 9" × 13" baking pan. Sprinkle evenly with graham cracker crumbs; stir lightly to blend and then layer chocolate chips, coconut flakes, then pecans. Drizzle evenly with sweetened condensed milk.

3. Bake for 25–30 minutes. Let cool and cut into squares to serve.

Hello Dolly Variations

These bars can have many variations. Replace the pecans with walnuts. Use half chocolate chips and half butterscotch chips. Peanut butter chips would add some nice flavor, too. Try replacing the graham cracker crumbs with cinnamon or chocolate graham cracker crumbs or crumble your favorite cookies or cereal. You could also mix 1 teaspoon of vanilla extract or your favorite flavoring into the sweetened condensed milk before drizzling it over the top.

Mississippi Mud Brownies

Rich and decadent, you can substitute walnuts for the pecans and add 1 cup of coconut flakes to the frosting if you like.

INGREDIENTS | MAKES 24

1½ cups butter, divided

7 ounces unsweetened chocolate, chopped, divided

2 cups granulated sugar

4 large eggs

1 cup all-purpose flour

Pinch salt

1 cup chopped pecans

½ cup evaporated milk

½ teaspoon vanilla extract

4½ cups powdered sugar

3 cups miniature marshmallows

Chocolate Bloom

Heat and humidity can cause chocolate to get a discoloration called bloom. The white bloom caused by heat does not change the taste of the chocolate, so you can still use it. The grayish bloom caused by high humidity does change the taste of the chocolate, and it is best to throw it away.

1. Preheat oven to 350°F. Grease a 9" × 13" baking pan.

2. Melt 1 cup butter in a medium microwaveable bowl and stir in 4 ounces chocolate until melted. Let cool.

3. Beat granulated sugar into chocolate mixture. Beat in eggs 1 at a time, beating well after each addition. Add flour and salt; blend until smooth. Fold in pecans. Spread into the prepared pan.

4. Bake for 25–30 minutes or until a toothpick inserted in the center comes out with only a few crumbs clinging to it.

5. Bring milk to a simmer in a small saucepan over medium-low heat; add remaining butter and chocolate, stirring until chocolate is completely melted. Let cool slightly. Add vanilla; beat in powdered sugar until icing is smooth but can still be poured.

6. Spread marshmallows over warm brownies and quickly pour icing over the top. Let cool and cut into bars.

Never-Fail No-Bake Chocolate Cookies

These cookies are so easy to make up at a moment's notice. It's a quick chocolate fix, too!

INGREDIENTS | MAKES 4 DOZEN

½ cup butter
½ cup whole milk or evaporated milk
2 cups sugar
1 cup semisweet chocolate chips
3 tablespoons peanut butter
3 cups quick-cooking rolled oats
1 teaspoon vanilla extract

1. In a medium saucepan over medium heat, combine butter, milk, and sugar. Cook, stirring occasionally, until mixture comes to a rolling boil. Boil for 1 minute.

2. Meanwhile, combine chocolate chips, peanut butter, oats, and vanilla in a large bowl. Pour hot mixture over the top. Stir until chocolate is melted and all ingredients are well blended.

3. Drop by teaspoonfuls onto waxed paper. When cooled and firm, store cookies in layers in airtight containers with waxed paper between layers.

Kentucky Bourbon Balls

These delicious and easy little bourbon balls are a holiday tradition in the South. Serve them around the Christmas and New Year's holidays.

INGREDIENTS | MAKES ABOUT 48

1½ cups finely crushed vanilla wafers
1 cup finely chopped pecans
2½ cups powdered sugar, divided
3 tablespoons unsweetened cocoa powder
5 tablespoons bourbon
2 tablespoons light corn syrup

1. In a large bowl, thoroughly blend vanilla wafer crumbs, pecans, 1½ cups powdered sugar, and cocoa powder.

2. In a small bowl, combine bourbon and corn syrup; stir into vanilla wafer mixture, blending well. Cover and chill for 2 hours.

3. Sift remaining powdered sugar onto waxed paper or a large plate. Shape chilled mixture into 1" balls and roll in powdered sugar.

4. Store bourbon balls in the refrigerator in tightly covered containers. Refrigerate for 1 or 2 days and then roll in powdered sugar again just before serving, if desired.

Southern Pecan Pralines

These delicious pecan praline candies are similar to the wonderful pralines you can find in New Orleans, and they're quite easy to make.

INGREDIENTS | MAKES ABOUT 36

1 cup granulated sugar

1 cup light brown sugar, packed

¾ cup evaporated milk

¼ teaspoon salt

2 tablespoons butter

1 teaspoon vanilla extract

1 cup chopped pecans

1. Butter the sides of a heavy, 2-quart saucepan. Add granulated sugar, brown sugar, evaporated milk, and salt. Stir to blend well. Cook over low heat, stirring constantly, until sugar is dissolved.

2. Increase heat to medium and cook until mixture begins to boil, stirring constantly. Reduce heat to medium-low and continue cooking until the temperature reaches 234°F (soft ball stage) on a candy thermometer. Remove from heat, add 2 tablespoons butter and vanilla, and let stand for 5 minutes.

3. Stir in nuts, then beat until mixture is no longer glossy and has thickened, about 2–3 minutes. Quickly spoon mixture onto sheets of waxed paper or lightly buttered baking sheets. If mixture becomes too stiff before you can finish, stir in very small amounts of hot water to make it workable. Let cool.

Rocky Road Fudge

This is such a delicious treat, and it makes a great holiday gift.

INGREDIENTS | MAKES ABOUT 2 POUNDS

1 cup miniature marshmallows

3 cups sugar

1 cup evaporated milk

3 ounces unsweetened chocolate

1 tablespoon light corn syrup

Dash salt

3 tablespoons butter

2 teaspoons vanilla extract

1 cup chopped pecans

Smooth Fudge

Before the first boil, while sugar is dissolving, use a pastry brush dipped in a little hot water to wash down the sides. This will help remove any sugar crystals from the sides of the pan. One single crystal of sugar clinging to the side of the pan could encourage more crystallization in the fudge.

1. Line an 8" square pan with foil, extending the foil over the edges of the pan. Butter the foil, and then sprinkle marshmallows evenly over the bottom. Place the pan in the freezer.

2. Butter sides of a large saucepan. Add sugar, milk, chocolate, corn syrup, and salt. Cook over medium heat, stirring with a wooden spoon, until chocolate is melted and mixture begins to boil. While heating mixture, dip a pastry brush in hot water and brush the sides of the pan to reduce the risk of sugar remaining undissolved. Reduce heat to medium-low and boil gently, without stirring, until mixture registers about 236°F–238°F on a candy thermometer.

3. Remove from heat; add 3 tablespoons butter and vanilla; let stand without stirring until it reaches about 110°F. Beat with a wooden spoon until mixture just begins to thicken. Add chopped nuts and beat until mixture begins to lose its gloss but can be poured.

4. Pour mixture over marshmallows in the pan. When partially set, score into squares. Let cool completely.

5. When fudge is firm, use the ends of the foil to lift it out of the pan. Cut into pieces. Layer fudge pieces in a tightly covered container with squares of waxed paper separating the layers. Store fudge in the refrigerator for up to 2 weeks.

Martha Washington Candy

This is a popular candy seen all over the South, and it's delicious! If you can't find paraffin, melt dipping chocolate or almond bark and dip the chilled candies in that.

INGREDIENTS | MAKES 48

2 pounds powdered sugar, sifted

1 (14-ounce) can sweetened condensed milk

1 teaspoon vanilla extract

2 cups sweetened coconut flakes

½ cup butter, softened

3 cups chopped pecans

3 cups semisweet chocolate chips

4 ounces paraffin wax

Is Paraffin Wax Safe to Eat?

Food-grade paraffin wax is widely used in chocolates and other foods. Although it is edible, it is not digestible; the wax passes through the digestive system. Paraffin is often used as a coating for fruits and vegetables, protecting them and making them shinier and more attractive. Paraffin is added to the chocolate to help it stay firm at room temperature and to give the chocolate a glossy finish. Though paraffin is rarely used in canning these days, it's usually found in the canning section of the food market.

1. Combine powdered sugar, condensed milk, vanilla, coconut flakes, butter, and pecans in a medium bowl. Blend well and shape into 1" balls. Chill in the refrigerator thoroughly until hardened.

2. In the top of a double boiler over simmering water, melt chocolate chips with wax. Using a fork or toothpicks, dip candy in chocolate mixture, coating thoroughly; let cool.

3. Store candy in airtight containers in the refrigerator for up to 2 weeks.

CHAPTER 15

Desserts and Sweet Sauces

Spiced Bread Pudding

This is a delicious classic version of bread pudding with spices and raisins. Serve it plain or with Vanilla Sauce or Bourbon Sauce (see recipes in this chapter).

INGREDIENTS | SERVES 6–8

3 cups whole milk
5 cups torn French bread pieces
1 tablespoon butter, softened
3 large eggs, lightly beaten
¾ cup sugar
½ teaspoon salt
1½ teaspoons ground cinnamon
1 teaspoon vanilla extract
½ cup raisins

1. Preheat oven to 350°F. Butter an 8" square baking dish.

2. In a small saucepan, heat milk over medium heat until just hot. Place bread pieces in a large bowl and pour milk over bread; stir in butter. Let stand for 2 minutes.

3. In a small bowl, beat eggs lightly; whisk in sugar, salt, cinnamon, and vanilla. Stir into bread mixture along with raisins.

4. Pour mixture into the prepared baking dish. Place baking dish in a larger baking pan and pour very hot water into the larger pan to a depth of about ½".

5. Bake for 20–30 minutes until set.

Peach Custard Bread Pudding

This wonderful bread pudding has it all! The diced peaches shine like jewels in this delicious dessert.

INGREDIENTS | SERVES 6

2½ cups diced fresh peaches
¼ cup peach nectar
4 cups soft bread pieces
2 tablespoons butter, melted
4 large eggs
½ cup sugar
1¾ cups whole milk
1 teaspoon vanilla extract
Old-Fashioned Butterscotch Sauce (see recipe in this chapter)

Bain-Marie

A bain-marie is a large pan containing hot water into which smaller pans are set to cook food or keep it warm. Cheesecakes and custards are often cooked in a bain-marie. The bain-marie will help prevent the top of a cheesecake from cracking and helps keep the custard or bread pudding from forming a top crust. On the stovetop, a bain-marie can simply be a bowl set over a saucepan of hot water, a very good way to melt chocolate.

1. In a small saucepan over medium heat, combine diced peaches and peach nectar; simmer for 5 minutes or until peaches are tender.

2. Preheat oven to 325°F. Butter a 2- to 2½-quart baking dish.

3. Arrange torn bread pieces in the prepared baking dish. Drizzle melted butter over bread. Add peach mixture and toss to combine ingredients.

4. In a medium mixing bowl, whisk together eggs, sugar, milk, and vanilla; pour mixture over bread and peach mixture and stir gently to combine ingredients.

5. Set the pan in a larger pan; pour very hot water into the larger pan to a depth of about ½"–1". Bake for 60–75 minutes or until pudding is set. A knife should come out clean when inserted near the center.

6. Serve with butterscotch sauce.

Sweet Potato Crème Brûlée

*This is a delicious way to enjoy sweet potatoes, and it makes
a beautiful dessert for a special occasion.*

INGREDIENTS | SERVES 6

1½ cups heavy whipping cream

2 teaspoons vanilla extract

5 large egg yolks

⅓ cup plus 2 tablespoons sugar, divided

1 teaspoon ground cinnamon

¼ teaspoon ground allspice

¼ teaspoon ground nutmeg

¾ cup cooked puréed sweet potatoes

Pecan halves

1. Preheat oven to 350°F. Place 6 (4- to 6-ounce) ramekins in a large baking pan with sides.

2. In a small saucepan, bring cream to a boil over medium-high heat. Remove from heat and stir in vanilla.

3. In a medium bowl, beat egg yolks with ⅓ cup sugar, cinnamon, allspice, nutmeg, and sweet potato. Whisk hot cream into egg yolk mixture. Ladle evenly into ramekins.

4. Place the pan with the ramekins on the oven rack, then fill the pan with very hot to boiling water about halfway up the sides of the dishes. Carefully slide the oven rack in, then bake for about 20–25 minutes. The centers will still be a little soft and will move just slightly. Use great care when filling and moving this pan of very hot water. You might want to first take the custards out of the water and then remove the pan of water from the oven. Use a spatula and potholder or oven mitt to lift each ramekin out to a wire rack to cool. Let the water cool, then empty the pan and dry thoroughly.

5. Once ramekins are cooled, put them back in the baking pan, cover with wrap or foil, and refrigerate for at least 4 hours.

6. Just before serving, sprinkle about 1½ teaspoons sugar over each crème brûlée. Slide ramekins under the broiler and broil for about 30 seconds. When sugar begins to melt and brown a bit, remove from the oven. Place a few pecan halves on each.

Peach Cobbler

The peach cobbler has become one of the stars of Southern cooking, whether it's made with fresh, frozen, or canned peaches, or a pastry crust, soft cake-like crust, or a delicious biscuit or dumpling topping. Serve peach cobbler warm, with whipped cream or vanilla ice cream.

INGREDIENTS | SERVES 6

4 cups sliced fresh peaches
1 cup sugar, divided
1½ teaspoons ground cinnamon, divided
1 large egg
⅓ cup half-and-half or whole milk
3 tablespoons butter, melted
½ cup all-purpose flour
2 teaspoons baking powder
½ teaspoon salt

What's a Cobbler?

The origin of the name of this American dessert is not known, but there is some speculation that it comes from the phrase "to cobble up," or to put something together quickly.

1. Preheat oven to 350°F. Lightly grease an 11" × 7" baking dish with butter.

2. Arrange peach slices in the baking dish; sprinkle with ½ cup sugar and 1 teaspoon cinnamon.

3. In a medium bowl, whisk egg with half-and-half or milk. Whisk in remaining ½ cup sugar and melted butter. Stir flour before measuring; add to egg mixture along with baking powder and salt.

4. Spoon the soft batter over peaches, covering as much of the top as possible. Sprinkle with remaining ½ teaspoon cinnamon

5. Bake for 30–40 minutes until crust is nicely browned.

Fresh Fruit Ambrosia

Here's a heavenly fruit ambrosia recipe, an old Southern tradition. It's lovely with whipped cream or a thick custard sauce.

INGREDIENTS | SERVES 6

3 oranges, peeled and sectioned

1 cup orange juice

1 (8-ounce) can pineapple chunks (undrained)

½ cup halved seedless red grapes

¼ cup halved seedless green grapes

½ cup sweetened coconut flakes

½ cup chopped pecans

1. In a large bowl, combine orange sections with orange juice, pineapple chunks, and grape halves. Refrigerate until serving time.

2. Just before serving, fold in coconut and chopped pecans.

Bananas with Rum Custard Sauce

This custard sauce is delicious served over sliced bananas, but you can also make the sauce to serve with bread pudding or other dessert or fruit.

INGREDIENTS | SERVES 8

8 large egg yolks

2½ cups half-and-half

5 tablespoons sugar

¼ teaspoon salt

1 tablespoon dark rum

1 teaspoon vanilla extract

8 medium ripe but firm bananas, peeled

Freshly grated nutmeg

1. In the top of a double boiler over hot water, combine egg yolks, half-and-half, sugar, and salt. Whisk until smooth. Cook over low heat, stirring constantly, until mixture is thick enough to coat a spoon. Strain through a fine-meshed sieve into a medium bowl; stir in rum and vanilla. Cover and chill thoroughly.

2. Slice bananas thinly and arrange in dessert dishes. Spoon some of the custard sauce over bananas and sprinkle each serving with a dash of freshly grated nutmeg.

Grilled Peaches with Pecans

Make sure to select peaches that are ripe, but still firm, for this recipe. If a peach is soft and overripe, it will simply fall through the grates when grilled.

INGREDIENTS | SERVES 4

1 tablespoon red wine vinegar
1 teaspoon honey
⅛ teaspoon kosher salt
6 firm freestone peaches
1 tablespoon canola oil
3 tablespoons light brown sugar
½ teaspoon ground cinnamon
½ cup chopped pecans
¼ cup caramel syrup

1. Preheat grill to medium-high or high. Whisk together vinegar, honey, and salt in a small bowl. Mix well.

2. Cut open 4 peaches and remove the pits. Set the other 2 peaches aside for later. Place peach halves on a baking sheet. Drizzle each with a little of the vinegar mixture. Place baking sheet in the refrigerator and let peaches marinate for 5 minutes.

3. Meanwhile, brush the grill lightly with canola oil. Remove peaches from the refrigerator and place on the grill, skin up. Turn peaches after 3 minutes. Let peaches grill, skin side down, for 2 minutes. Remove peaches from grill and place on a baking sheet. Sprinkle grilled peaches with brown sugar and cinnamon.

4. Slice open the 2 reserved peaches and remove pits. Dice raw peaches and place in a mixing bowl. Gently stir pecans into diced peaches.

5. To serve, cut each grilled peach half into quarters. Split grilled peach quarters between 4 dessert bowls. Sprinkle pecan mixture over each. Drizzle a little caramel syrup over the top and serve.

Blackberry Stew with Sweet Biscuits

This easy-to-assemble dessert is a cross between shortcake and cobbler. For a dramatic presentation, cut the biscuits into decorative shapes.

INGREDIENTS | SERVES 6

1 cup granulated sugar
½ cup water
6 cups blackberries
1 teaspoon lemon juice
2 cups all-purpose flour
½ teaspoon salt
1 tablespoon baking powder
1 cup powdered sugar
½ cup very cold butter
¾ cup light cream

1. In a large saucepan, combine granulated sugar and water. Bring to a boil over medium-high heat, stirring constantly. Remove from heat; carefully add blackberries and lemon juice. Return to medium-high heat and bring to a boil. Immediately reduce heat to medium-low; simmer for 15 minutes.

2. Preheat oven to 400°F. Cover a baking sheet with foil and spray foil with nonstick cooking spray.

3. In a large bowl, combine flour, salt, baking powder, and powdered sugar; stir with a whisk to blend. Add butter; cut in with a pastry blender or 2 knives until mixture resembles coarse crumbs. Stir in cream to make a soft dough.

4. Coat your hands and a work surface with flour. Knead dough briefly; roll out to 1" thick. Using a biscuit or cookie cutter, cut into 8 biscuits. Place on prepared baking sheet, at least 1" apart. Bake for 10–12 minutes or until biscuits are light brown on top.

5. Ladle blackberry stew into shallow bowls; top each bowl with a hot biscuit.

Country Apple Hand Pies

Bits of tart, fresh apple make a delicious filling for these portable pies.

INGREDIENTS | SERVES 8

2 Granny Smith apples, peeled, cored, and finely chopped

½ teaspoon ground cinnamon

¼ cup sugar

2 tablespoons cornstarch

2 Flaky Butter Pie Crusts (see recipe in Chapter 13), unbaked

1 large egg, beaten

Hand Pies Into Fried Pies

Any hand pie made with a fruit filling can be made into a fried pie with a few simple modifications. First, do not cut a steam vent. The vent will allow oil to seep into the pie. Second, try to press out any air in the pastry before crimping. Fry the pies in oil heated to 350°F until puffed and golden.

1. In a medium bowl, combine apples, cinnamon, sugar, and cornstarch until well mixed. Allow to stand for 5 minutes.

2. Preheat oven to 425°F and line a baking sheet with parchment paper.

3. Cut pastry into 8 rounds or squares. Place about ⅓ cup filling on each piece of pastry, slightly off center; brush the edges of pastry with beaten egg and fold dough over filling. Pinch or crimp with a fork to seal. Place pies on the prepared baking sheet and brush with beaten egg. With scissors or a sharp paring knife, cut vents in pastry so that steam can escape.

4. Bake for 15 minutes. Reduce heat to 350°F and bake for 25 minutes or until pastry is golden brown and juices are bubbling. Let cool to room temperature before serving.

Apple Pecan Crunch

This is a nutty versions of an apple crisp. Serve it warm with ice cream or a vanilla sauce.

INGREDIENTS | SERVES 6

5 large apples, peeled, cored, and sliced
½ cup pecan pieces or halves
3 tablespoons water
¾ cup all-purpose flour
1 cup sugar
1 teaspoon ground cinnamon
½ teaspoon salt
½ cup butter, softened

1. Preheat oven to 350°F. Lightly butter an 8" square baking dish.

2. Arrange apple slices in the baking dish; sprinkle with pecans. Add water.

3. In a small mixing bowl, combine flour, sugar, cinnamon, and salt. Cut in butter with a pastry blender until mixture resembles coarse crumbs. Sprinkle crumb mixture over apples.

4. Bake for 35–45 minutes or until apples are tender.

Fresh Strawberry Sauce

This is a delicious sauce for topping ice cream, or you can use it on pound cake, angel food cake, or as a topping for a cheesecake.

INGREDIENTS | SERVES 8

1 pint fresh strawberries
½ cup sugar
¼ cup water
Juice and finely grated zest of ½ medium lemon
2 tablespoons butter

1. Rinse and hull strawberries. Cut small strawberries in half and slice large berries.

2. In a small saucepan, combine sugar, water, and lemon juice and zest; stir over medium heat until sugar is dissolved and mixture just begins to boil. Add butter and stir until melted. Add strawberries and heat through. Do not cook the sauce.

3. Chill sauce thoroughly before serving.

Old-Fashioned Butterscotch Sauce

*This delicious butterscotch is wonderful on a bread pudding,
or you could use it as a topping for ice cream.*

INGREDIENTS | MAKES ABOUT 2 CUPS

1 cup light brown sugar, packed
2/3 cup light corn syrup
1/4 cup butter
1/8 teaspoon baking soda
2/3 cup evaporated milk
1 teaspoon vanilla extract

1. Combine sugar, corn syrup, and butter in a small saucepan over medium heat. Bring to a full rolling boil, stirring constantly. Continue cooking, without stirring, at a full rolling boil for 1 minute.

2. Remove from heat and let stand for 5 minutes. In a small cup, dissolve baking soda in milk and add vanilla; stir into sauce. Stir until smooth.

3. Pour into a 1-pint canning jar or two 8-ounce jars. Store sauce in the refrigerator for up to 2 weeks.

4. To reheat sauce, put jar in a pan of warm water.

Bourbon Sauce

*This rich and delicious bourbon sauce is perfect for bread pudding. You can also
substitute dark rum and use this sauce over bananas, ice cream, or other desserts.*

INGREDIENTS | MAKES 2 CUPS

2 cups heavy whipping cream
2/3 cup sugar
4 large egg yolks
2 teaspoons vanilla extract
1/4 cup bourbon

1. Combine cream and sugar in a heavy medium saucepan. Heat over medium-low heat until mixture is hot and it begins to steam.

2. In a small bowl or 2-cup measure, whisk egg yolks. Whisk about 1/3 of the hot mixture into yolks, then stir yolk mixture into cream mixture in the saucepan. Reduce heat to low and continue cooking until mixture coats a spoon. Do not boil.

3. Remove from heat and stir in vanilla and bourbon. Strain through a fine-meshed sieve into a small bowl and serve warm.

Vanilla Sauce

This makes a delicious sauce for berries, pudding, or gingerbread.

INGREDIENTS | MAKES 1½ CUPS

2 cups water

1 cup granulated sugar or vanilla sugar

2 tablespoons cornstarch

¼ cup butter

1 tablespoon vanilla extract

Dash salt

Vanilla Sugar

Vanilla sugar is wonderful to flavor coffee or other beverages, and it can be used in any recipe calling for granulated sugar. It also makes a wonderful, unique food gift. Cut 1 vanilla bean into 1" pieces and then combine them with 3 cups of granulated sugar; cover and let stand for 2 weeks. Pour the sugar, with the pieces of bean, into ½-pint or 1-pint jars and give as gifts, or use it for desserts, beverages, or cookie decorating. Remove beans when using in a recipe.

1. In a medium saucepan, bring water to a boil over high heat. Combine sugar and cornstarch in a small cup, blending well, and then stir mixture into boiling water. Reduce heat to medium. Cook sauce, stirring constantly, until thickened.

2. Remove from heat and add butter, vanilla, and a dash of salt. Stir until butter is melted.

3. Store sauce in a jar or tightly covered container in the refrigerator for 1–2 weeks.

Butter Pecan Ice Cream

Rarely will you find an ice cream parlor that doesn't have butter pecan on the menu, as it is the most popular flavor after chocolate, vanilla, and strawberry, and certainly the most popular ice cream with nuts. This recipe is easy to pull together and is packed with nutty, buttery flavor.

INGREDIENTS | MAKES 1 QUART

1 cup chopped pecans
2 tablespoons butter
1 cup whole milk
1¾ cups light brown sugar, packed
Pinch salt
3 large egg yolks, beaten
2½ cups heavy cream
1 tablespoon vanilla extract

1. Sauté pecans in butter in a medium skillet until aromatic and lightly browned. Set aside; do not drain any remaining butter.

2. Combine milk, brown sugar, and salt in a medium saucepan and warm over medium heat until sugar is dissolved. Do not allow to boil.

3. In a small bowl, whisk egg yolks. Once milk mixture is hot, temper eggs by adding half of the milk mixture to eggs, whisking constantly. Return mixture to saucepan and heat until thickened.

4. Pour heavy cream and vanilla extract into a large mixing bowl over an ice bath. Strain cooked custard into cream, stirring until cooled. Add pecan mixture. Stir and place in the refrigerator until thoroughly chilled, about 5 hours or overnight.

5. Once chilled, add to an ice cream maker and follow manufacturer's instructions for freezing.

Blueberry Peach Sherbet

The combination of blueberries and peaches makes one of the tastiest sherbets available. It screams of summer, but can be made in the dead of winter from frozen fruit, should you need a quick vacation!

INGREDIENTS | MAKES 1 QUART

1 cup fresh or frozen blueberries
2 peaches, peeled and chopped
Juice of 1 medium lemon
1¼ cups sugar, divided
1 cup water
⅓ cup heavy whipping cream

1. Rinse blueberries but do not dry. Add to a medium bowl with chopped peaches. Drizzle with lemon juice and 2 tablespoons sugar. Cover and set aside while making the syrup.

2. Place remaining sugar and water in a medium saucepan; stir over medium heat until all of the sugar is dissolved. Allow to cool.

3. Place blueberry-peach mixture in a food processor and purée until smooth. Press through a fine-meshed sieve to remove seeds if desired. Stir into sugar syrup.

4. In a medium bowl, whip cream to stiff peaks, then fold into blueberry-peach mixture.

5. Add to an ice cream maker and follow manufacturer's instructions for freezing.

CHAPTER 16

Beverages

Southern-Style Ice Tea

When you're in the South, you'll quickly learn that if you want unsweetened tea, you should say so! Sweetened or not, ice tea has been a Southern tradition since the nineteenth century, around the time ice became available to most people.

INGREDIENTS | MAKES 1 QUART

3 cups water

3 heaping teaspoons fresh orange pekoe bulk tea

4 cups cold water

Lemon slices

1. Add 3 cups water to a nonreactive saucepan and bring to a boil over high heat. Reduce heat to low and add tea. Cover and let simmer for 5–8 minutes or to desired strength.

2. Strain through a fine-meshed sieve into a large pitcher; add cold water. Refrigerate to chill thoroughly. Serve with lemon slices.

Nonreactive Pots

It's always a good idea to have a nonreactive pot and skillet in your arsenal of cooking tools. Certain acidic foods can react to some materials, including aluminum, copper, and iron. Good nonreactive pot and skillet materials include glass, stainless steel, enamel or an enamel-lined pan (with no chips), or glazed ceramic.

Orange Cooler

Easy, nutritious, and delicious, this is a drink the kids will love. A sprig of mint, a straw, and a long ice-tea spoon make this drink look extra special.

INGREDIENTS | SERVES 6

3 cups cold orange juice

6 large scoops orange sherbet

Ginger ale, chilled

6 sprigs fresh mint

1. Pour ½ cup of orange juice into each of 6 tumblers. Add a generous scoop of orange sherbet to each glass, then fill with cold ginger ale.

2. Stir slightly and serve with ice-tea spoons and straws. Garnish with a sprig of mint.

Watermelon-Mint Aqua Fresca

Literally "fresh water," aqua fresca is a water-based drink infused with fruit.

INGREDIENTS | SERVES 6

¾ cup sugar

2 cups water, divided

½ cup fresh whole mint leaves

1 (6-pound) seedless watermelon, cubed

Make Watermelon "Ice Cubes"

Cut a watermelon into 1" cubes. Place on a baking sheet in a single layer. Freeze until solid. Use to cool down your drinks without watering them down.

1. In a small saucepan, bring sugar, 1 cup water, and mint to a boil over high heat. Stir to dissolve sugar.

2. Strain out mint and discard. Allow mixture to cool.

3. Place watermelon and sugar mixture in a food processor. Pulse until smooth. Strain through a wide wire mesh sieve into a pitcher. Stir in remaining water.

Hot Spiced Cider

This is an easy and delicious drink, perfect for cold winter nights and holiday gatherings. If you're having an adult get-together or New Year's Eve party, offer this with a little rum or bourbon. Serve with a cinnamon stick in each mug for a decorative touch.

INGREDIENTS | MAKES 2 QUARTS

2 quarts apple cider

¼ cup light brown sugar, packed

8 whole cloves

6 whole allspice berries

1 (6") cinnamon stick

⅛ teaspoon freshly grated nutmeg

Dash salt

1. Combine all ingredients in a large saucepan. Bring to a boil over medium-high heat.

2. Strain through a fine-meshed sieve and serve hot in mugs.

Bourbon Vanilla Milk Punch

*A wonderful combination of flavors, this bourbon milk punch makes a beautiful beverage
for a relaxing summer party or get-together with good friends and neighbors.*

INGREDIENTS | SERVES 8

2 quarts vanilla ice cream

1 cup good-quality Kentucky bourbon

2 tablespoons vanilla extract

Freshly grated nutmeg

1. In a blender, combine ice cream, bourbon, and vanilla. Blend until smooth.

2. Pour into cups or small tumblers and grate a little nutmeg over each serving.

Where Did Bourbon Originate?

Bourbon is as American as apple pie. It's whiskey in a distinctly Southern blend, made with at least 51 percent corn, along with rye and other grains. Bourbon evolved in the late 1700s in Bourbon County, Virginia, an area that would later become part of Kentucky. Today, bourbon is produced exclusively in Kentucky and is exported all over the world.

Kentucky Mint Julep

*Serve mint juleps in a traditional silver julep cup, if you have one; otherwise, a glass will
do just fine! Stir the ice a bit to frost the julep cup, or serve in frosted glasses.*

INGREDIENTS | MAKES ABOUT 20

2 cups sugar

2 cups water

¼ cup fresh mint leaves

Small ice cubes or crushed ice

5 cups Kentucky bourbon

Fresh mint sprigs

1. In a medium saucepan, combine sugar and water; heat over medium-low heat until hot and clear. Remove from heat. Put mint leaves in a cup and bruise by gently pressing leaves against the sides of the cup with a spoon. Stir leaves into syrup and let steep for about 20–25 minutes.

2. Fill a julep cup or glass with ice, then add 1 tablespoon of the syrup and 2 ounces of bourbon.

3. Garnish each serving with fresh mint sprigs.

Mint Citrus Cooler

*This is a beautiful citrus beverage for a special summer occasion or gathering.
You can also make a big pitcher full for a family cookout.*

INGREDIENTS | SERVES 12

1½ cups sugar
2½ cups water
1 cup fresh mint leaves
Juice of 2 medium oranges
Juice of 6 medium lemons
1 heaping tablespoon finely grated orange zest
Thin lemon and orange slices
Fresh mint sprigs

1. In a medium saucepan, combine sugar and water. Bring to a boil over medium-high heat. Reduce heat to medium-low and simmer for 5 minutes. Remove from heat and let cool for 10 minutes.

2. Place mint leaves in a medium bowl; add slightly cooled syrup, orange juice, lemon juice, and orange zest. Cover and let steep for about 1 hour. Strain into a 1-quart container. Cover and refrigerate until serving time.

3. For each tall glass, mix ⅓ cup syrup with ⅔ cup cold water. Add a few ice cubes, a thin orange or lemon slice, and a sprig of mint.

Cranberry Party Punch

Here's a festive and flavorful fruit punch for the holidays, perfect for a party or family gathering. This recipe can be doubled quite easily if you're expecting a crowd.

INGREDIENTS | MAKES 1 GALLON

6 cups cranberry juice
4½ cups apple juice
Juice of 5 or 6 small lemons (about ¾ cup)
1 medium lemon, thinly sliced
1 (8-ounce) can pineapple tidbits (undrained)
6 cups club soda

1. Combine cranberry juice, apple juice, and lemon juice in a large pitcher. Add lemon slices and undrained pineapple tidbits.

2. Chill thoroughly, then pour into a punch bowl. Add club soda just before serving, along with ice cubes or an ice ring.

Georgia Peach Shake

This delicious peach shake hits the spot on a hot summer day, and it's a great way to use those juicy ripe peaches. The kids will adore it!

INGREDIENTS | SERVES 4

2 cups sliced fresh peaches, peeled and pitted

½ cup pineapple juice

½ cup sugar

1 quart vanilla ice cream

1½ cups whole milk

1. Using an electric blender, blend together sliced peaches, pineapple juice, and sugar until smooth. Add ice cream and blend until soft and blended; pour in milk and pulse just until combined.

2. Pour into tall chilled glasses and serve with straws.

Perfect Peeled Peaches

If you need perfectly smooth peeled peaches, plunge them into boiling water for a few seconds, then immerse quickly in ice water. Under running water, use your fingers to scrape or peel away the skin. Cut peaches in half to remove the pit, then slice or dice. Peeling peaches this way is especially nice for recipes that use whole peaches or uniform halves or slices.

Strawberry Ice Cream Soda

This is an ice cream soda you'll make again and again. The whole family will be asking for this one, and not only during hot weather months. Luckily, fresh strawberries are available almost year-round these days!

INGREDIENTS | SERVES 2

2 heaping tablespoons strawberry jam

4 tablespoons mashed fresh strawberries

4 tablespoons heavy whipping cream

4 generous scoops strawberry ice cream

Club soda

Sweetened whipped cream

Sliced strawberries

Sweetened Whipped Cream

To make sweetened whipped cream, whip 1 cup of heavy whipping cream until almost stiff, then add about 3–4 tablespoons of powdered sugar and 1 teaspoon vanilla extract. Beat until the whipped cream holds peaks. Be careful not to whip the cream too long or you'll end up with butter!

1. In each of 2 tall 16-ounce glasses, add 1 heaping tablespoon jam, 2 tablespoons mashed strawberries, 2 tablespoons heavy whipping cream, and 1 generous scoop of strawberry ice cream. Fill each glass about ⅔ full with club soda, then add another generous scoop of strawberry ice cream.

2. Top each soda with a dollop of whipped cream and sliced strawberries. Serve with a long ice-tea spoon and a straw.

Old-Fashioned Hot Cocoa

If you have a utensil or machine specially made for frothing, fill cups about ¾ of the way and make that beautiful foamy top. You could almost skip the marshmallows.

INGREDIENTS | SERVES 4

3 tablespoons unsweetened cocoa powder

¼ cup sugar

4 cups whole milk

¼ teaspoon vanilla extract

Miniature marshmallows or marshmallow creme

Scalding Milk

Many recipes call for scalded milk just because that was how bacteria was killed before the days of pasteurization. You still might want to heat or scald milk if you need to dissolve sugar in it or melt butter or other fat, or if you use raw milk. Scald milk by heating it in a saucepan over low heat, stirring occasionally, just until small bubbles begin to form around the inside edge of the pan. The milk will form a slight skin on top, which you will notice when you stir, and it will begin to steam.

1. In a small bowl, combine cocoa and sugar, blending well.

2. In a medium saucepan, heat milk to scalding (see sidebar). Stir about ½ cup hot milk into cocoa and sugar mixture, then pour hot cocoa mixture into hot milk in the saucepan. Stir until well blended, then stir in vanilla.

3. Serve in cups with miniature marshmallows or a dollop of marshmallow creme.

Glossary of Southern Food and Cooking Terms

Adjust Seasoning
To taste the dish near the end of cooking, before serving, to judge the need for salt and pepper, spices, herbs, or other seasonings.

Au Jus
A French term meaning "served with its own juice," used in reference to beef or other meat.

Bacon Drippings
Also known as bacon grease, this is the fat rendered from cooked bacon.

Bain-Marie
This French term, also known as a water bath, is a cooking technique used for sauces and custards, cheesecakes, and other egg-based dishes. The dish is cooked or baked in a larger pan of warm water, which helps keep the sauce from separating and helps to prevent cracks forming in cheesecake. A water bath is also used to keep some foods warm.

Baste
To brush or spoon liquid, butter, or other fat over food as it cooks.

Batter
The uncooked base mixture of most baked items and a mixture used to dip foods in before frying. Batter is usually made from a combination of flour, eggs, and liquid, and is thin enough to be stirred or whisked.

Beat
Beating by hand is to rapidly stir in a circular motion; 100 strokes equals approximately 1 minute with an electric mixer.

Beignet
A deep-fried New Orleans pastry, served hot with a generous dusting of powdered sugar.

Bisque
A thick, creamy soup, often made with seafood.

Blacken or Blackened
A method of cooking in which meat, poultry, or fish is seasoned with a spicy seasoning mixture, then fried in a very hot cast-iron skillet until crisp and blackened or very deeply browned on both sides.

Blanch

Blanching is a cooking process in which food is briefly plunged into boiling water and then submerged in very cold water to stop the cooking. Blanching peaches and tomatoes for 20–30 seconds makes them easier to peel.

Blend

To mix 2 or more ingredients together until combined, using a spoon, whisk, blender, mixer, or other implement.

Braise

To brown food in a small amount of fat, and then cover and cook it slowly over a long period of time in a small amount of liquid, such as water, wine, or broth, until done.

Broil

To cook food directly under or over the heat source, usually in the oven under the top element, or on the grill. In the oven, the standard broiling temperature is usually 550°F unless the recipe specifies otherwise.

Brown

To cook food over medium to high heat until the surface is browned. This can be done on the stovetop or under the broiler.

Butterfly

To cut a food, such as shrimp or pork tenderloin, down the center, but not quite through, leaving both sides attached. The food is then spread to resemble a butterfly.

Cajun Cooking

This is a blend of Southern and French cuisines; a country-style cooking method using animal fats and dark roux. Cajun seasoning blends tend to be spicier than Creole seasoning, but both Cajun and Creole cuisines typically use the "trinity" of chopped onion, celery, and bell peppers, and both use filé powder.

Capers

A small edible flower bud of a bush, usually grown in Mediterranean countries. Capers are dried then pickled in a vinegar and salt brine. Capers add piquant flavor to many sauces and condiments, such as rémoulade sauce, and are sometimes used as a garnish.

Caramelize

To heat sugar until it melts, liquefies, and then turns golden brown. This technique is used to make candy, frostings, and topping for desserts such as crème brûlée.

Casserole

This term actually pertains to the baking dish as well as the ingredient combination it contains. Casseroles can be made with meat, poultry, vegetables, fish or seafood, and just about any combination, and they are often made with a bread crumb or shredded cheese topping.

Chili Sauce

This is a ketchup-like sauce that is spicier and usually sweeter tasting. Often used in sauces, you'll find it near the ketchup in most supermarkets.

Chop
To cut into small pieces.

Chunk
To cut into bite-sized pieces, usually 1" or larger.

Chutney
A condiment that usually contains fruit or vegetables, sugar, vinegar, and spices. Chutney makes a nice addition to various spreads and sandwich fillings.

Clarified Butter
Butter that has been melted, then skimmed of milk solids. Clarified butter is used to sauté foods and will withstand much higher heats than whole butter.

Cobbler
A baked dessert dish consisting of a fruit filling covered with sweetened soft dough, biscuit-like dough, or rolled pie pastry.

Country Ham
Country ham is a distinctly Southern product, dry cured following federal guidelines that require at least 18 percent of the ham's weight be lost during the curing and aging process; the ham must also contain at least 4 percent salt.

Crawfish
Freshwater crustaceans that look like very small lobsters, with claws. About 3"–6" in length, they're particularly popular in Louisiana and some other parts of the South. They are sometimes called crayfish in other countries and areas outside of Louisiana.

Creole Cooking
Creole cuisine, a cooking style found chiefly in New Orleans, is generally a blend of French, Spanish, and African cuisines. Creole cooking is thought to be somewhat more sophisticated than Cajun cooking, which uses more pork fat and spices compared with Creole cooking's emphasis on butter, cream, and tomatoes. One thing both cuisines have in common is the "trinity" of chopped onion, celery, and bell peppers, and both use filé powder. You'll find a variety of Creole seasonings on the market to give dishes a distinctive Creole flavor.

Croquettes
Ground or minced cooked food, such as chicken, salmon, or other meat, bound with a thick sauce and formed into shapes or patties, usually coated with bread crumbs, and fried.

Cube
To cut into cubes, usually about ½"–1" in size.

Cut In
To incorporate solid fat into dry ingredients using a pastry blender, fork, or 2 knives. A food processor is sometimes used to cut in fats.

Dash
A dash is a measurement less than ⅛ teaspoon.

Deep-Fry
To cook in hot fat that is deep enough to cover the food.

Dice

To cut food into small cubes, from ⅛" to less than 1" in size.

Dough

A mixture of flour, liquid, and other ingredients that is too stiff to pour and is usually worked or blended by hand.

Drizzle

To pour a liquid or thin mixture over something, such as a glaze for a cake or bread, or butter over a food just before baking.

Fatback

The layer of fat found along the back of a pig. Fresh (unsalted) fatback is used to make lard and cracklings.

Filé Powder

A seasoning and thickener made of sassafras leaves. Filé is traditionally used to flavor and thicken Cajun and Creole dishes, such as gumbo.

Fillet

A boneless piece of meat, poultry, or fish, sometimes spelled *filet*.

Fold

To gently combine a light item or mixture with a heavier mixture, such as egg whites into a cake or pancake batter or berries into a batter. A rubber spatula is usually used to fold ingredients or egg white mixture into a batter. The spatula is cut into the batter then brought across the bottom of the bowl and up the side. The bowl is rotated slightly as the motion is repeated until the ingredients are combined.

Fritter

A sweet or savory deep-fried cake. A fritter may incorporate food into the batter, or single pieces of food may be dipped in batter.

Fry

To cook food in fat over medium to high heat.

Garnish

To decorate food or the dish on which the food is served. Examples of garnishes include lemon or citrus zest on a dollop of whipped cream, chopped parsley on a casserole, and lemon slices with cooked fish fillets or seafood.

Giblets

The heart, liver, and gizzards of poultry.

Glaze

To coat food with a thin sweet or savory coating that becomes smooth and glossy after setting or cooking.

Grate

To cut things into small shreds or pieces, using a hand grater or food processor grater attachment.

Grease

To spread fat on a cooking pan or utensil to keep food from sticking. To grease and flour describes greasing a pan then dusting with a coating of flour, which is shaken to distribute evenly before inverting and discarding excess flour.

Grill

To cook on a rack over hot coal, gas, or other heat source.

Grind

To reduce food to very small particles, as in ground beef or sausage, spices, or coffee. Coffee grinders, a mortar and pestle, a food processor, meat grinder, and pepper mill can all be used to grind different types of foods.

Grits

Any coarsely ground grain, but commonly used in reference to hominy grits, made from dried corn kernels.

Gumbo

A Creole-style stew, usually made with tomatoes, okra, and other vegetables and meats. Gumbo usually starts with a roux as the thickener, and filé powder is often added just before serving.

Half-and-Half

A milk and cream mixture with about 11 to 18 percent milk fat. Substitute evaporated milk or equal amounts of milk and cream.

Ham Hock

The ham hock is the lower part of a hog's hind leg, usually cut in 3" lengths. Ham hocks are usually cured and smoked and make a good flavoring for beans, greens, and other dishes.

Headspace

The amount of space left in the top of a jar of home-canned food or container of frozen food.

Heavy Cream

Cream with at least 36 percent fat content. Often labeled "heavy whipping cream."

Hog Jowl

From the cheek of a hog, this is cured and smoked, and can be cut into slices and used as bacon. Usually found only in the South, hog jowl is used to flavor beans, greens, and other dishes.

Hoppin' John

A dish of black-eyed peas cooked with pork fat and seasonings and usually served with rice and cornbread. This is a traditional Southern New Year's Day dish, eaten to bring good luck.

Hush Puppies

A deep-fried cornmeal dumpling, often containing chopped green onions.

Jambalaya

A very versatile Creole dish, jambalaya is a combination of cooked rice and a variety of other ingredients. It may include tomatoes, onion, green pepper, meat, poultry, a variety of spices, and/or shellfish.

Jus

The French word for juice, as in beef au jus, or beef with natural juices.

Key Lime

This lime, from Florida, is much smaller and yellower than the more common Persian lime.

Knead

A baking technique used to mix and work dough using the hands. Dough is pressed with the heels of the hands while stretching it out, then it's folded over itself and the motion is repeated several times, as the recipe directs.

Lard

Lard is rendered and clarified pork fat. The best lard is made from the fat around the pig's kidneys, called leaf lard. Lard makes tender and flaky pastry and biscuits.

Marinate

To let food soak in a seasoned liquid to make it more flavorful or more tender.

Mince

To cut food into very small pieces, using a knife, food processor, or other chopping utensil. Minced food is cut into smaller pieces than chopped food.

Mint Julep

A Kentucky specialty drink made with bourbon and mint, and usually with sugar syrup and crushed ice. The mint julep is a Kentucky Derby tradition and is sometimes served in a silver julep tumbler.

Nonreactive Pan

A nonreactive pan is made of a nonpourous material that does not produce a chemical reaction when it comes into contact with acidic foods. An aluminum pan is reactive, while stainless steel, glass, and enamel and enamel-lined pans are not.

Okra

Okra pods, brought to the southern United States by Africans during the days of the slave trade, are green and tapered pods with ridges. Okra is often sliced and fried, pickled, or cooked with tomatoes. Sliced okra is also used for its thickening properties in stews and gumbo.

Oysters Bienville

A New Orleans dish, created in the 1930s by the famous Antoine's Restaurant, named after the city's founder. The dish is made with oysters on the half-shell topped with a sherry sauce, along with garlic, mushrooms, and minced shrimp. The oysters are topped with a bread crumb and grated cheese mixture and baked on a bed of rock salt.

Oysters Rockefeller

Another famous New Orleans dish created by Antoine's, this dish was named after John D. Rockefeller. The dish is commonly made with oysters on the half-shell topped with spinach, butter, bread crumbs, and seasonings, baked on a bed of rock salt.

Pain Perdu

A New Orleans French toast, pain perdu literally means "lost bread," because it is a way to revive stale bread that would otherwise be lost.

Pilau

Also called pilaf and sometimes perloo, this dish is a combination of rice that has been browned in fat, along with chopped vegetables, meat, poultry, or seafood, and seasonings.

Pimiento

The pimiento is a large sweet red pepper, about 4" × 3" in size, and chopped pimientos or strips are commonly used in pimiento cheese spread or other spreads and dips, and many casseroles. The pimiento is sweeter than red bell peppers, and green olives are often stuffed with pimientos. They are found in supermarkets in small jars or cans, usually chopped or cut in strips.

Po'Boy or Poor Boy Sandwich

A New Orleans specialty sandwich made with split French bread rolls, mayonnaise, shredded lettuce and other vegetables, and sliced meat, fried oysters, or other fried seafood, and sometimes cheese or gravy.

Powdered Sugar

Also called confectioners' sugar, powdered sugar is sugar that has been crushed into a fine powder and combined with a small amount of cornstarch to keep it from clumping.

Pulled Pork

Barbecued pork roast, usually shoulder, which is slow cooked (usually in a pit or pit-type barbecue) until very tender and then shredded and mixed with sauce or served with a sauce. The sauce varies from one region to another.

Ramekin

A small baking dish, usually round, used to make custards, individual desserts, or individual servings of other dishes.

Reduce

To reduce a mixture is to boil a sauce mixture, juices, wine, or broth until reduced in volume through evaporation, making the sauce more flavorful and somewhat thicker.

Render

To extract the fat from meat or poultry by cooking over low heat. Rendered fat is strained after cooking.

Roast

As a verb, to cook a food in the oven in an uncovered, shallow pan with no liquid; much of the surface of the food is surrounded by heat.

Rolling Boil

A fast boil that cannot be slowed by stirring or whisking.

Roux

A mixture of fat and flour that is blended and cooked slowly over low heat until the desired consistency or color is reached. Roux is used as a base for thickening stews, gumbos, and sauces.

Salt Pork

Salt-cured pork that is essentially a layer of fat from the pig's belly or sides; it is similar to bacon but much fattier. Salt pork is used to flavor beans, greens, and other dishes.

Sauté

To cook food quickly in a small amount of fat, commonly in a sauté pan or skillet.

Scald

To heat a liquid such as milk to just below the boiling point. Scalding milk is not necessary these days, because of pasteurization, but you still might want to scald milk or heat it if you need to melt fat or dissolve sugar in it, or if you use raw milk. Scald also means to plunge a food into boiling water to loosen the peel.

Scallop

A dish cooked in a thick sauce, such as scalloped potatoes or corn scallop. A scallop is also a mollusk with fan-shaped shells, and can also mean to form a decorative "scalloped" edge along the edge of pie dough or other food.

Scant

A "scant" teaspoon, tablespoon, or other measurement is not quite full to the rim.

Score

To cut shallow slashes, usually in a decorative pattern, in ham or other food. Scoring might be done to decorate, to allow excess fat to drain, or to help tenderize a meat.

Sear

To brown meat quickly over high heat. Meat, poultry, or fish might be seared under a broiler, in a skillet, or on the grill.

Shred

To cut food into narrow strips or particles; shredding may be done using a knife, a food processor, a grater, or 2 forks.

Simmer

To cook in liquid at a temperature just below the boiling point, when very small bubbles just begin to break the surface.

Skillet

A long-handled pan, also called a frying pan, made with low sides. A skillet should have a heavy bottom for high heat.

Slow Cooker

An electric cooker with a crockery insert and a glass or plastic cover, made to cook foods at a low temperature for a long period of time using moist heat. The heating element is usually built into the sides of the cooker to surround the food with heat and avoid scorching.

Soften

To make a food, such as cream cheese or butter, softer by letting it stand at room temperature or by wrapping it and submerging in warm or hot water.

Springform Pan

A round cake pan that is a little deeper than a standard cake pan. Springform pans have a clamp on the side that releases the sides from the bottom, leaving the cake undisturbed. Springform pans are commonly used for cheesecakes and tortes.

Succotash

A Southern dish, usually made with a combination of seasoned lima beans and corn, sometimes with the addition of chopped onion, peppers, or cream.

Sweet Onion

Sweet onions have a higher amount of natural sugar, and can be found almost year-round. Varieties include a Southern favorite, Vidalia, from Georgia, along with the Hawaiian Maui, Washington's Walla Walla, Texas Sweets, Mayan, Grand Canyon, and others.

Tabasco Sauce

A fermented hot sauce, made in Louisiana, that is commonly used to flavor a wide variety of dishes and beverages.

Vinaigrette

An oil and vinegar sauce or dressing, usually used on salads or other vegetables. Vinaigrette might also contain seasonings, grated onion or shallots, garlic, mustard, or other ingredients.

Whipped Topping

An imitation whipped cream product, found frozen and ready to thaw and use, or made from a dry mix by adding milk. Many of these products are lower in fat and a quick substitute for whipped cream.

Whipping Cream

Whipping cream, also called light whipping cream, can contain from 30–36 percent fat.

Whisk

A whipping utensil of varying shapes made with looped wires joined at the handle, used to whip or blend sauces, eggs, and other ingredients. As a verb, whisk means to whip or blend ingredients with a whisk.

Zest

Zest is the colorful thin outer layer of citrus fruit, such as lemons, not including the white inner layer, or pith. Use a zester, sharp paring knife, vegetable peeler, or fine grater to peel or grate this aromatic layer from the fruit.

Standard U.S./Metric Measurement Conversions

VOLUME CONVERSIONS

U.S. Volume Measure	Metric Equivalent
⅛ teaspoon	0.5 milliliter
¼ teaspoon	1 milliliter
½ teaspoon	2 milliliters
1 teaspoon	5 milliliters
½ tablespoon	7 milliliters
1 tablespoon (3 teaspoons)	15 milliliters
2 tablespoons (1 fluid ounce)	30 milliliters
¼ cup (4 tablespoons)	60 milliliters
⅓ cup	90 milliliters
½ cup (4 fluid ounces)	125 milliliters
⅔ cup	160 milliliters
¾ cup (6 fluid ounces)	180 milliliters
1 cup (16 tablespoons)	250 milliliters
1 pint (2 cups)	500 milliliters
1 quart (4 cups)	1 liter (about)

WEIGHT CONVERSIONS

U.S. Weight Measure	Metric Equivalent
½ ounce	15 grams
1 ounce	30 grams
2 ounces	60 grams
3 ounces	85 grams
¼ pound (4 ounces)	115 grams
½ pound (8 ounces)	225 grams
¾ pound (12 ounces)	340 grams
1 pound (16 ounces)	454 grams

OVEN TEMPERATURE CONVERSIONS

Degrees Fahrenheit	Degrees Celsius
200 degrees F	95 degrees C
250 degrees F	120 degrees C
275 degrees F	135 degrees C
300 degrees F	150 degrees C
325 degrees F	160 degrees C
350 degrees F	180 degrees C
375 degrees F	190 degrees C
400 degrees F	205 degrees C
425 degrees F	220 degrees C
450 degrees F	230 degrees C

BAKING PAN SIZES

U.S.	Metric
8 × 1½ inch round baking pan	20 × 4 cm cake tin
9 × 1½ inch round baking pan	23 × 3.5 cm cake tin
11 × 7 × 1½ inch baking pan	28 × 18 × 4 cm baking tin
13 × 9 × 2 inch baking pan	30 × 20 × 5 cm baking tin
2 quart rectangular baking dish	30 × 20 × 3 cm baking tin
15 × 10 × 2 inch baking pan	30 × 25 × 2 cm baking tin (Swiss roll tin)
9 inch pie plate	22 × 4 or 23 × 4 cm pie plate
7 or 8 inch springform pan	18 or 20 cm springform or loose-bottom cake tin
9 × 5 × 3 inch loaf pan	23 × 13 × 7 cm or 2 lb narrow loaf or pâté tin
1½ quart casserole	1.5 liter casserole
2 quart casserole	2 liter casserole

Index

Note: Page numbers in **bold** indicate recipe category lists.